In this timely, provocative and lively book Sara Mills opens up the study of stylistics to feminist enquiry. Combining insights from literary and linguistic theory she provides a rationale for the interrogation of texts from a feminist perspective. Through an examination of both literary and non-literary texts; newspapers, pop songs and advertisements, she highlights such issues as sexism, political correctness, reader-positioning, agency and meaning.

Feminist Stylistics presumes no prior knowledge of either feminist or stylistic theory. Each chapter includes a short expository section which shows how the issue has been discussed by literary and linguistic theorists and then goes on to provide a feminist theoretical framework or critique.

Numerous books have been written on feminist literary theory and feminist linguistic analysis but this is the first sustained account of feminist stylistics. The book includes an extensive bibliography, and provides its readers with a 'tool-kit' with which to expose the gender bias of both canonical and 'popular' texts. *Feminist Stylistics* will be essential reading for all students of literature and language.

Sara Mills is Research Professor in English, Sheffield Hallam University.

The INTERFACE Series

> A linguist deaf to the poetic function of language and a literary scholar indifferent to linguistic problems and unconversant with linguistic methods, are equally flagrant anachronisms. – Roman Jakobson

This statement, made over twenty-five years ago, is no less relevant today, and 'flagrant anachronisms' still abound. The aim of the INTERFACE series is to examine topics at the 'interface' of language studies and literary criticism and in so doing to build bridges between these traditionally divided disciplines.

Already published in the series:

The Series Editor
Ronald Carter is Professor of Modern English Language at the University of Nottingham and was National Coordinator of the 'Language in the National Curriculum' Project (LINC) from 1989 to 1992.

Feminist Stylistics

Sara Mills

London and New York

First published 1995
by Routledge
2 Park Square, Milton Park, Abingdon, Oxon OX14 4RN

Simultaneously published in the USA and Canada
by Routledge
270 Madison Ave, New York, NY 10016

Reprinted 1998

Transferred to Digital Printing 2006

Typeset in Baskerville by Florencetype Ltd, Stoodleigh, Devon

British Library Cataloguing in Publication Data
A catalogue record for this book is available from the British Library

Library of Congress Cataloguing in Publication Data
A catalogue record for this book is available from the Library of Congress

ISBN 0-415-05027-8 (hbk)
ISBN 0-415-05028-6 (pbk)
Printed and bound by CPI Antony Rowe, Eastbourne

To Tony and Gabriel

Contents

Preface

This book has had a rather chequered career: I began writing it on my own, but after I had completed about half of it, Shan Wareing and I decided that our interests were sufficiently close to warrant our writing it together. For two years we worked together on the project, during which time we both started new jobs and began to have numerous other commitments. Finally, because of pressure of work, we decided that I should finish the book alone. Shan's contribution to the book not only consists of the sections of the text which she initially wrote, but also of the enthusiasm and verve that she brought to the whole process of collaborative working. I have revised the book substantially both in terms of the structure and the text, but I have acknowledged the sections in the text which are more Shan's than mine. I would like to thank Shan for permission to publish her contributions in revised form; some of her contributions appear in modified form in Wareing 1994. I would also like to thank her for reading through the manuscript.

Acknowledgements

I would like to thank Deirdre Burton for inspiring me with her work in feminist text analysis, and Ron Carter for his support and encouragement in this project. Staff and students at the Programme in Literary Linguistics, Strathclyde University, and the English and Drama Department, Loughborough University, have also played a key role in the development of the ideas in this book. Tony Brown has discussed the ideas in this book on innumerable occasions and made constructive comments on drafts of chapters. I would like to thank the following people in particular for reading and commenting on versions of this book: Nigel Fabb, Lynne Pearce, and members of the Feminist Research Group, Loughborough University. I would also like to thank Julia Hall, Emma Cotter and Jenny Overton of Routledge for their help with a rather unruly text.

The author and the publishers are grateful to the following for permission to reproduce material: the *Sun* for the photograph reproduced on p. 41; WWF UK Ltd for the leaflet reprinted on p. 92; the *Leicester Mail* for the text reprinted on p. 132; and International Creative Management, Inc. for material reprinted on pp. 185–6, taken from Toni Morrison's *Sula*, © 1973 Toni Morrison.

Introduction

This book aims to describe a form of analysis which I have termed 'feminist stylistics'. Both the 'feminist' and the 'stylistics' parts of this phrase are complex and may have different meanings for readers. Nevertheless, the phrase itself is one which best sums up my concern first and foremost with an analysis which identifies itself as feminist and which uses linguistic or language analysis to examine texts. Feminist analysis aims to draw attention to and change the way that gender is represented, since it is clear that a great many of these representational practices are not in the interests of either women or men. Thus, feminist stylistic analysis is concerned not only to describe sexism in a text, but also to analyse the way that point of view, agency, metaphor, or transitivity are unexpectedly closely related to matters of gender, to discover whether women's writing practices can be described, and so on. By close reading, using techniques from a range of linguistic and literary backgrounds, my aim is to present readers with a vocabulary to describe what is going on in texts and what is going on in the readers themselves when they read. When we read we do not always read suspiciously; we are used to certain types of messages and they often do not strike us as necessarily oppressive or pernicious. We often view language simply as a tool or as a vehicle for ideas, rather than as a material entity which may in fact shape those ideas. As David Lee states:

> Given that language is an instrument for the assignment of the phenomena of human experience to conceptual categories it is clearly not simply a mirror that reflects reality. Rather it functions to impose structure on our perceptions of the world. Language is . . . highly selective, and in this sense . . . the process of linguistic encoding involves a significant degree of abstraction away from 'reality'.
>
> (Lee 1992: 8)

It is because some texts bear messages which work on us in a way of which we are not necessarily aware that I feel it is important to analyse texts carefully in terms of the systematic language choices which have been made. Close analysis may help the reader to become aware of the way that language choices may serve the interests of some people to the detriment of others.

Norman Fairclough states in his book *Language and Power* that his objective is 'to help increase consciousness of language and power, and particularly of how language contributes to the domination of some people by others' (Fairclough 1989: 4). In many ways I would agree with this aim, since analysis of language can help the reader be aware of ideologies of gender difference which are oppressive. But this is not my only aim, since ideologies of gender are not solely oppressive, and they are not simply imposed on women by men. Women and men construct their own sense of self within the limits of these discursive frameworks, and build their pleasures and emotional development, often in conscious resistance to, as well as in compliance with, these constraints (Haugg 1988; Smith 1990; S. Mills 1992a). Thus, analysis of images and texts representing gender difference enables us to trace the options available to subjects in terms of the construction of subject positions or roles. As Rajan states, 'our understanding of the problems of "real" women cannot lie outside the "imagined" constructs in and through which "women" emerge as subjects. Negotiating with these mediations and simulacra we seek to arrive at an understanding of the issues at stake' (Rajan 1994: 10). What I would like to capture in this book is the way that the meanings of gender are represented so that it is possible to contest those representations, or reinterpret them; but I would also like to 'make strange' the way gender is represented in our culture, so that perhaps we might be able to think of ways in which it could be represented differently and more productively, both for women and men. I am concerned in this book with the representation of gender difference, that is, the way being a woman or being a man, being straight or being gay, being white or black, is represented both in words and images.

The book is designed as a toolkit; that is, I feel that there is a range of questions which can be directed at any text and which will enable the reader to find out more about the underlying messages of the text. Asking systematic questions and concentrating on particular aspects of texts can tell you a great deal more about the text than a simple reading which focuses on the subject-matter of the text alone. Much feminist criticism, as I show later, has acted as a fundamental critique of the way that texts are written and the way that women are represented or described. This critique is extremely important but it sometimes focuses only on the content of the text and does not provide the reader with a set of strategies which can be employed when facing other texts. It is the generalizable quality of language analysis which is important here. (See Durant and Fabb 1989, and Montgomery *et al.* 1992 for skills-based approaches to text analysis.)

The book does not assume any knowledge of feminism or mainstream stylistics. It simply assumes an interest in language and a healthy suspicion of texts – a suspicion both of those texts with which a reader sympathizes and those with which she doesn't. I have tried to explain new terms within the text in a non-academic language, and I have listed these terms in the glossary at the end of the book. I have also included numerous textual examples so that the form of analysis is as clear as possible. I believe that this book is necessary because, although many stylistics books exist, there are few which deal with gender issues in a thorough manner (see, however, Wales 1994). In fact, very few of them refer to gender at all. It seems a pity that a field where language skills are focused on is not one where these skills are put to good use, as part of a raising of consciousness about the ways that we as readers are acted upon by texts.

FEMINISM

Feminism (or, more accurately, feminisms) is difficult to define because of the many different kinds of feminism which exist today. This introductory summary is therefore not to be considered as comprehensive but rather as attempting to posit some form of common denominator of a rich and varied theoretical field. (For introductory guides to feminist thought, see S. Mills *et al.* 1989; Tong 1989; Warhol and Herndl 1991.) Most feminists hold a belief that women as a group are treated oppressively and differently from men and that they are subject to personal and institutional discrimination. Feminists also believe that society is organized in such a way that it works, in general, to the benefit of men rather than women; that is, that it is patriarchal. This does not imply that all men benefit equally from the way that society is structured, since society also oppresses men in different degrees, nor does it imply that all men take part in the continuance of the system, since men can decide to oppose the oppression of other groups. But it does imply that there is a general difference in the way that men and women are treated in society as a whole and in the way that they view themselves and others view them as gendered beings. Many feminists are aware of the difficulties of assuming that all women or all men are the same, and particularly during the last ten years such feminist theory has been concerned with analysing the way that different forms of oppression and/or discrimination, such as racism and homophobia, may overlap and interact with forms of sexism. Feminists are very aware of the dangers of making simplistic analyses, based on the assumption that 'women' form a homogeneous group. So many differences exist between women – differences of class, race, age, education, wealth – that the very category 'woman' is difficult to maintain, since there appear to be perhaps as many differences amongst women as there are differences from men (see Butler 1990; Fuss 1990). As Butler states (1990: xi), in recent years feminism itself has had to deal with the tricky question of 'What new shape of politics emerges when identity as a common ground no longer constrains the discourse on feminist politics? And to what extent does the effort to locate a common identity as the foundation for a feminist politics preclude a radical inquiry into the political construction and regulation of identity itself?' It is this view of feminist inquiry which is concerned with how women and men are constructed at a representational and at an actual level, and how certain views of women are favoured at the expense of others, which informs this book. And although I would not attempt to assert that all women are the same, most feminists would still maintain that women are systematically discriminated against as a group, albeit in a variety of ways. Feminism implies commitment to changing the social structure to make it less oppressive to women, and, for that matter, to men. This commitment to change I feel should inform feminist analysis and teaching practice.

Feminism is not alone in supporting pedagogic methods which emphasize the teaching of skills, and in encouraging people to fundamentally question received wisdom; other pedagogies are also based on these ideals – Paolo Freire's work in Brazil, for example. However, academic work can sometimes pose itself as a neutral study, whereas as Burton notes: 'I take it as axiomatic that *all* observation, let alone description, must take place within an already constructed theoretical framework of socially, ideologically and linguistically constructed reality, whether the observer/describer of observations is articulately aware of that framework or not' (Burton 1982: 196). For Burton, it is 'essential to distinguish between work which supports an oppressive dominant ideology and work which challenges it, and to state clearly which it is that you are doing' (ibid.: 197). Feminist analysis has always been clear on what it aims to do and has made its theoretical position very clear to readers. I believe these ideals are intrinsic to feminist thought. Feminism sets itself in opposition to the kind of academic work which aims to mystify the uninitiated and to keep out all but a select few. Feminist research aims to be accessible, to enable others, to equip women with the skills and knowledge they need or want (see Bowles and Klein 1983; Stanley 1990). These principles informed my intentions in writing this book.

STYLISTICS

Stylistics has been defined as the analysis of the language of literary texts, usually taking its theoretical models from linguistics, in order to undertake this analysis. As Simpson states, stylistics uses 'linguistic analysis to provide a window on the devices which characterize a particular work' (Simpson 1992: 48). Carter and Simpson make a distinction between linguistic stylistics and literary stylistics; for them linguistic stylistics is where 'practitioners attempt to derive from the study of style and language a refinement of models for the analysis of language and thus to contribute to the development of linguistic theory' (Carter and Simpson 1989: 4); literary stylistics is more concerned with providing 'the basis for fuller understanding, appreciation and interpretation of avowedly literary and author-centred texts. The general impulse will be to draw eclectically on linguistic insights and to use them in the service of what is generally claimed to be fuller interpretation of language effects than is possible without the benefit of linguistics' (ibid.: 7). Thus both forms of stylistic analysis draw on a range of linguistic models, from Noam Chomsky's generative grammar and Michael Halliday's systemic linguistics to John Searle's speech-acts and Malcolm Coulthard's discourse analysis. However, the difference lies in their objectives in undertaking analysis.

Geoffrey Leech and Michael Short supply a fuller definition:

> in general, literary stylistics has, implicitly or explicitly, the goal of explaining
> the relation between language and artistic function. The motivating questions
> are not so much *what*, as *why* and *how*. From the linguist's angle, it is '*why* does
> the author here choose to express himself [*sic*] in this particular way?'. From
> the critic's viewpoint it is '*how* is such-and-such an aesthetic effect achieved
> through language?'
>
> (Leech and Short 1981: 13)

Feminist stylisticians have other questions, in addition to these posed by Leech
and Short; for example, we place less emphasis on the *artistic* function of language
than on other aspects of language, since it is clear that there are regularities in
representations across a range of different texts. The beauty of form and language
in a poem is less important than perhaps that the same techniques are employed
in the poem as in pornography. But feminist stylistics is concerned with the
general emphasis outlined by Leech and Short, that is, why authors have chosen
certain ways to express themselves rather than others, and how certain effects
are achieved through language.

Stylistics developed as an alternative, more objective form of analysis, in
contrast to the type of literary analysis which had developed within educational
institutions.[1] Short characterizes this type of literary work as essentially concerned
with the subjective, individualistic process of interpreting literary texts; he says:

> it is true that each reader will to some extent interpret a text differently
> from others, merely as a consequence of the fact that we are all different
> from one another, have had different experiences, and so on. But it should
> be obvious that such a subjectivist view of literary understanding runs
> counter to the presuppositions of stylistic analysis, whose proponents assume
> that our shared knowledge of the structure of our language and the processes
> for interpreting utterances in our community imply a relatively large degree
> of common understanding, in spite of differences in individual response.
> For the stylistician, the major fact to be explained is that, although we are
> all different, we agree to a remarkable extent over the interpretation . . .
> the range of interpretations which have been produced for even the most
> discussed texts is remarkably small compared with the theoretically infinite
> set of 'possible' readings.
>
> (Short 1989: 2–3)

Many linguists have been dissatisfied with the unjustified assertions which they
felt were made about literary texts in English literature departments, and many
felt a need to provide their students with a range of skills and techniques which
could be employed when analysing and reading literary texts. By focusing on
the language of texts, it was felt that it would be possible to make a rigorous,
objective analysis of the text, rather than a subjective appreciation of literary
worth, an activity against which stylisticians were reacting (Steen 1989). The

early Russian Formalists aimed to establish a scientific study of literature 'which would seek to define the literariness of literature, that is, isolate by rigorous scientific means the specifically literary forms and properties of texts' (Carter and Nash 1990: 31). But it is clear that this concern with rigorous analysis need not limit itself simply to the analysis of literariness; rather it can be a stepping-stone for an analysis of text which can help us to interpret and understand what the text means to us as individual readers, at the same time as ensuring that the analysis which we perform is replicable by other readers/analysts.

Traditional stylistics sets out to analyse literary texts in a seemingly scientific way, drawing on linguistics. This is what distinguishes it from other literary analysis more frequently taking place in English literature departments. But stylistics has also retained the traces of its association with literary analysis and this sometimes leads to a disjunction within analyses, as Sol Saporta states:

> Terms like value, aesthetic purpose, etc., are apparently an essential part of the methods of most literary criticism, but such terms are not available to linguists. The statements that linguists make will include reference to phonemes, stresses, morphemes, syntactical patterns, etc. and their patterned repetition and co-occurrence. It remains to be demonstrated to what extent an analysis of messages based on such features will correlate with that made in terms of value and purpose.
>
> (Saporta 1964: 83)

This issue of being located partly within traditional literary criticism and partly in linguistics has led to members of both camps expressing dissatisfaction with what stylistics can achieve. For example, one of the claims which stylisticians make for their approach to texts is objectivity. In contrast to the subjectivity of a Leavisite approach, which evaluates literary texts according to criteria unique to the critic, stylisticians pride themselves that their analyses are replicable, that is, if other theorists did the same analysis, they would come to the same results. Many stylisticians include graphs and diagrams in their work and emphasize the process of quantifying specified components of texts (see Sinclair 1966). In extreme cases, stylistic studies have perfected quantification at the expense of interpretation, or have treated linguistic forms as if they contained meaning without reference to the context in which they occur. Work of this kind has fuelled the arguments of sceptics who attack stylistics for being primarily concerned with counting the number of verbs and nouns in a passage, for no better purpose than to find out how many verbs and nouns there are.

Not all stylistics has been concerned with 'counting' to the exclusion of all other considerations (as it has sometimes been stereotyped). Indeed, as I have suggested (p. 4), there have been distinct schools of stylistics, each with its own aims and methods. For example, much early stylistic work was concerned to analyse those elements of a particular style which made the writer's prose identifiable and idiosyncratic. This school of stylistics clearly believed that individual writers developed 'idiolects' which could be traced in their work.

Grammatical analysis made it possible to state that certain authors tended to use a particular range of syntactic structure; much of this analysis focused on the description of the style of those writers who seemed to write in a very distinctive way; for example, Gerard Manley Hopkins or e. e. cummings.[2] Other stylisticians have been concerned with the quality of 'literariness'. They analysed canonical texts, held to be of great literary value because of their skilful crafting and density of patterning (Mukarovsky 1970; Jakobson 1960). Texts were analysed which seemed to deviate from a norm of 'ordinary' language. The task of the stylistician was envisaged as justifying the categorization of a poem as great literature, or trying to define the special nature of literature as a whole, by drawing attention to the difference of literary language. Literary language was therefore seen as a different register or type of language, which it was the task of the stylistician to describe. This concern with literature has continued in much present-day stylistics so that Leech can claim 'stylistics may be regarded simply as the variety of discourse analysis dealing with literary discourse' (Leech 1973: 151). Yet there is a sense in which stylistics is now using the knowledge and skills derived from close textual analysis of literary texts to investigate more fully the construction and effect of non-literary texts (Fairclough 1989).

As I mentioned earlier, stylistics was often used during the early period of its development to back up intuitions about the meaning of the text under analysis. However, this provoked something of a reaction among other stylisticians such as John Sinclair who tried to show that linguistics should not be used as an aid to interpretation. In Sinclair's essay, the aptly named 'Taking a poem to pieces', he suggests that linguistics could analyse only the linguistic structure of the text – its deviance from a norm, for example (Sinclair 1966: 68–81). In his analysis of a poem by Philip Larkin, 'First sight', he shows that there is a preponderance of a certain linguistic feature in the poem, which defeats the reader's expectation of what is to follow. However, he makes no claims to interpreting the poem on the basis of his analysis. For Sinclair, it is sufficient for the linguist to describe the structure of the text without suggesting that there is any link between the formal structure and the meaning of the poem. This is the type of linguistics which most characterizes stylistics for many people, and it is this approach which students sometimes find discouraging – they assume that stylistics is only concerned with clause-counting. I feel that, in fact, stylistics can offer numerous interesting and valuable ways of approaching texts, and can be used to elicit far more worthwhile information than the total number of nouns in a text. It can make readers aware of aspects of texts, for example, grammatical choices or lexical choices, which skew the interpretation of a text, something which a simple close reading cannot do.

Some linguists such as Leech have tried to use linguistics as a way of providing a toolkit or shared vocabulary for students of literature. This approach has been adopted by the writers of *Ways of Reading* (Montgomery *et al.* 1992) and also by Durant and Fabb (1989) who aim to provide a battery of questions with which a reader can examine a text, and their own reading process, in order to become aware of how a text comes to have meaning, and of the way that readers begin to formulate interpretations. Norman Fairclough, in a similar way, is concerned to provide readers with a range of questions to ask a text in order to investigate the way that ideology informs the production and reception of texts (Fairclough 1989). In this book, I am concerned to meld this task-based, question-oriented approach to text analysis with a wider concern with the way readers form interpretations which are related to their gender – where the process of interpretation rests on cues in the text which have a different significance, or are significant to a different extent, depending on the reader's gender-identity.

Whilst stylistics enjoyed a certain vogue in the 1960s, within the last twenty years it has undergone a profound revolution. Many have asserted that because of the advent of literary theory, stylistics as a study has died. However, stylistics seems to be remarkably resilient and has taken on board some of the findings of literary theory and critical linguistics, albeit in a rather piecemeal fashion.[3] It has now moved into the area of 'literary linguistics', 'poetics and linguistics', 'contextual stylistics' and 'discourse stylistics' (see Toolan 1992; Carter and Simpson 1989).[4] The focus of analysis has changed from an analysis of the text in itself to an analysis of the factors determining the meaning of a text in its social context. This new concern is perhaps most clearly signalled by Roger Fowler when he states: 'There is a dialectical interrelationship between language and social structure: the varieties of linguistic usage are both *products* of socio-economic forces and institutions – reflexes of such factors as power relations, occupational roles, social stratifications, etc. – and *practices* which are instrumental in forming and legitimating these same social forces and institutions' (Fowler 1981: 21). Carter and Simpson's edition of essays, *Language, Discourse and Literature: An Introduction to Discourse Stylistics*, tries to put these ideas into action so that stylistic analysis is not simply limited to word-counts; they argue that stylistics should be concerned with occupying 'the territory beyond the level of the sentence or the single conversational exchange' and with examining 'those broader contextual properties of texts which affect their description and interpretation' (Carter and Simpson 1989: 14). Despite this revolution, it should be remembered that this change involves a very small group of stylisticians – and many are still working within the same frameworks as twenty years ago, and even within the more 'radical' sections of stylistics, feminism and gendered analysis have not had much impact.[5]

While there has been much work done in stylistics, within the schools described above, and in other areas, which has been creative and useful, and which has furthered understanding of how certain textual effects are achieved, stylistic analysis is often conducted within a framework of assumptions that must be disputed. Stylistics largely inherited its theoretical foundations from contemporary literary criticism and linguistics. These fields have moved on, and stylistics needs to respond to the new ideas which have emerged from both fields in recent years. For example, many of the early stylisticians mentioned above assumed that it is possible to analyse a text in isolation, as a self-contained entity, which has a meaning independent of any external considerations. This is an outdated inheritance, and has been questioned in modern traditions of literary criticism and linguistics. It has often been assumed by stylisticians that the meaning of the text is contained in its language, and that the text generates only one reading – the one accessed by the stylistician. This view is seriously jeopardized by theories of pragmatics, which deal with the extent to which the meaning of language is context-dependent (Levinson 1983; Brown and Yule 1983). For some stylisticians, the language of the text is discussed in relation to a linguistic system, and that linguistic system is treated as stable, natural, undisputed and shared by all native speakers – as if we were part of a homogeneous speech community, all using language in the same way. Extensive work in linguistics, sociolinguistics and literary theory has contradicted this view of language, revealing it to be unstable, the site of conflict, and exploding the myth of a homogeneous speech community (Hymes 1971; Pratt 1987). Stylistics has traditionally not considered a text in the context either of its production or its critical reception (see Chapter 1). Factors such as gender, race and class have not entered into the analysis, any more than the text's status within the canon has occasioned comment from the stylistician. And in fact, stylisticians have often regarded these variables as a distraction from real linguistic analysis: as Carter and Simpson state, for many working in stylistics, a concentration on factors such as gender, class and ideological position:

> can push language description to limits where analytical procedures from other disciplines have to be conjoined. It is at such points that the relative discreteness of linguistic description may be compromised. Of course, compromise is a necessary feature of interdisciplinary work . . . but without the 'scientific' procedures, and without the development of 'models' with predictive power, it becomes difficult to undertake analysis which is sufficiently principled to promote linguistic descriptive progress, and to prevent the kind of integration with other disciplines which is absorption rather than mutually productive support.
>
> (Carter and Simpson 1989: 15)

This book attempts to integrate the study of texts from a view of textuality informed by both linguistics and literary theory, which is focused precisely on these factors which are seen to be so dangerously 'compromising'.

The above limitations represent a serious flaw in the field of stylistic analysis to date. The concentration on a very limited set of texts for analysis and the ignoring of context and factors such as race, class and gender seriously undermines stylistics' claim to scientific/unbiased analysis, on which much store has been set. I aim both to show how important it is to consider these extratextual aspects in any textual analysis, and to suggest ways of doing so. I am mainly concerned with the issue of gender, and how this can be incorporated into stylistic analysis, but it it necessary to avoid some of the theoretical impasses which might be encountered. When gender has been addressed as a variable by stylistics to date, analysis has been on a fairly banal level, typically centring around the discussion of 'the female sentence' or the way that women supposedly write (see Chapter 2). I am not going to be using stylistics in the ways outlined above, to analyse the style of an author, or to count the number of verbs or nouns, or to examine the artistry of a poem. Instead I will be drawing on theories in linguistics and literary theory which encourage a focus on a different range of issues and questions, specifically those of relevance to the concerns of feminists, so that the analysis of language serves our interests.

CRITICAL LINGUISTICS

My aim in proposing a feminist stylistics, which relates the language of texts to extra-textual political processes, has a precursor in critical linguistics and it is for this reason that I would now like to describe the analyses and language models which have been formulated by critical linguists and critical discourse analysts. Critical linguistics is the study of texts from an avowedly political perspective. In the words of Hodge and Kress: 'Critical linguistics is a theory of language whose aim [is] to provide an illuminating account of verbal language as a social phenomenon, especially for the use of critical theorists . . . who [want] to explore social and political forces and processes as they act through and on texts and forms of discourse' (Hodge and Kress 1988: vii). In a similar vein, Roger Fowler states: 'critical linguistics simply means an enquiry into the relations between signs, meanings and the social and historical conditions which govern the semiotic structure of discourse, using a particular kind of linguistic analysis' (Fowler 1991: 5). Not only is critical linguistics a description of underlying ideological messages in texts but, as Fowler and Kress state, it 'is a critique of the structures and goals of a society which has impregnated its language with social meanings, many of which we regard as negative, dehumanising and restrictive in their effects' (Fowler et al. 1979: 196). As these quotations show, these critical linguists generally view the effect of the sociohistorical situation on language as something of a one-way traffic; that is, that social structures determine the form and content of language. This view has been challenged in recent years, most notably by Kress and Fowler themselves (Hodge and Kress 1988; Fowler 1991). Linguists such as Norman Fairclough, Roger Fowler, Gunther Kress, Robert Hodge, Tony Trew and others have challenged conventional views of textuality and meaning, focusing instead on the conditions of the text's production and reception and the interrelation between language and sociohistorical context (Fairclough 1989; Fowler et al. 1979; Hodge and Kress 1988; Fowler 1991). Critical linguists such as Hodge and Kress have shown that meaning does not simply reside in a text but is the result of a process of negotiations and a set of relations between the social system within which the text is produced and consumed, the writer and the reader (Hodge and Kress 1988). They draw on explicitly political theorists such as Valentin Voloshinov and Michel Pecheux to focus on how language can be a motivating force in the way that people define themselves and are defined by others (Voloshinov 1973; Pecheux 1982). They go on to show that this process of using language to define oneself can have effects on the language system as a whole and ultimately on the way that society is structured.

For all of these linguists, language is not a transparent carrier of meanings, but is a medium which imposes its own constraints on the meaning which is constructed. Language is seen very much as a social phenomenon. As Fowler and Kress state, 'The forms of language in use are a *part of*, as well as *a consequence of*, social process' (Fowler *et al.* 1979: 26); and they go on to say that 'the linguistic forms of speech and writing express the social circumstances in which language occurs. The relationship of style to situation is very precise and functional, so that an analysis of linguistic structure reveals the contexts of language with considerable accuracy' (Fowler *et al.* 1979: 26). In contrast to many sociolinguists, critical linguists are concerned not simply to describe the link between society and language but to see language being used as a form of social control; for them 'language serves to confirm and consolidate the organizations which shape it, being used to manipulate people, to establish and maintain them in economically convenient roles and statuses, to maintain the power of state agencies, corporations and other institutions' (Fowler *et al.* 1979: 190). This is all distinctly unfashionable in the post-Marxist 1990s – and yet a modified version of the above view does have the advantage that it is possible to teach people to regard language-use as part of relations of power within society and to intervene in those relations. For many critical linguists, not only is language tied into notions of restriction on linguistic expression but continued use of particular styles of speech and writing will change and determine cognitive processing. Fowler and Kress state that 'social groupings and relationships influence the linguistic behaviour of speakers and writers, and moreover . . . these socially determined patterns of language influence non-linguistic behaviour including, crucially, cognitive activity. Syntax can code a world-view without any conscious choice on the part of a writer or speaker' (Fowler *et al.* 1979: 185).

Hodge and Kress concern themselves in part with what they term gender systems, that is, the way that gender differences are encoded within texts (by using this term 'systems' they mean to show that these differences are not simply the product of individual texts but rather part of larger-scale social processes). They state that 'one aspect of a gender system is a classification of reality which projects social meanings about men and women onto the non-human world, inscribing an ideology of sex roles and sex identities into the language itself' (Hodge and Kress 1988: 98). This is crucial for the overall project of this book, which is concerned not only to chart the way sexist attitudes manifest themselves in individual language items, but also to analyse the larger-scale systems whereby reality is organized along gendered lines.

Central to critical linguistic analysis is the notion of ideology, as Tony Trew states: 'To the extent that the concepts in a discourse are related as a system, they are part of a theory or ideology, that is, a system of concepts and images which are a way of seeing and grasping things, and of interpreting what is seen or heard or read. All perception involves theory or ideology, and there are no "raw" uninterpreted, theory-free facts' (Trew in Fowler *et al.* 1979: 95). It is the prime focus of critical linguistics to unmask those ideologies which seem to be hidden within language-use which poses itself as natural.

The essays in the 1979 collection by Fowler *et al.*, *Language and Control*, are one of the best examples of a systematic attempt to locate ideological messages at the level of sentence structure, in such elements as passivization, nominalization, transitivity and thematization. Tony Trew states most clearly the relationship between the analysis of ideology and the analysis of language: 'Linguistic theory can be used in such [analytical] work, because discourse is a field of both ideological processes and linguistic processes, and because there is a determinate relation between those two kinds of process' (Trew in Fowler *et al.* 1979: 154). However, the very concept of ideology has been the subject of development and interrogation of late, particularly in the work of Hodge and Kress, and many other theorists of ideological critique. They criticize earlier work: 'Theories of ideology tend to treat ideology as a once-for-all category whose immutable forms confront pre-ideological individuals, assigning them the only social roles and meanings they can have, allowing no space or time in which negotiation or divergence or resistance could occur' (Hodge and Kress 1988: 259). I shall be drawing on this more constructive approach to ideology, one where formulating and developing strategies of resistance is as important as recognizing oppression. I shall also be adding to this view of ideology a notion that ideologies are in a process of change, rather than viewing them as static and fixed, as many earlier theorists did. Martin argues for a more dynamic view of ideology since he states that 'ideology can be interpreted more as a type of language dependent on the use to which language is put. Here we are looking at ideology in crisis, undergoing a process of change during which speakers take up options to challenge or defend some worldview that has prevailed to that point in time' (Martin 1986: 228). Seeing ideologies as always and necessarily in crisis allows for the possibility that speakers and hearers can resist the effects of those ideologies and bring about change in the way such issues are viewed.

A further element which is important for critical linguists is the notion that the language which is used by speakers and writers is part of a system which presents certain choices to them within a set of restricted parameters. The writer/speaker assumes that she has choice, but the language system pre-exists her and determines what can be stated, mostly without the person's being aware of any restriction. As Fowler and Kress state: 'Any text embodies interpretations of its subject, and evaluations based on the relationship between source and addressee. Those interpretative meanings are not created uniquely for the occasion; the systematic use of these linguistic structures is connected with the text's place in the socio-economic system, and hence they exist in advance of the production of text and our reception of it' (Fowler *et al.* 1979: 185). Therefore, although certain language choices feel very personal – for example, when we express emotion, or when we coin a phrase to express ourselves – it is necessary to recognize that, nevertheless, our choices are determined by social forces rather than individual ones.

I shall also be drawing on Hodge and Kress's notion that it is not enough simply to analyse language; they state that 'meaning resides so strongly and pervasively in other systems of meaning [other than verbal language] in a multiplicity of visual, aural, behavioural and other codes, that a concentration on words alone is not enough . . . no single code can be successfully studied or fully understood in isolation' (ibid. vii). It is for this reason that I have analysed a number of visual images, when analysing texts, since this at least does try to present texts within their context and in their entirety. Furthermore, Kress and Fowler stress that the meaning of sentences cannot be reduced to their constituent parts; for example, they say: 'Our analyses suggest . . . that lexical items, linguistic forms and linguistic processes carry specific meanings. When they are realized in a coherent discourse, systematic options from sets of alternatives are exercised, and the total and interacting effect of these carries a meaning over and above that of the items and processes in isolation' (Fowler et al. 1979: 186). I would argue that gender difference is one of the larger elements which is transmitted to the reader in a great number of texts at present.

Hodge and Kress are concerned with other aspects than gender, as is Norman Fairclough. He has been concerned to develop a critical discourse analysis, which takes account of power relations in its analyses of texts. His work has included a study of Margaret Thatcher's use of language, showing how an individual might select from available discourses, to construct a subject position which is advantageous to their goals. In particular, Fairclough looks at how Thatcher's interview technique derives from a blend of features associated with white middle-class femininity, and the traditional 'authoritative expressive elements' used by male politicians (Fairclough 1989: 191). This kind of analysis, which considers what discourses are available to which speakers, and their relative authority within a society, is an important element of my feminist stylistics framework. Fairclough has also considered how texts address readers, and how readers are positioned in an interactive framework by a text, which as we will see is highly relevant to the analysis of texts such as advertisements (Fairclough 1989: 132–3). Much of this work is based on Michael Halliday's systemic linguistics, which is a system which is concerned with the relation between language and social forces; indeed, within this grammatical system the distinction between language and society seems false, since language is perceived as very much a part of society and as a form of social action. Social forces determine language and language in turn has an impact on society, in the sense that it may reaffirm the status quo or challenge it. Halliday, rather than assuming that sentences can be looked at in isolation, considers the various functions that sentences and texts have. In this way, he demonstrates his awareness of the social quality of language, that language and texts are integrated into our social world and that they serve purposes in the world. As Fowler and Kress state: 'language serves to confirm and consolidate the organizations which shape it, being used to manipulate people, to establish and maintain them in economically convenient roles and statuses, to maintain the power of state agencies, corporations and other institutions' (Fowler et al. 1979: 190). However, as a feminist it is necessary to stress that as well as keeping people in their place, language can also be one of the many ways that they can question their position; awareness of the ways in which language is used as a stabilizing mechanism, can be a step in the direction of liberation.

I will use the systems developed by Halliday and critical linguists in a selective way, since there are certain insights which I would like to build on. The notion that linguistics should be critical in all of the senses of that term is one which informs this book as a whole (S. Mills 1989b). However, I have found that especially in the early work, some of Halliday's analyses are based on misapprehensions concerning the analysis of language in texts, and furthermore, there are few systemic analyses which concern themselves with gender. Therefore, I would now like to consider feminist text analysis which has concerned itself explicitly with questions of gender and suggest ways in which this book will be both drawing on this work and fusing its concerns with those of critical linguistics.

FEMINIST ANALYSIS OF TEXT

Feminist literary theorists have made many attempts to consider the language of texts in some detail. From Virginia Woolf's pioneering work on sentence structure and gender to Kate Millett's groundbreaking analysis of language and sexism, language has been focused on in the suspicious readings of feminism (Woolf 1979; Millett 1977). In current French feminist literary and psychoanalytical theory, language is a key issue in literary analysis. Within psychoanalytical theory and much literary theory, language is perceived as the medium through which the self is formed and which shapes the way that we think about the world. According to this view, analysis of language can thus tell us a great deal about the production of the self or subject (see Millard in S. Mills *et al.* 1989).

However, this concern with the linguistic level of texts does not pervade feminist criticism as a whole. Much Anglo-American feminist theory, for example, has been concerned with representations of women and relating those representations of female characters to a generalized female self-identity and experience (see Moi 1985 and S. Mills *et al.* 1989 for a discussion of Anglo-American criticism). These feminist critics tend to focus on content analysis alone, and this is perhaps one of their greatest shortcomings, since their claims are often based on untenable theoretical positions. Their approach seems like a return to the subjectivity of traditional literary analysis and it bears all the theoretical disadvantages of that type of criticism. Furthermore, this approach reduces the theorist to evaluating the text; either 'This is a good representation because it accords with what I consider to be woman's experience', or 'This is sexist because it produces a false representation of women'. When critics take on this kind of evaluative role, they position themselves very much within the domain of the phallocentric literary criticism (that is, criticism which generally tends to privilege male opinions and writers), which feminist theory aims to criticize and displace. By focusing on content analysis, the critic has to assume a single meaning for the text. In this way it is possible to claim whatever interpretation you like for a text – it becomes extremely difficult to prove that a reading is not in fact 'correct' or 'adequate', because the discussion is reduced to comparing subjective readings, with no agreed criteria for assessing how one reading might be 'better' than another. Although content analysis is important, as I will show in this book, it needs to take place alongside, and not instead of, analysis of the language of a text in the context of its production and reception process.

For many feminists teaching and reading, our own suspicious reading of texts may take the form of close reading (Kamuf 1980). Close reading techniques work on the assumption that the reader analyses the language of a text to support her intuitions; the process consists of spotting language items in texts and, having identified a preponderance of certain items, using these data to back up an original hunch about the text. In these circumstances, language analysis is used as a way of justifying an initial reaction felt by the reader. However, this is a rather haphazard method of paying attention to language items, and it can be argued that this kind of close reading can really be used to justify any argument the reader may have about the text, since the language items for analysis are selected *after* a judgement has been passed on the text. In such a situation, data that counter the original hypothesis can easily be ignored. Furthermore, although the reader is paying close attention to details of language, because she has not necessarily theorized how she reads in the first place, there is a danger that aspects of the text will still evade her, as apparently being 'commonsense', or natural. My proposed approach to texts aims to raise consciousness and awareness of the means whereby texts present certain information or material as it if were commonsense, hopefully to a greater extent than an untheorized close reading can do (for a discussion of feminist close reading, see S. Mills 1992c). The reader thus has a means of distancing herself from naturalized reading strategies. If we as readers rely on our intuition about a text, we may fall in with the ideology from which the text was produced. A further problem with untheorized close reading is that each reader comes to the text with her own set of background assumptions. She does not consider the notion that background assumptions may differ between different groups of readers, and influence their reading of the text, and she will therefore have no way to explain why several close readings may reach different conclusions about the same text. Therefore, what is needed is to develop a model of analysis which will enable close, suspicious readings that will be replicable; that is, the model of analysis will not change overly from reader to reader and from text to text.

Any work on gender and text analysis has to take into account contemporary feminist work in sociolinguistics, the major figures in British sociolinguistics being Deborah Cameron and Jennifer Coates (Cameron 1985; Cameron 1990a; Coates 1986; Coates and Cameron 1988). Both these linguists approach their work with the assumption that there are features in language which can be explained only by reference to gender. Coates's work has analysed discourse differences in women's and men's conversation styles, identifying features of all-female group discussions which differ from those found in mixed or male-only discussion groups. There has also been considerable work done on differences – real or imagined – in pronunciation, syntax and lexis between men and women. This is an increasing area of research, which embraces a wide spectrum of approaches. (See, for example, R. Lakoff 1975; Edelsky 1977; Spender 1980; Cameron 1990a). Two aspects of this area of work which are of particular relevance to feminist stylistics are the strength of the stereotypes and beliefs regarding what is 'typical' male or female usage, and the difference in interactive norms found in all-female and all-male groups. Edelsky's (1977) research shows that at an early age children have internalized ideas of what is a 'typical' word for a man to use rather than a woman (e.g. strong swear words), or for a woman to use rather than a man (e.g. milder expletives such as 'oh dear'), showing how ingrained are stereotypes of gendered language. Coates, on the other hand, has investigated the differences in the way all-woman groups handle topic selection and development, and turn-taking, amongst other features of talk. These studies show how gender is a variable affecting both our language competence and our beliefs and expectations about language-use.[6]

Cameron's work includes analyses of the way women and men are represented in language, investigating terms such as 'false generics', i.e. the use of the general term to refer to a specific sub-group of that word, as in this example from the *Guardian*: 'A coloured South African who was subject to racial abuse by his neighbours went berserk with a machete and killed his next-door neighbour's wife' (cited in Cameron 1985: 85). In this example, the generic word 'neighbour' – which is usually thought to include male and female – clearly refers only to the male neighbour; otherwise, the additional term 'wife' would not have been necessary. Close language analysis such as this feminist work emphasizes the importance of studying language and 'commonsense' views of it, and of taking gender issues into account when constructing theories of what language is and how it works.

Deirdre Burton's work supports an approach which places gender issues at the centre of academic study. In an essay which has been of fundamental importance in the effort to construct a feminist stylistics, Burton produces an analysis of the transitivity choices in a passage from Sylvia Plath's *The Bell Jar* (Burton 1982).[7] Burton explores the ways in which language can be used to produce the sense of a character being powerless: how the linguistic form of the verbs contributes to the protagonist's apparent feeling of lack of control over her own life. The essay concludes with examples of students' rewritings of the passage from Plath, experimenting with the ways in which changes in grammar can be made to reverse this effect, to confer greater power and control on a literary character and also, more importantly, on the reader. Burton's view is that *no* analytical work can be conducted which is truly apolitical – all work either supports or challenges the existing social order: '*All* knowledge is contained and produced within an ideological framework' (Burton 1982: 197). She extends this argument to point out that methodologies used in the analysis of data are governed by the theoretical framework which also governs the data collection, and to make sense of any work, the researchers must be explicit about their political affiliations: 'As all method-ological components of theories are intricately related to the goal of those theories, responsible academics must continually state and refer to both the lower-order and higher-order constraints of the particular work they are doing, in order to make sense of that work' (Burton 1982: 197). It is Burton's work, more than any other, which has influenced my work within feminist stylistics.

SUMMARY

Feminist Stylistics aims to make explicit some of the untenable assumptions under-lying conventional stylistics and, by not simply adding gender to its list of interesting elements to analyse, to take stylistics into a new phase. It aims to lead stylistics away from analysis of the language of the text, as if that language were simply *there*, to an analysis of socioeconomic factors which have allowed that language to appear, or which have determined its appearance, or which have determined the type of interpretations of that text which are possible. Thus, it will be shown that women's writing within western European culture may or may not be written in ways different from men's writing, but the important fact remains that it often *means* differently from men's work, and that there is a range of factors which determine that difference. It is produced under largely different circumstances and marketed/packaged in significantly different ways.

Feminist Stylistics also aims to show that gender is foregrounded in texts at certain key moments and is usually dealt with in ways which can be predicted. These moments often appear to be commonsense but foregrounding them enables us to read them differently. In this way, the book intends to look at texts which appear to be explicitly dealing with gender issues; for example, love scenes in books, differential usage of terms for men and women, sexism and so on. But it will also analyse those elements which do not at first sight seem to have anything to do with gender; for example, metaphor, narrative and focalization.

I argue explicitly for stylistics to move away from the analysis of literary texts to an analysis of literature in the context of other forms of writing; for example, advertising, newspaper reports and so on. Since literature is one of many forms of writing which play a role in the constitution of the subject, and the production of messages about what women and men are like in this society, and since there are similar processes at work in other forms of signification, the analysis of the similarity within rather than the difference between these processes seems more productive (for example, the similarity in fragmentation/representation in pornography and love poetry discussed in Chapter 6). This is particularly impor-tant in feminist stylistics where 'woman' is the object of a great many discourses besides literature. As I stated at the outset of this introduction, the book aims to provide readers with the tools (terminology, skills, questions to ask) to identify and deal with sexism and gender bias in texts. I aim to raise awareness of the way that gender difference works in a broad range of texts.

The set of social and linguistic relations with which I will be concerned will be those based on gender. I will be using the notion of gender here in a very wide sense, not assuming that all women are the same or that all men are the same. An acknowledgement of differences within the terms 'woman' and 'man' is one of the key aspects of this analysis. Gender is a term which has a number of theoretical problems, most notably it can run the risk of effacing political edge, because it assumes that men and women are different and that that difference is the same for both groups. Thus, the way that women are oppressed by patriarchal systems is not considered, or is considered only in relation to the way that men are oppressed by the same systems. However, gender is a useful term, since it foregrounds the fact that men and women and femininity and masculinity are produced as different, even though there are elements which women and men share. It also foregrounds the fact that the grouping 'women' makes sense only in relation to, and in contradistinction from, the grouping 'men'. Thus, I will here be using the term 'gender' to mean difference between women and men in a relational and not an oppositional way. I will be concerned with specificity here, with the specific variables which are at work within gender, most notably race and class.

This is a form of analysis which both women and men can do: although there is a great debate about whether men can be feminists or not, it is quite clear that *anyone* can read using a feminist critique, if they are asking interesting questions and have an awareness of the debates going on in the field. There is clearly a difference between men doing feminist critique and women doing it. First, despite the large proportion of female students who take English Studies, successful published writers, literary reviewers and those in the senior academic positions in English departments at all levels of education, are still predominantly male. Second, what is at stake for the researcher differs, depending on their gender. That certainly does not mean that men should be excluded from feminist knowledge, as long as they do not seek to appropriate that knowledge (see Jardine and Smith 1987). It simply means that men should consider the reasons why they are doing feminist analysis: to gain street credibility, to appear to be a New Man, to oppose patriarchal ideologies, to find out something about masculinity and so on. There is some excellent work being undertaken by men into masculinity at present, and this draws productively on feminist studies (Abbott 1990; Boone and Cadden 1990; Middleton 1992). Furthermore, research by gay and lesbian theorists has also drawn on feminist theory and currently influences the types of models of gender identity which are being formulated (Dollimore 1991; Shepherd and Wallis 1989; Hobby and White 1991; Bristow 1992).

A feminist analysis of the language of texts is essential since so many things in western culture are sex-differentiated: from spectacles to cardigans, from deodorants to nappies, from birthday cards to weight training; all of these elements are differentiated according to gender and this difference is marked and maintained in the language used. I would argue that, along the lines of Lévi-Strauss's theories on totem, this difference is perpetuated through language-use (Lévi-Strauss 1967).

Lévi-Strauss asserted that some social groupings which he investigated used totems – that is, insignia representing animals – to represent their groupings; thus one grouping used the lion and another the lynx to characterize their groups.[8] Lévi-Strauss argues that the groups themselves were no different one from the other, and it is because of this essential similarity that the groups used animals where difference was clearly marked to symbolize themselves, so that they could emphasize the difference which they wished to stress. Western European cultural systems attach great importance to gender difference, and it is signalled at every possible moment, in situations where sex differences are irrelevant. Let us consider as an example of this tendency the advertisement for Guess perfume on page 20.

This advertisement is promoting two products: a perfume aimed at men and one aimed at women.[9] It has a representation of two naked people locked in an embrace: the woman engages the eye-contact of the reader and the man seems to be looking more at the woman. Both the man and the woman are represented as stereotypically heterosexually feminine and masculine: the woman has long hair, is wearing makeup and is classically attractive. Her look, pout and tousled hair are sexual. The male is also stereotypically represented since he is rugged in appearance: he has an unkempt beard and moustache and is frowning. He is also holding the woman tightly in his flexed muscular arms, whereas her arm is gently laid on him. What is naturalized in this representation is the commonsensical and unmarked nature of both heterosexuality and whiteness: these two idealized representations affirm, by the very fact that it does not need to be referred to, the hidden message that all males and all females will aspire to heterosexual relations on this model and that males and females are white. Blackness and homosexuality are implicitly designated as marked forms of identity in comparison with this seemingly 'normal' image of relationship.

In order to market two fragrances for two different target audiences, the advertisers have chosen to demarcate these audiences as clearly as possible: men and women here are globally different. This is signalled by the use of two different terms for the same substance: '*parfum*' for women and 'fragrance' for men. The word '*parfum*' signals sophistication and sexuality, since in English the use of French often signals these qualities. But in addition, 'perfume' is seen to be a word which is necessarily within the zone of female experience. It is considered in general to be a word which is not used for males. Therefore the advertisers have chosen to use the word 'fragrance', in much the same way that other manufacturers choose to use the term 'aftershave' instead of 'perfume' when describing products for males. Thus, here one could assume in fact that the fragrances are the same, or even that the products themselves are the same, but that the manufacturers and advertisers find it necessary to differentiate them in a fairly extreme way. Thus, this type of feminist stylistic analysis is concerned to examine the way that gender difference is encoded in texts.

Feminist analysis is not simply concerned with the analysis of difference either, since not all of the elements which go to make up those differences are equally weighted; discrimination and differential access to power and rights need to be

considered. It is clear that a representation of a Black woman would not mean the same as the representation of a white woman in the context of this advertisement for perfume, simply because of the sexual qualities which racist discourses have written into such representations (see Wetherell and Potter 1992; Ware 1992). It is the aim of this book to foreground those sometimes hidden differences, since very often the difference is one which is naturalized; that is, because it is so prevalent within our society it appears to be 'normal' or 'commonsense'. Language analysis can help to challenge these notions of 'normality' by showing alternative choices within the language and explaining the way that these alternatives can lead to different and more productive meanings.

From the experience of teaching, I have found that students sometimes find this approach difficult. It can feel to them as if the process of analysis dissects and destroys the pleasure they derived from the text when they read it unanalytically. While I do not want to make light of the changes linguistically informed feminist awareness can make to someone's reading habits and way of thinking, I should stress that it is possible to gain pleasure from critique as well. I would argue that this approach to texts can intensify the pleasure to be gained from reading, by making us more aware of how that pleasure is produced.

STRUCTURE OF THE BOOK

Each chapter of the book is concerned with one or more elements of feminist stylistic analysis. These are interrelated, as I hope will become clear. The book begins by considering some theoretical issues; that is, first which model of text we are to use and how this model can determine the type of interpretation that we then go on to develop. I then move on to consider the question of whether men and women write in different ways, and finally I consider the role of the gender in the process of interpretation of texts. The second part of the book is concerned with analysis of texts at three levels: of the word, of the phrase or sentence and of discourse. It is clear to me that it is not sufficient to analyse language simply at the level of the word, because words have meaning only in terms of their context. However, it is also evident that certain words concerning gender difference do seem to reflect an overall gender bias and for this reason they may be analysed in relative isolation. It is because of this concern that I then turn to the analysis of words in their relations to other words and larger-scale structures, and finally I consider the discourse elements which determine the use of the language items which I have so far described. By this I mean that there are larger structures within texts such as narrative, plot, focalization and schemata which can be seen to determine those smaller-scale elements.

The book as a whole does not aim to cover every aspect of text production and reception in relation to gender difference, because that is clearly beyond the scope of one study. It is the aim of this book rather to ask questions about our commonsense notions of gender and text and to help to create a productive suspicion of all processes of text interpretation.

Part I

General Theoretical Issues

Chapter 1

Feminist Models of Text

This chapter discusses the different models of text which are available to feminist text analysis. In order to do any analysis of text, we need to be clear about the type of model that we are using, because that has serious implications for how we analyse the text and what our interpretations are.[1] This does mean that, unlike most stylistics textbooks, we cannot plunge straightaway into an analysis of texts, but that we have to consider our assumptions about texts and the relation they have with context and readers, since frequently it is here that assumptions about gender are most at work. In this chapter, I focus mostly on literary texts and the models which have been drawn upon in their analysis, because stylistic analyses have in the main concentrated on literary texts; however, these models of analysis need to be considered when discussing any type of text.

MODELS OF LANGUAGE AND TEXT: IMPLICIT AND EXPLICIT

In stylistic analysis in general, the model of text and language which is used is rarely made explicit. That is, the text itself is assumed to exist in some self-evident state whereby it *contains* meanings which the critic and reader discover or uncover; the critic does not need to explain this to the reader, because it is taken as commonsense knowledge about texts in general which both the reader and the critic share. As I argued in the Introduction, many of the stylistic analyses which have been undertaken have used a text-immanent model of meaning; that is, they have assumed that what the critic 'finds' in the text is located in the text itself, rather than perhaps being more the result of a negotiation between the reader and the text. In a similar way, traditional stylisticians rarely discuss the model of language that they are drawing upon in order to come to their analysis of the text. There are various models of language; for example, language can be seen as a form of information transfer – the most commonsense and simplistic view; language can be viewed as a form of social networking or social bonding, or as the site where power relations are negotiated and enforced; language can also be seen as a set of mutually exclusive choices in a closed system. The fact that there is this diversity of language models is certain to affect the form of the analysis (see Crystal 1988 and Lyons 1981 for a discussion of some of these models).

Furthermore, few stylisticians address the question of why they are using a particular linguistic system. Although the question of which linguistic model is to be used has been an issue in debates around stylistics for the last twenty years, in individual studies of texts it has rarely been considered necessary to state why the critic is using a particular system at all. Because the type of analysis undertaken is assumed to be objective, little attention is paid to questions such as gender, race and class, which, stylisticians assume, would necessarily bias the analysis. Stylistic analysis is thus posed as outside such questions, constituting a 'neutral' form of reading. Feminist linguists and literary critics who would like to engage in linguistic analysis of texts are often torn between the academic respectability which they attain if they use the seemingly scientific methods developed by linguists and stylisticians, and the realization that these methods, rather than producing readings which are neutral, produce analyses which are themselves biased in favour of the value-systems of white middle-class males. Very often feminist critics have drawn upon the same models of language and textuality as patriarchal critics, which leads to fundamental problems in the type of analysis engaged upon, as Deborah Cameron has shown (Cameron 1985).

Critics often do not state why it is that we should be analysing texts at all; the purpose of the analysis is rarely made clear and the function of the critic and the analysis produced by the critic are rarely discussed. We might ask what the reader of the stylistics article or textbook is supposed to do with the knowledge which is produced, since very often there is an underlying assumption that readers are supposed to learn the techniques and skills described in order to be able to come to perform 'better' readings than they currently do. This lack of explicitness about the assumptions an analysis is based upon, is a serious failing in much traditional stylistic work.

It is the aim of this chapter to explore two models of text, one the traditional stylistic model and the other a feminist model of text, to show what differences the choice of model makes on analysis. These are not the only models of text available to stylisticians or feminists, but they exemplify limit-cases of the models drawn upon, and may be seen to represent tendencies in various types of analysis.[2]

CONTRASTING MODELS: A TRADITIONAL MODEL OF TEXT

The first model to be described is a traditional stylistic one, which is based on a model of language and communication used in linguistics. This has been termed the code model of understanding (see Crystal 1988). Here, language is seen as largely about transaction, the exchange of information between two people (see Figure 1).

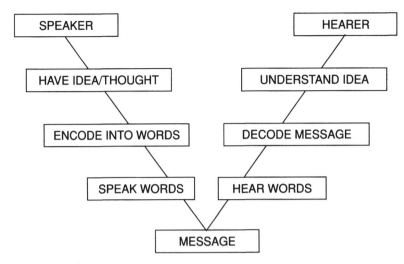

Figure 1 Code model of language

One of the participants, the speaker, has a thought which s/he encodes into words; this message is then transmitted through speech, which the other participant hears and decodes. As Sperber and Wilson point out: 'the view of linguistic communication as achieved by encoding thoughts in sounds is so entrenched in western culture that it has become hard to see it as a hypothesis rather than a fact' (Sperber and Wilson 1986: 6). I would like now to attempt to unearth some of the assumptions underlying this model, since this model implicitly forms the theoretical basis for many theories of literary production. First, it is assumed that thought precedes the production of words and speech, that thought is somehow separate from language and exists outside language. Second, it is assumed that the message which is encoded in language is exactly the same as the message which is decoded, that is, that there are no impediments to communication and there are no misunderstandings. This is an idealized form of communication where words have meaning in an unproblematic and simple way. In the same way that we all assume a shared knowledge for words such as 'table', we are to assume that, within this model, when we say words with more abstract meanings, such as 'democracy' or 'freedom', we can be sure that we will be understood by the hearer as we intended. Third, it is assumed that the normal mode of language-use is between two participants, speaking face to face, one of whom is the speaker and one of whom is the listener. It is fairly obvious that in most conversations, these roles are not so clearly allocated (except for within very stratified power relations, we normally shift from speaker role to hearer role with great facility).[3] Finally, it is assumed that the speaker has perfect control over language and can choose to express whatever s/he wishes; there are no pressures or constraints which the language exerts on what can be said. Language here is seen simply as a transparent medium which is used for the transmission of thoughts or information. The role of the listener is also unproblematic in that she decodes the message and achieves perfect understanding of the information transmitted; her role is essentially passive – she is simply a decoder. (See S. Mills 1991 and LeCercle 1990 for an alternative view.)

There are several problems with this model as is evident from these comments; first, although most people do manage to make some sense of what is said to them, perfect communication is rarely achieved. Most speakers and readers tolerate a remarkable amount of 'fuzziness' in both their production and reception of speech and writing. Second, the listener plays an active role in trying to make sense of what the speaker is saying and makes hypotheses and inferences as the conversation progresses, rather than being a passive recipient of a message from the speaker. Finally, it is clear that speakers produce meanings within the confines of their linguistic system; whilst each speaker has a measure of control over what s/he says, the degree of flexibility and 'freedom' is limited. The linguistic system fixes the parameters of the meanings available to the speaker and hearer.

Whilst it is clear that there are a number of problems with the code model itself, it has often been drawn on in stylistic analysis as an implicit basis for a model of literary texts. According to this model, the text is seen as a repository for the thoughts of an author, who is seen to be an exceptional individual, at the same time as s/he is seen to be partly influenced by the society in which s/he lives (see Figure 2).

Figure 2 Conventional model of text

The author takes on the role of the speaker, and as such is seen as a producer of ideas which are encoded in the text. The role of the reader in this model is passive: she is simply the receiver and decoder of the ideas contained in the text. The text is taken as a given; it is treated as if it existed in its own right and is analysed with little reference to factors or constraints outside it – the socio-economic factors of gender and race, for example. The text is also seen, yet again, as a transparent medium which 'carries' the ideas of the author. Language is recognized as having a material identity only when it is considered by stylis-ticians to be the result of conscious choices on the part of the author to 'play' or experiment with the medium itself. Within this model of text, the author is in control of the material s/he produces, that is, there are patterns and effects within the text which the author decides upon and which it is the job of the stylistician to detect.

In addition to the problems with the code model of communication itself which I have described, there are further problems when this model is used as the basis for a model of literary texts. These concern the implicit assumptions that this model entails when one comes to examine the role of the author, the critic and perhaps most importantly context and the reader. First, the writer is clearly *not* in complete control of her/his material. In larger discourse terms, as Michel Foucault has shown, there are constraints on the way we use language and organize information, which derive from large-scale rules and regulations which are part of the changing nature of discursive formations and structures (Foucault 1972). We do not simply write anything we wish, but we write within the context of those elements which are considered appropriate within our society; all writings which fall outside these parameters are labelled 'mad', 'deviant', or 'unreadable'. As Foucault states: 'On the basis of the grammar and of the wealth of vocabulary available at a given time, there are, in total, relatively few things that are said' (Foucault 1972: 118). Furthermore, as many literary theorists such as Jonathan Culler, Harold Bloom and Roland Barthes have shown, there is a range of literary conventions which structure the possibilities of expression at a given time (Culler 1975; Bloom 1975; Barthes 1977). Authorial choice is made within a limited set of parameters. Not only are there literary conventions which determine, for example, the type of poetry which can be written at a given time (the explicit rules governing the structure and format of a sonnet) but there are also constraints which determine what is a fitting subject for a literary work. That is not to say that authors, like all users of language, do not experiment and play with these conventions, but that individual choice and experimentation are fairly tightly limited by a range of parameters which critics like Foucault have seen it as their task to describe.

A second problem with this model of literary texts is associated with the role of the critic. A linguistic model is simply taken by the stylistician and 'applied' to the text as an aid to interpretation. The analysis is notably small-scale, focusing on words and possibly clauses; rarely does analysis of language go beyond the level of the sentence. As Martin Montgomery states: 'Stylistics has traditionally been concerned pre-eminently with the differences between or within texts, and those differences have commonly been explored in terms of the formal parameters of lexico-grammar' (Montgomery 1988: 2). It is only recently with the advent of discourse stylistics that there seems to be a move in the direction of the analysis of context and the relations between features within texts and extratextual factors (Carter and Simpson 1989; Coupland 1988; Toolan 1992). Discourse stylistics is concerned with descriptions of features within the text which are not limited to relations between clauses. However, I would argue that even discourse stylistics, despite its concern with elements of text larger than the sentence, is saddled with a very traditional model of the text and the critic.

The critic in the traditional stylistic model of text is placed in the position of attempting to describe the intentions of the author in producing the text. However, proving that the writer intended the patterns and effects which the reader succeeds in tracing is impossible. Stanley Fish has argued that, in fact, these patternings, which seem to the stylistician to be so much an inherent part of the text itself and its structure, are largely a result of an analytical process which the reader puts into effect when reading texts which have been labelled 'literary'. This literariness is less something to be found in texts, but rather something we as readers perform on texts, that we find in texts through our reading process (Fish 1980). We might ask therefore what the status of the critic is; is the stylistician simply a more active reader who reads in a more skilled way than the assumed passive reader implied by this model?

A third problem with the model is that there is little reference to context, and even where context – the extratextual – is referred to, it is largely in terms of the processes of production (that is, focused on the author). Stylistic analysis has so far shown itself to be largely uninterested in the world outside the text except for the role of the author who plays a determining role in the production and explanation of the linguistic devices which are 'discovered' in the text. Furthermore, analysis of context rarely includes the role of the reader, which is obviously a more significant factor in the process of interpretation than this model will allow. However, whilst it is important to see the reader as playing a major role in the construction of the meaning of the text, it is not necessary to adopt the type of approach, developed by critics like Stanley Fish, which places the reader in the position of creator of the text, usurping that of the author. (For a discussion of readership, see Chapter 5, and also S. Mills 1994.)

It is because of this difficulty in discussing the extratextual that this type of traditional stylistic analysis is so gender-blind: because the critic cannot, within this framework, discuss factors outside the text – what I have been referring to in a broad sense as context. The very nature of the text and its process of production and reception cannot therefore be described. To give a straightforward example, stylisticians do not ask questions about the status of the text they are analysing in relation to the canon. Most texts focused on in stylistic analyses are canonical – that is, they are drawn from a limited number of texts which are seen to have literary value (for example, D. H. Lawrence, Shakespeare, Pinter, Beckett and so on). Many feminist critics have shown (Moi 1985; Showalter 1978) that women's texts have often been excluded from canonical status, by the process termed phallocentric criticism – that is, texts have been judged according to a set of male-oriented criteria (see Montgomery et al. 1992). This obviously has some effect on the statements that the critic can make about the text in question, since there is an underlying assumption that texts which are of value are most likely to be those which are male-authored (see Battersby 1989 for a discussion of the relation between gender and genius). Within such a model, it is difficult to make statements about gender and textuality, since gender is seen to be a factor which lies outside the text – part of its context – and therefore outside the concerns of reader/critic, and yet assumptions about gender play an important role in the choice of which text to analyse.

Feminist stylistics is a move away from text-immanent criticism to a theorized concern with those factors outside the text which may determine, or interact with, elements in the text. Used in this sense, the term 'context' itself needs revision, since even though gender can be seen as extratextual, it can also be viewed as part of the text, as leaving a *trace* within the text, in much the same way as any other constraint or determinant inevitably leaves a trace on the text. This idea that the productive process leaves traces in the text is formulated by Norman Fairclough: 'The formal properties of a text can be regarded on the one hand as *traces* of the productive process, and on the other hand as *cues* in the process of interpretation' (Fairclough 1989: 24). The assumption that the context of its production will leave signposts on the unglossed text, and that this should be significant to the critic, may sound like a rediscovery of traditional literary criticism's concern with sociohistorical context. However, I wish to present a case for context being handled in a more interesting theoretical way than has so far been the case with the analysis of literary texts. An emphasis on lexical items and the way they interact with their context can help the reader to avoid some of the over-generalized cause–effect relations posited by traditional stylistic critics and also to integrate a concern with gender into her critical practice.

CONTRASTING MODELS: A FEMINIST MODEL OF TEXT

The following model of the text avoids some of the problems described and broadens our definition of context (see Figure 3).[4]

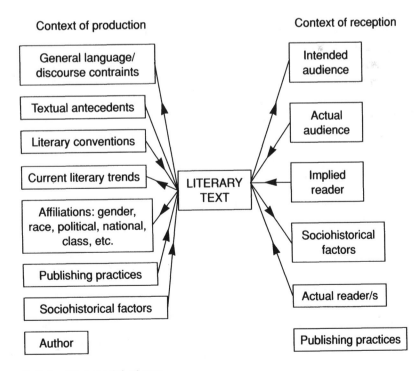

Figure 3 A feminist model of text

There are two facets to context within this model: that of production and that of reception. On the context-of-production side of the model are listed some of the many factors which go into the production of a text, literary and non-literary. First, there are the large-scale general language and discourse constraints, mentioned earlier as limiting the range of ideas which can be expressed within each sociohistorical conjuncture, and also the form which these ideas can take when expressed. Literary conventions governing form, and also choice of language and genre, clearly have considerable influence over the type of text produced. So, for example, the highly stylized poetic forms and lexical choices of the Augustan period were largely discarded in the Romantic period that followed, when the publication (1802) of *The Lyrical Ballads* by Wordsworth and Coleridge marked a shift in ideas about the suitable formal dimensions, appropriate lexis, grammatical structures and content of poetry. Many of these conventions have been made explicit in textbooks which analyse literature (such as Leech 1973) but many more are not fully brought to conscious analysis (see Culler 1975 for the first attempt at analysing conventions in a systematic way). There are clearly literary trends which affect which writers are published and what type of writing is published; writers in the 1990s know that epic poetry is unlikely to be published, whereas novels are marketable commodities. Writers also have a fairly clear notion of what subject-matter is likely to be acceptable to the publishing world at a particular time; serious novels about menstruation are unlikely to be published at the time of writing (1994) by mainstream publishers, neither are analyses of racism.

Another factor on the production side of the model is that of affiliations: the conscious links which individuals make to situate themselves as individuals; for example, as Black, as straight, as a member of a political party, and so on. There is a range of affiliations which an individual writer can make, drawn from the affiliative possibilities which are signalled within each society at the local or the national level. Since the publishing, reviewing and teaching of literature are implicitly informed by the notion of 'this text speaks to us', affiliative statements in the text may signal to 'gatekeepers' of literature that this text is or is not written by one of 'our kind'. This makes a great deal of difference in terms of whether a writer is published, who publishes her/his work, whether the book is reviewed and where it is reviewed.

Publishers particularly in the 1990s can affect the way that books are written, since they can often ask for books to be reworked and they certainly play a major role in the process of editing the text, either at the draft or the final manuscript stage. Publishers have clear ideas about what they can market and are likely to try to fit the works within their 'list' to this notion of what can be sold. Constraints on publishers, because of the nature of multinational ownership of publishing firms by companies whose main interests are not in literature or writing, can also have a great effect, so that profit motives are at the fore in the choice of which authors to engage and which not. Furthermore, the type of publicity which is given to a book will determine to a large extent the way that it is read. Books which mysteriously appear on the Booker prize shortlist are from those which publishers have suggested for inclusion and they are thus marketed to a particular audience with this prize in mind.

Sociohistorical factors can also affect the production of texts, since in times of repression, certain types of writing are more likely to appear; for example, the samizdat publications, or suppressed writings, in the former Soviet Union. Furthermore, in times of high economic inflation, it is more unlikely that minority experimental writing will be subsidized by the publishing industry's profits on bestsellers. The economic, social and cultural background of the production of text is vital to the construction of a text, since so much of the commonsense knowledge of that period is contained in the book either to be unconsciously included by the author or to be resisted. It is not possible to be fully aware of all of the factors which influence what is included in a book, but it is clear that the author is not the determining factor, as has often been assumed. However, the author has a major input in the production of the text; theorists such as Roland Barthes and Michel Foucault have described the 'death of the author' and Foucault has relegated the place of the author to the 'author function', that is, the author is simply that complex of ideas which we as critics of texts use to bind a group of disparate texts together (Barthes 1977; Foucault 1980), but neither of these theorists would assert that the author plays little part in production. Whilst the role of the author has to be set in the context of the range of factors here mentioned, the author has a certain limited range of choices about what can and cannot be resisted or accepted. Texts are not simply repetitions of other texts or reaffirmations of ideological positions.

On the reception side of the model, there is the intended audience, the general community of readers to whom the book will be marketed. In some ways this needs to be also listed under the production side, since it is a factor which is borne in mind by authors and publishers alike. The implied reader of the text is the position to which the text is directed. The implied reader may be a single 'person' or 'position' or it might shift during the course of the work. This projected dialogic 'other' of the text determines the shape and style of the text itself. The actual audience – the people who buy and/or read the book, which may not match the people for whom the book was intended – also exerts pressure on the way that a book is produced and received. For example, books on the Booker prize list may have been intended for a select audience (such seems to be the case with *Possession*, A. S. Byatt's very 'literary' winner of the 1990 prize) but the book may, because of its position on the list, ultimately be read by a very wide range of people. Sociohistorical factors also affect the way that the book is received and read; for example, general trends in buying, lending in libraries and reviewing may determine the availability of books, and also may determine the views that readers have about the books and the readings that they make of the books.

The factors on the side of production should not be seen in isolation from factors on the side of reception; it is clear that there is a complex interchange between the process of production and that of reception, and it is equally clear that the literary text is not simply influenced by these factors. It is a two-way process whereby the text itself determines the type of constraint on production which exerts an influence on future texts.

One question which may be posed is why this model is necessary at all; it seems like an unnecessary problematizing of what is a fairly simple transaction between the author and the reader. First, in the traditional 'code' model, it is not possible to describe the processes of discrimination which affect the way that a text is produced; for example, some female writers may feel constrained to write in particular ways or to write on particular subjects because of what they perceive are society's views of them as women and as writers. Second, in the traditional model, the author is seen to be responsible for what is in the text and therefore if, for example, the text contains elements of sexism, that is simply a problem with the individual author. It is not possible to look at larger processes at work in a wide range of texts. Third, the reader is seen in the traditional model as isolated and as producing an individual response to the text. It is necessary for feminist readers to be able to produce a range of readings which a particular reading community is likely to have, and to see the reader as being offered choices in the hypotheses they formulate about the text. As readers, we are all influenced to a greater or lesser extent by our affiliations to various groups, and the extent to which we perceive ourselves as members of these different groups is a vital aspect of our identity. So while we may all be female, we will perceive ourselves as more or less in other categories too – more or less feminist, more or less trade union members, more or less educated, and so on. We see ourselves as members of ethnic groups, religious groups, class groups, families. Our readings of a text will in part be formed by the extent to which we identify with a variety of possible social categories, and one of the tasks a feminist critic will set herself is to look at how texts cue certain readings for certain readers. For example, Jeanette Winterson's novel *Written on the Body* (1992) has a protagonist of unspecified gender. Readers, however, according to the author, impose gender on the character: women reading the text assume it to be a woman while men reading the text assume the character to be a man.[5] Fourth, for the feminist reader it is important to see the text not as a container of meanings but as a site for negotiation; the language which is used is not in that sense fixed, but rather is a series of potentially ambiguous traces which are left and which the reader then has to interrogate. As I mentioned above, Norman Fairclough uses the notion of traces to describe the formal properties a text possesses as a result of the process of production, and which also act as cues for the reader in the process of interpretation (Fairclough 1989: 24). Fairclough views the productive and interpretative processes as 'an interplay between properties of texts and a considerable range of "member's resources" which people have in their heads and draw upon when they produce or interpret texts – including their knowledge of language, representations of the natural and social worlds they inhabit, values, beliefs, assumptions, and so on' (Fairclough 1989: 24). Thus, rather than the meaning being located within the text, meaning can now be seen to be more of a negotiation between assumed knowledge or members' resources which the author posits that the reader will take for granted.

As feminist readers, therefore, we need two kinds of information to construct the possible readings of a text which might be arrived at. First, we need to make a close textual analysis of the text, identifying certain features of form – literary conventions, syntax, lexis, genre and so on: the cues to interpretation. Second, we need to make some generalized predictions about groups of readers' background knowledge – of language, of literary conventions – and of their models of the world. By uniting these two kinds of information, it should be possible to build up a picture of how specified social groups might read a text. This gives the readers far greater control over their own reading process: the text addresses the reader but the reader can negotiate with that address, by being able to identify which cues – formal properties in the text – are influencing their reading, and what in their own background knowledge is determining their reading. Ideally, the feminist reader will be able to locate other possible readings of the text; this flexibility in reading strategies gives the reader more scope for intervention, since they are now in the position of being able to see *around* their own, and others', reading of the text.

The advantage of this model is that textual production and reception are considered not simply as the context of production, which is the way in which texts are conventionally analysed. Rather the reception of the text is part of context. A second advantage is that the reader's role is given more prominence: it is clear that the reader is addressed by the text, and that s/he is affected by and can influence the interpretation of the text. S/he is an active participant, negotiating with the meanings which are being foisted on to her/him, and resisting or questioning some of those meanings. This is in direct contrast to the passive recipient of the text in Figure 2.

I am not proposing a model of text which is 'open' in Umberto Eco's usage; that is, the text can mean anything and it is totally up to individual readers to impose their meanings upon the text (Eco 1979). The reader is positioned by the text in a range of ways which can be accepted or resisted. If there were no dominant reading/s, that is, no coherent message which the text seems to be offering to the reader in a self-evident way, then there would be no consensus whatsoever as to what texts might mean. Each word, for example, could be taken in its polyvalence, that is, the multiplicity of its potential meanings, and be taken to mean something different by each reader. As readers, we can observe the difference between the way we approach a text which deliberately exploits the polyphony of words, and so defies the reader to find a self-evident, coherent message in it, and a text which is apparently written without questioning the process of the creation of meaning. Let us take two examples to illustrate this point; the first is from Margaret Atwood's *Surfacing* (1979) and the second is from Celia Dale's *A Personal Call* (1986).

I can't believe I'm on the road again, twisting along past the lake where the white birches are dying, the disease is spreading up from the south, and

I notice they now have sea-planes for hire. But this is still near the city-limits; we didn't go through, it's swelled enough to have a bypass, that's success.

(Atwood 1979: 7)

As had been his custom for the thirty-odd years he had been in business, Mr Frederick Peebles bought an evening newspaper at Waterloo. And after successfully battling for a seat he settled down with more than usual satisfaction to digest the day's happenings; for not only was it a dank and nasty November evening, not only was he weary after his day's work, not only was there a full report of Manchester City vs Yorkshire Wanderers, but there was also a double column account on page one of the latest and as yet unsolved murder. And Mr Peebles, mild-mannered, shining-pated little ledger clerk of St Mary Axe, loved a good murder.

(Dale 1986: 33)

This first example, by Atwood, is much more difficult to read, since as readers we find it difficult to make connections and to find the relevance relations between one statement and another. Although each clause is superficially related to the next because it is simply joined to it by a comma or by 'and', in fact the relation between the clauses is not self-evident. For example, we may find it difficult to work out the logical relation between the fact that the narrator is concerned about the spread of a disease affecting birches, and the fact that she observes that there are sea-planes for hire, although these clauses are linked together by 'and'. In a similar way the use of 'But' in the following clause does not seem to set up a relation of contrast, since we are not sure at all what the contrast relates to. Nor for that matter can the reader be sure of who 'we' refers to in the next clause, or whether 'success' is being used here ironically or in a straightforwardly literal way. In short, this opening passage from Atwood's novel sets the reader a number of problems: either we assume that the narrator is deranged and this lack of connection between clauses is a signpost to the reader of this fact, or we might consider this a depiction of a poetic sensibility whereby visual images simply trace a path across the narrator's awareness in a stream-of-consciousness manner. Or we might assume that this passage is setting up problems which the following text will resolve; we therefore store our inability to process the text one way or another to have the problem resolved later in the text.

With the text by Celia Dale the reader is on much safer ground and can interpret in a much more straightforward way. The text sets out a classic paradox (the fact that Peebles is a quiet mild-mannered man who nevertheless enjoys reading about murders) as the opening gambit in a detective plot. We as readers can predict what is going to happen in this story in a way which we cannot do for the Margaret Atwood text. Thus, it is evident that different types of texts can be seen to have different relations to the construction of dominant readings. Although it must be stated that there is a wide range of readings which a text can have, nevertheless the possibilities for dominant readings are certainly not endless. (See Chapter 3 for a full discussion of positioning and dominant readings.)

This feminist model takes into account the interactional nature of the relation between texts and their context. By using such a model, it is possible to discuss the ways in which texts are determined by a wide range of pressures on their processes of production and reception, and also how they have an effect on their audience and on the processes of production of further texts. It is clear that with a more complex model such as this, it becomes more difficult to make the straightforward statements beloved of stylistics. If we consider for a moment the proposition in much stylistics that a particular formal pattern leads the reader to a particular interpretation of a poem, it is possible to see that this assertion is very difficult to justify completely. For example, one proposition which is frequently put forward in much early stylistics work on both prose and poetry is that there are sounds or sound patterns within the text which lead the reader to a particular interpretation. It is important to ask ourselves whether readers register these supposedly onomatopoeic words and phrases, without being cued by the content of the text, and other features of the context. Geoffrey Leech and Michael Short use an example from D. H. Lawrence to demonstrate onomatopoeia: they first cite Lawrence's text and then go on to analyse it:

> 'The small locomotive engine, Number 4, came clanking, stumbling down from Selston with seven full wagons.'
>
> The sense of listening to and 'feeling' the motion of the locomotive is created by a combination of the rhythm (the trochaic regularity of 'clanking, stumbling down from Selston'), the dragging effect of the consonant clusters (/cl/, /nk/, /mbl/, /lst/), and the actual qualities of the consonants them-selves (e.g. the hard effect of the stop consonants /c/, /k/, /t/, /b/).
>
> (Leech and Short 1981: 45)

A full linguistic analysis renders untenable the presumptions which underlie this process of interpretation. First, studies of so-called onomatopoeic sounds in a variety of languages suggest that, in fact, it is very rarely that two separate language communities produce the same lexical item to refer to a non-linguistic sound which exists in both, although members of both speech communities claim that their world is onomatopoeic. Dogs in English, for example, say 'bow wow', but in Japanese say 'wan-wan'. Both items are thought to imitate the noise to which they refer. However, the relationship between the non-linguistic sound and the word used to refer to it, which is naturalized within the speech community, is less apparently onomatopoeic to a non-speaker of the language – as speakers of English are less likely to think 'wan-wan' resembles the noise a dog makes, and presumably Japanese speakers are less likely to recognize 'bow wow' as onomatopoeic. Second, a claim that some formal property of language has a single, self-evident meaning (for example, that consonant clusters have a 'drag-ging' effect) presupposes a direct connection between form and function, which is a position impossible to sustain in the light of work conducted in the field of pragmatics. This type of analysis also presupposes a homogeneous readership, where every reader will find the same meaning in a text as every other, ignoring the differences in interpretation across readers of different cultural backgrounds and political affiliations.

This type of interpretation of sound patterning in texts is emblematic of many other types of stylistic analysis; there are fairly sound pedagogic reasons for doing so, since it is essential to provide workable models of textual analysis which can be replicated on a wide range of other texts. In this sense, the need to teach skills to students overrides the fundamental theoretical problems which are entailed with assuming that certain meanings are contained within the texts and certain elements in the text lead to a single interpretation.

Instead, therefore, of general claims about the 'meanings' of texts, more modest statements can be made about, for example, the way that the text might be addressing the reader and the limits of resisting that address, or the associations which seem to be presented in a text which might be determined by certain discursive constraints and pressures. Within this more theorized model, the critic is more concerned with charting a range of possible readings which the text negotiates with a reader and which that reader accepts or resists.

The literary text in this feminist model is quite different from that often used by traditional stylisticians. In this model, the integrity of the text has been breached; by that I mean that the text no longer has such clear boundaries (it is no longer always obvious what is part of the text and what is not). If the way that the text is constructed is partly a result of factors out of the control of the author, it is more difficult to state clearly what is *in* the text and what falls outside. Thus, gender is clearly outside the text and yet it is also very much a part of its integral structure. This difficulty is signposted clearly in the model in Figure 3 by the fact that the arrow leads in two directions, both to and from the context and literary text; these signal the bidirectional relationship between context and text, that is, the text is not simply the product of a sociohistorical context and the author, but rather the text in fact asserts itself upon the author and upon the context. Similarly, the context of reception will assert itself upon that of production and upon the text itself. If a community of readers decides to read a text in a particular way, the meaning of the text will have changed in some sense; thus, Kate Millett's famous intervention into reading D. H. Lawrence's work, where she foregrounded the sexism of the depiction of female characters, has irrevocably changed the meaning of that text for countless readers, even if they do not agree with the reading she has proposed (Millett 1977). Similarly, those texts which are bought by many readers will have an effect on the way that texts are marketed in the future and which texts it is thought will be successful.

This is not a model of texts which all feminists will agree upon, nor is there something intrinsically feminist about it. However, it is one which a number of feminists use, if only implicitly, because of their dissatisfaction with conventional models which limit the ways we can talk about reading texts. This model simply offers a structure within which to view a considerable amount of work which has been done by feminist theorists. It makes space for the possibility, and in fact the necessity, of integrating notions of gender, race and class, and also socio-historical and economic factors, into the analysis, and indeed into the definition of the text itself. This model is one influenced by current poststructuralist literary theory, and is one which has greater explanatory power. By taking into account the determinants of a text's construction and the constraints on a text's reception, it will be possible to analyse the language of a text in a more productive way.[6] This model is particularly open to gendered analysis – it helps to explain, for example, why it is that women's writing is read in a certain way, why some women writers use similar language and why certain features of a text produce a gendered address to the reader. Rather than assuming, for example, that all women write in a similar way, because they are women, and using the discovery of similar metaphorical patterns in some women's writing to justify this claim (see Horner and Zlosnick 1990), the critic might consider what factors in the production and reception context might lead the reader to trace similar factors in women's texts. For example, it is the case in 1990s' reviewing and publishing that women's texts are grouped together, whereas men's writing is not, or at least not grouped under the conceptual heading 'men's writing'. This leads to a tendency in critical writing to consider women's writing as formally distinct and to focus on those factors which justify such an argument (see Chapter 2 for a fuller discussion of gender and writing). This questioning of the process of reception of texts may move the analysis away from essentialist notions that men and women write in fundamentally different ways, and rather focus attention upon the factors in the context which might lead to their work being marketed and read in different ways; this may in turn lead to a move towards analysing men's writing or specific groups of women's writing.

This book intends to exemplify this model of text to feminist ends. The difference in the model used can be seen even to have a bearing on the role of the analyst her/himself. Where the traditional stylistician tends to efface his or her presence, the feminist foregrounds herself, drawing attention to the political necessity of this type of analysis. Stylisticians rarely make clear why they are doing an analysis. Feminist critics usually have a very clear idea of why feminist analysis must be done and why it is necessary to develop tools to do so; since, as I mentioned in the Introduction, feminists are concerned not only to analyse texts but to change social relations through that analysis and through other forms of action. Feminist text analysis, like critical linguistics, can develop into a form of consciousness-raising, a 'making aware' of that which seems to be self-evidently normal or neutral, a 'making strange' of the ordinary, and forcing readers to re-examine the text in the light of a consideration of gender. For those who work in educational institutions, this is an essential part of our task as teachers and lecturers, that we attempt not only to impart skills in text analysis which are of interest in themselves, but also to make students aware of or enable them to describe effects in texts for whose description they previously lacked the vocabulary. In this sense, feminist stylistics is not simply an academic exercise, it is primarily political; a way of empowering people so that they are not the dupes of texts, so that they can analyse texts and in that analysis become aware of some of the factors which work on all individuals in the present society (for a full discussion see S. Mills 1991, on feminism and institutions).

As an example to illustrate the difference between the two models, consider the text on page 41. This text appeared in the *Sun* newspaper during the Gulf crisis in January 1991. All of the semi-nude models who were used by the *Sun* during this period appeared wearing some form of military uniform. It is highly unlikely that a conventional stylistician would include this text for analysis, although certain other stylisticians have concentrated on the analysis of texts from other media (Fairclough 1989; Fowler 1991). A conventional analysis of this text using the traditional first model would simply discuss the word-play in the text, drawing attention to the constant punning on military and sexual lines (the references to 'train your sights', 'cruise', 'striking', 'fully equipped', 'frontal assault', 'desert storm', 'sure-fire', etc.). The critic might concern herself with discussing *doubles entendres*, and the linkage between references to breasts and euphemisms within the text ('frontal assault', 'fully equipped', 'at the front', etc.).[7] This analysis would assume that these meanings are in the text itself and are simply waiting for the stylistician to analyse them. Using the feminist model of text, it would be necessary to perform a more complex and intensive analysis of the text. First, the history of Page Three 'girls' would have to be taken into account; that is, the way that these images are often a form of display of solidarity amongst certain males – they are frequently consumed and discussed within group contexts. The critic would also have to consider the way that humour is very often used to defuse a potentially difficult or taboo subject (see Chapter 5 on sexism and humour). In this sense the humour is less self-evident, but something which is determined by the context. Rather than simply taking offence at this representation and its supposed humour (although that is not to say that offence is not a valid response), the feminist theorist would examine the ways that this text has been produced to make sense. It is only comprehensible or coherent with reference to a larger social construction of a male sexual obsession with women's breasts (see, for example, so-called soft pornography such as *Mayfair*, *Penthouse*, etc.) and to the way that the sight of breasts is here positioned as being linked in some way to the Gulf conflict, as a form of 'support' for the soldiers. The feminist reader might also draw on the notion of 'logonomic system' developed by Hodge and Kress (1988). A logonomic system is 'a set of rules prescribing the conditions for the production and reception of meaning' (Hodge and Kress 1988: 4). They suggest that there are larger systems of meaning-production which determine the way that individual statements are produced and the way that we as readers are expected to decode them and receive them. In the case of statements about women, Hodge and Kress state: 'when a logonomic system allows a statement offensive to women to be read as "a joke", this signifies a particular structure of gender relations, one in which males are dominant as a group in relation to females but need to mask their hostility and

aggression towards them' (Hodge and Kress 1988: 5; see Chapter 6 for a fuller discussion on larger frameworks).

The theorist would also examine the ways that the text attempts to force the reader to collude in the production of this knowledge as self-evidently natural, as in the use of questions which the reader is supposed to be asking/being asked; for example, 'Cruise a lovely girl, then?'. Rhetorical questions invite the reader to participate either in posing the question, or in supplying the answer, which the text constructs as self-evident. In this case, the dominant reading is obviously that Gaynor Goodman is a lovely girl. In supplying this answer, the reader is adopting what Fowler calls the public idiom of the newspaper – that is, the newspaper style is a 'copy' of the type of language the reader is supposed to use (Fowler 1991). The woman's first name is also used – Gaynor – as if 'we' know this person and this seeming intimacy functions as a form of power relation (see the discussion of T/V forms in Chapter 4). This woman is presented as 'ours' – 'ours' here functions inclusively, implying a homogeneous group comprising the people who produce the newspaper and the readers, although female readers must find their relationship to this 'our' strange, to say the least. Inclusive 'our' also appears in the phrase 'our brave boys'; once the 'our' has been accepted by the reader, the braveness of the soldiers has to be accepted. The term 'boys' also draws on the ethos of 'matey solidarity', involving readers in a spirit of camaraderie and encouraging them to regard the actions of these men as playful, as if they were indeed boys. The use of 'your' in the headline and the phrase 'any fella with intelligence' also address the male reader and make him part of the collusive message. The male reader, in much the same way as the female reader, does not necessarily have to collude with the type of representational practices and language used here, but he is certainly encouraged to do so. The overall cohesion of the text, produced by devices such as the lexical collocations with warfare (all the words which are associated with arms and fighting), and the repeated references to the model, means that the different forms of address – first person 'our', second person 'your', third person 'any fella' – can all be read as referring to the reader. The gaze of the model also directly addresses the reader in a way which, in the context of this type of representation, is interpreted as sexually inviting. This look could be interpreted in a wide range of ways (for example, as forceful, as assertive) but because of the context, it will probably be assumed to be sexual.

The feminist stylistician, drawing on this model of text, would also look outside the text itself to the context in which this text is consumed. She would examine the way that the text is used as a form of male bonding amongst certain sectors of the male population, so that the representation is not generally read by isolated individuals, but often forms part of male leisure talk, being the focus of comments about the merits of this particular model in relation to other Page Three 'girls'. Thus the representation itself serves as a vehicle for the establishing of relations of friendship and status; as Dorothy Smith argues, newspaper and magazine texts themselves are often central in the process whereby we affirm and contest our adoption of the roles of masculinity and femininity (Smith 1990). The feminist critic might also examine the way that the text is authored so that it is significant that the author's name is not given; we assume that it was written by a group of writers or that the skill in producing the text was not sufficient to consider including the name of the writer; whereas the photographer is named.

For the feminist theorist, this text need not be forced to make sense, in the way that most stylistic analysis assumes that analyses of texts, just like texts themselves, need to be coherent – in fact, it is its incoherence as text which is most interesting. Humour in this newspaper is often a result of extended metaphors which are not logical under sustained analysis. The phrase 'Cruise a lovely girl, then?' makes little sense if the reader ignores the word-play and tries to extract a literal meaning. Interpretation depends on the reader recognizing the phrase 'Who's a lovely girl then' – a phrase which might be more suitably addressed to a budgerigar than a woman – and supplying that phrase while simultaneously superimposing on it 'cruise' (as in missile), a rhyming word from the lexicon of war. Similarly, 'train your sights on our Gaynor' is a phrase generally used in the context of aiming a gun at a target or victim. Here perhaps more than at other places the mixture of references to war and references to sexual activity is most incongruous.

If analysed in detail, the meanings of particular items become less self-evident. The text's primary purpose is entertainment of male readers, rather than information-transfer, and its referential meaning is ambiguous or obscure (for further analysis of page three, see, for example, Davies *et al.* 1987 and Gamman and Marshment 1988). Standard stylistic procedure would involve identifying and quantifying the language elements contained within the text. As theorists, it is more interesting to explore how the meaning of the text depends on the knowledge of certain catch-phrases, the assumption that sex and warfare can be somehow connected, and the readers' ability to slot themselves into or resist the various forms of address.

Thus, it is clear from the analysis of this text that the choice of a model of language and textuality is not simply a question which is of theoretical interest, but is also important in terms of the type and scale of the analysis which is made. The type of analysis which feminist models of text allow is of greater complexity and explanatory power than those conventionally used in stylistics. Whilst stylistics is clearly in the process of developing new ways of analysing texts, it is to be hoped that an awareness of the model of text which is used in analysis will aid stylisticians to ask themselves questions about their own practice and to develop more theoretically challenging analyses of texts, particularly in relation to gender.

Chapter 2

The Gendered Sentence

One of the debates which is of long standing within feminist literary analysis is concerned with whether women writers produce texts which are significantly different in terms of language from those of males.[1] This debate began with the work of Virginia Woolf when she asserted that there was a sentence which women writers had developed which she termed the 'female sentence' or the 'sentence of the feminine gender' (Woolf 1929 [1966]). For Woolf, certain women writers crafted a new type of sentence which is looser and more accretive than the male sentence. This view that women's writing is fundamentally different from men's seems to be echoed in the more recent statements by French feminists such as Luce Irigaray and Hélène Cixous (Irigaray 1985; Cixous 1976). Both Woolf and some French feminists assert that there is a difference between men's and women's writing, but their discussions frequently remain at a rather abstract level, since they rarely give concrete examples.

In this chapter, I aim to examine this question of whether there is a gendered sentence. First, I consider work by linguists into whether women's speech is different from men's to draw an analogy with work on writing. Then I consider the analyses by Woolf, Cixous and Irigaray which propose that there is a 'women's writing' which is distinct from 'men's writing' and then I examine the work which has been done by linguists, which attempts to prove that male writing and female writing are different in terms of their formal linguistic constituents. Then, drawing on Monique Wittig's work, I question the notion that men and women write in substantially different ways. But rather than simply dismiss the notion of gender as a determinant in textual production, I consider Sandra Gilbert and Susan Gubar's term 'female affiliation complex' to describe the way in which we might divide women writers into those who consciously align themselves with a main-stream/malestream tradition and those who are attempting to align themselves with a female 'minority' tradition (Gilbert and Gubar 1988; Deleuze and Guattari 1986). This affiliative difference can be traced in a number of textual cues which appear in the text and seems to be a way in which women can consciously situate their texts as female-authored. Finally, I consider the fact that women's writing is judged in a different way from men's writing and this is amongst the factors which may account for the notion of clear-cut difference between women's and men's writing.

It is rare that Virginia Woolf and French feminists are discussed together, but I would argue that their assumptions about language, writing and gender are surprisingly similar, and the elisions which they make, although in different terms, result in a similar confusion about sexual/gender difference and writing.[2] A great deal of theoretical work has been predicated on defining the female/feminine in terms of lack in relation to the male/masculine. This is certainly true when the female sentence is discussed. Most theorists have focused on descriptions of the female sentence alone, as if the male sentence were an implicit norm. This practice of describing things associated with women as if they were deviant from a male norm can be termed phallocentric (see Ellman 1968 for a full discussion). Phallocentrism is the practice of placing the male at the centre of theoretical models, and assuming that 'male' is in fact coterminous with 'human'. As Monique Wittig says: 'There are not two genders. There is only one: the feminine; the masculine not being a gender. For the masculine is not the masculine but the general' (Wittig 1983: 2).

WOMEN'S SPEECH?

It might be useful, at this point, to consider an example of phallocentrism in linguistic research on women's speech. Many theorists, both feminists and anti-feminists, have attempted to prove that women speak in a different way from men (note again that men are the norm and women defined in relation to them); women's speech is thus seen as a deviation from the norm: the human, i.e. the male. Even in descriptions of languages other than English, such as Koasati, where men lack certain vocabulary items which women use, the issue is still discussed in terms of women's language being deviant (see Cameron 1985 and Cameron 1990a). Much of the early research on speech by liberal feminists, such as Robin Lakoff (1975), and radical feminists, such as Dale Spender (1980), attempted to prove that women in fact speak quite differently from men, that there is such a thing as a 'women's language', a sex-preferential usage or genderlect which is determined by the power difference between males and females. Lakoff and Spender characterize women's speech as more hesitant, less fluent, less logical, less assertive than men's speech. Women, in their view, are more silent, interrupt less frequently than men, use tag-questions and modal verbs more than men, use co-operative strategies in conversations rather than competitive ones, and so on.[3] It is interesting to note that this type of research has never defined, except by implication, the male norm from which female speech is supposed to deviate.[4]

More recent work by feminist linguists such as Deborah Cameron (1985) and Jennifer Coates (1986) has shown that in the sort of research just mentioned, feminists simply followed the ground-rules laid down by male linguists before them. They implicitly accepted that research into sex difference should try to prove that women are, in fact, inadequate males. Cameron says: 'Many sex difference studies are simply elaborate justifications of female subordination' (Cameron 1985: 50). The findings of many of these studies have since been questioned; it would seem that these researchers simply concentrated on data which confirmed their preconceptions and ignored evidence which suggested that male speech also contains elements of hesitancy, deference and irrationality. Another important flaw in this type of research is that where specifically female elements can be identified in speech, they will usually be classified negatively. Thus, Peter Trudgill, based on his work analysing dialect usage in a working-class community in East Anglia, asserts that British working-class women attempt to use language elements from a higher class position than their own and can therefore be classified as essentially conservative in their speech habits; working-class males, however, maintain dialect-use more and attain 'covert prestige' through this usage (Trudgill 1972). Here the interesting factor is that male language-use is classified in a positive way and female usage is classified negatively. In Madagascar, however, where the men are seen as linguistically conservative, conservatism magically transforms into a positive quality (see Cameron 1985: 50 for a full discussion). Deborah Cameron suggests that in many sociolinguistic studies, sexism is operating at the level of hypothesis formation and at the level of interpretation of the results (see Chapter 3 on sexism). In this type of linguistic analysis, phallocentrism is clearly at work, whereby male speech is considered to be positive or the norm and women's speech is classified as deviant. This is analogous to the situation which obtains in the analysis of women's writing.

FEMALE SENTENCE/*ECRITURE FÉMININE*

To turn now to the male and female sentence in literature, I will first discuss the views of Virginia Woolf, as she has perhaps defined the terms within which the debate has been argued, and she is also one of the first to describe the female sentence in positive terms. She states that

> it is still true that before a woman can write exactly as she wishes to write, she has many difficulties to face. To begin with, there is the technical difficulty – so simple apparently; in reality, so baffling – that the very form of the sentence does not fit her. It is a sentence made by men; it is too loose, too heavy, too pompous for a woman's use. Yet in a novel, it covers so wide a stretch of ground, an ordinary and usual type of sentence has to be found to carry the reader on easily and naturally from one end of the book to the other. And this a woman must make for herself, altering and adapting the current sentence until she writes one that takes the natural shape of her thought without crushing or distorting it.
>
> (Woolf in Cameron 1990a: 37)

Here, Woolf seems to be prefiguring Dale Spender's statement that language is literally 'man-made', that somehow women cannot fit their ideas and expressions into a language which has been constructed according to the needs of males (Spender 1980). Therefore, for Woolf it is necessary that women craft their own type of language. When writing about Dorothy Richardson, Woolf claims that Richardson invented 'the psychological sentence of the feminine gender' (Woolf in Cameron 1990a: 72). She defines this female sentence as 'of a more elastic fibre than the old, capable of stretching to the extreme, of suspending the frailest particles, of enveloping the vaguest shapes' (Woolf 1965: 204–5).

Woolf also suggests that the male sentence was insufficient for women writers: the example of the male sentence which Woolf gives is 'The grandeur of their works was an argument with them not to stop short but to proceed'. Here Woolf seems to be arguing that males write in a more formal mode than women, using nominalizations (grandeur, argument) rather than verbs or adjectives; the parallel phrasing of 'not to'/'but to' also has a very formal feel to it. It is also a very impersonal statement partly because of the use of nominalizations which lead to the omission of agency. However, Woolf's analysis of this sentence as male seems to be confusing the public/formal sphere with maleness, and although the two are often elided, it is important to recognize that it is formality that she is locating and not a gender difference.[5]

However, Woolf's position on the gendered sentence is ambiguous, for whilst stating that there is such a thing as the 'female sentence', and praising Emily Brontë and Jane Austen for using it, she also condemns Charlotte Brontë for writing as a woman. She says: 'It is fatal for anyone who writes to think of their sex' (Woolf 1977: 99). She suggests that writing about one's sex in anger at inequality leads to poor writing: Shakespeare was great, as he 'had no desire to protest, to preach, to proclaim an injury, to pay off a score' (Woolf 1977: 99). It is a fairly widely held view that writing should be androgynous or sexless; for example, as Joyce Carol Oates states: 'If there is a distinctly "female voice" – if there is a distinctly "male" voice – surely this is symptomatic of inferior art? Of course the serious artistic voice is one of individual *style* and it is sexless' (Oates 1986: 208). Here, both Woolf and Oates seem to propose an androgyny or a sexlessness for the good writer which is in essence male.[6] In considering Woolf's view of the differences between the male sentence and the female sentence, it is interesting to consider what she says about how women *should* write. The standard which Woolf suggests women should be aiming for could be interpreted as that of the stereotypical male sentence: 'She will write in a rage where she should write calmly. She will write foolishly where she should write wisely. She will write of herself where she should write of her characters. She is at war with her lot' (Woolf 1977: 99). That is, the supposedly neutral but in fact male sentence is implicitly described as calm, wise and apparently objective and impersonal.

The difference in type between these sentences is due in part to sentence structure but it must be noted that Dorothy Richardson's style is very much a product of her time and of avant-garde writing in general. When Woolf describes the female sentence it seems to be less a matter of style or language and more a question of content and subject-matter. A further ambiguity, which she shares with some of the French feminists, is that she states that men can in fact use this type of sentence too. At other points in her writing she suggests that the best type of writing is androgynous, not sexless but bisexual writing, which, as we will see, is very close to the position of Hélène Cixous.

Turning now to the French feminists, it is interesting to note how, even though they are working within an entirely different theoretical framework, they have still reached a position similar to Woolf's. Many French feminists work in the tradition of, and in reaction to, Jacques Lacan's theoretical work. As Ann Rosalind Jones remarks: 'Lacanian theory reserves the "I" position for men. Women because they lack the phallus, the positive symbol of gender, self-possession and worldly authority around which language is organised, occupy a negative position in language' (Jones 1985: 83). Feminists such as Hélène Cixous consider that this negative position in language can be celebrated; they term this position *écriture féminine*. Hélène Cixous reacted against the Lacanian idea of women as lack, and asserted women as plenitude, turning qualities assigned to women by society, such as hesitation and irrationality, into virtues. She stresses the multiple physical capacities of women: gestation, birth, lactation, etc.; and she has also elaborated the notion of a specifically female writing which reflects this multiplicity. Her definition of *écriture féminine* is essentially reactive, as she is recuperating an earlier derogatory definition of it which encompassed women writers who wrote about women's experience in a way which did not challenge French male stereotypes. It is these qualities of writing, the subjective and the formless, which are often the ones which men desire in women's writing and in women, but would not want for themselves. (See for a discussion of some of Cixous' ideas Helen Wilcox *et al.* (eds) *The Body and the Text* [1990]).

In some ways, by transforming this male definition of *écriture féminine* we are still trapped within the notion of women's language being deviant, powerless and submissive, and male language being normal, no matter how much we assert the contrary. However, this type of language is seen by Cixous in an entirely positive light, as being revolutionary. As she says: 'we are living through [the] very period when the conceptual foundation of a millennial culture is in the process of being undermined by millions of species of mole as yet not recognised' (Cixous 1981b: 93). These moles referred to here can be taken to be the women who are slowly eroding the fixed ideas and even sentence structures of patriarchy through subversive writing. She goes on to say 'The [political] economy of the masculine and the feminine is organised by different requirements and constraints, which, when socialised and metaphorised, produce signs, relations of power, relationships of production and of reproduction, an entire immense system of cultural inscription readable as masculine or feminine' (Cixous 1981b: 93). She states that if there were changes in these structures of political economy, there would also be changes in what we consider masculine and feminine, so she is not, as she at first appears, attributing unchanging categories of behaviour and character to females.

Cixous, like Luce Irigaray, has achieved a fusion of the critical and the creative in her own writing, putting *écriture féminine* into practice: in this *mélange*, she uses the dreams of her students, the journals of patients in psychoanalysis and liturgical passages. However, she says: 'It is impossible to *define* a feminine practice of writing, for this practice can never be theorised, enclosed, encoded – which doesn't mean that it doesn't exist. But it will always surpass the discourse that regulates the phallocentric system' (Cixous 1981a: 253). In her later writing Cixous shifts her position slightly so that, like Woolf, she states that men and women can both write this type of feminine sentence, but that women are more likely to use it. She says that writing must be bisexual (which recalls Woolf's notion of androgyny): 'There is no invention of other I's, no poetry, no fiction without a certain homosexuality' (Cixous 1981b: 97).

Luce Irigaray employs many elements of Lacanian psychoanalysis in her work. She describes women's writing as *parler femme*: 'her language in which "she" goes off in all directions and in which "he" is unable to discern the coherence of any meaning. Contradictory words seem a little crazy to the logic of reason, and inaudible for him who listens with ready-made grids, a code prepared in advance' (Irigaray 1985: 103). Again, we can see a recuperation of qualities which are attributed to women by men. She believes that women are able to use this type of language because, as she says, our sexual morphology is multiple and based on contiguity, in contrast to male sexuality which is unitary; thus she locates the difference in writing. She states: 'One must listen to her differently in order to hear an "other meaning" which is constantly in the process of weaving itself, at the same time ceaselessly embracing words and yet casting them off to avoid becoming fixed, immobilized. . . . Her statements are never identical to anything. Their distinguishing feature is contiguity. They touch *upon*' (Irigaray 1985: 84).

Irigaray herself has turned from writing on philosophy and psychoanalysis to writing short experimental prose passages; she is opposed to the authoritarian subject/object division of conventional syntax; she leaves out verbs, making her style almost telegraphic in structure; her writing is full of puns: for example, the title of one article is 'Ce Sexe qui n'en est pas un' ('This sex which is not *one* sex', i.e. which is multiple, but also 'This sex which is not a sex at all'). The structure of her texts is repetitive, cumulative rather than linear, using double or multiple voices, often ending without full closure.

Julia Kristeva, like Cixous and Irigaray, works from within an essentially Lacanian framework, but she is strongly opposed to the notion of *écriture féminine*. Nevertheless, she uses the term 'the semiotic' to refer to the pre-linguistic stage of development of the child; the semiotic is an area of rhythmic pulsions in active opposition to the symbolic, the stable system of language. The semiotic is described as anarchic and as an area of rhythm, colour and play in language. The semiotic breaks through into the symbolic from time to time; for example, in poetic writing. The semiotic is associated with the pre-Oedipal stage of unity with the mother, and is repressed into the unconscious on entering the symbolic order of the Father, the Law. Kristeva thinks that women, because they do not have a proper place within the symbolic, have a special relationship with the semiotic. Thus, although she rejects *écriture féminine*, women, for her, still have a privileged access to the semiotic, and are more likely to exploit this in writing. (For a discussion of the problems of a Kristevan position in analysing avant-garde writing, see S. Mills 1989b.) It is, therefore, rather paradoxical that when studying the rupture of the semiotic in literature, she studies male writers such as Céline, Mallarmé and Lautréamont. Perhaps we can understand this when she suggests that this type of writing is available to all speaking subjects prepared to take on bisexuality: 'All speaking subjects have within themselves a certain bisexuality which is precisely the possibility to explore all the sources of signification, that which posits a meaning as well as that which multiplies, pulverises and finally revives it' (Kristeva 1981: 165). This seems very similar to statements by Woolf, Cixous and Irigaray which attempt to state that women's writing is different from men's, whilst being unable to ignore the fact that men have written in this experimental fashion, and have perhaps been more renowned for this type of writing than women. This is not to suggest that women have not written in an experimental way, and in fact this type of analysis can be used when analysing their writing.[7]

Kristeva believes that the use of the semiotic in literature is potentially revolutionary for she says: 'To the extent that any activity resists the symbolic (or in the case of semiotic signifying, occupies it in a hit and run fashion), it is revolutionary' (Kristeva 1981: 166). Thus, in the same way as Irigaray and Cixous, she holds that significant political action can be undertaken in language itself. And she goes on to say: 'In a culture where the speaking subjects are conceived of as masters of their speech, they have what is called a "phallic" position. The fragmentation of language in a text calls into question the very posture of this mastery' (Kristeva 1981: 166). Thus, for Kristeva, the invoking of the semiotic in literature will shake the foundations of this phallic position.

To sum up what I have said about Woolf and the French feminists, it is possible to see that all of them begin with a position of stating that female writing is radically different from male writing in terms of linguistic structure and content. None of them, however, with the exception of Woolf, really goes on to define the male sentence as such. Woolf gives one example of the male sentence but does not describe its linguistic components in general. The French feminists give no examples, and do not define the male sentence, assuming perhaps that it is a commonsense 'naturalized' category to which we all have access. They all also state that male writers can use the female sentence when they have achieved a form of bisexuality or androgyny. They give no guidelines on situations when or if women can use the male sentence. Finally, they do not make clear whether this use of a 'feminine' sentence is part of unconscious processing to which all women have access or whether its use is a conscious artistic decision.

LINGUISTIC ANALYSES OF DIFFERENCE

There have been a number of linguistic analyses which have tried to test empirically claims that women and men have different styles of writing. Mary

Hiatt chose to focus on a range of elements which it is claimed differentiate women's writing from men's (Hiatt 1977). However, throughout her analysis of one hundred passages from popular fiction and non-fictional writing, Hiatt consistently confuses content analysis and linguistic analysis, and bases her analysis largely on stereotypes of what women are supposed to be like. For example, she states that 'The aim of . . . women apparently is to please, to be charming, witty and amusing. This aim can fairly be said to be a manifestation of approval-seeking behaviour of which women in general are accused. They "win" by cajoling, a subtle sort of seductiveness, by pretending that they aren't serious' (Hiatt 1977: 24). This interpretation of her results is clearly informed by phallocentrism. She asserts that in her set of passages from books by males and females, she found that there were significant differences between the writing styles. For example, she states that women writers in general use shorter sentences, which she assumes are structurally less complex than longer sentences – a value-judgement in itself. She goes on to claim that, because of a perceived lack of variety in sentence length, 'fewer of the female writers possess a noteworthy style than do their male counterparts' (Hiatt 1977: 32) and, although she claims that the female fiction writer's style is in fact complex and varied, 'their stylistic complexity is far less individualized than is that of the men. Perhaps it is just that they do not "dare" as does a Mailer' (Hiatt 1977: 34). Here, Hiatt is confusing an analysis of the feminine with an analysis of the female, in that what she seems to be describing is a style of writing which *could* be categorized as feminine and which only a limited number of women writers actually employ.

   In addition to sentence length, she analyses the frequency of use of exclamation marks and parenthetical statements, both of which she assumes would be stereo-typically more characteristic of female writing. Finding that the women writers in her sample use parenthesis more frequently than the men, she interprets this in the following way: 'if parentheses indicate non-essential material, then the women non-fiction writers certainly seem to feel that more of what they have to say is in a sense disposable' (Hiatt 1977: 45). She also considers logical connectives such as 'however', 'because', 'so', etc. On the basis of this evidence, she argues that women use a less authoritative style than men. In her discussion on the type of adverbs used by men and women she states: 'There is an apparent active quality to the men's fiction as opposed to the emotive quality of the women's' (Hiatt 1977: 99). She claims that women use 'really' more often than men, and this she states is indicative of a lack of assertiveness; however, one might be led to ask whether an over-use of 'really' might not indicate an excess of assertiveness (especially if it had occurred within men's writing). She concludes by asking:

> One might ask *why* is the way women write more moderate, consistent and evenhanded than the way men write? The chief reason is doubtless that women are a minority group, more likely to conform than to dare. . . . Under the circumstances, it is to be expected that they seem at times unsure

that anyone will believe them, reluctant to arrive at conclusions, a bit over-determined to present a cheerful face.

(Hiatt 1977: 136)

She goes on to say: 'The women's style is also more perceptive than that of the men [since] they are denied access to a world of actions' (Hiatt 1977: 137). However, before accepting Hiatt's arguments that on linguistic grounds there are clear distinctions to be made between male and female writing, it must be noted that Hiatt frequently overinterprets on the basis of minimal differences in style, and frequently labels elements which she feels occur within women's writing as negative. (See Cameron 1990b for a useful discussion of the interpretation of results in sociolinguistics.) Similarly, she does not consider that her categorization of texts into male and female might be at all problematic. Feminist theory has been concerned in the last twenty years with the differences within the term 'woman', far more than it has been concerned with making global statements about 'woman'. (For a review of these developments see S. Mills 1992d; S. Mills and Pearce 1993; Fuss 1990; and Butler 1990.)

Susan Leonardi is another critic who has analysed the gendered sentence in terms of its language components, this time in relation to Woolf's fictional writing; she shows that the gendered sentence can be analysed in terms of sentence structure/syntax, subject-matter, completion and logic or reference. In terms of sentence structure, Leonardi says that Woolf wanted to reject the man's sentence which she defines as 'the hierarchical sentence of the literary tradition she inherited, a sentence which, with its high degree of subordination, makes so clear the judgement about what is more important and what is less' (Leonardi 1986: 151). David Tallentire (1986) has carried out a statistical analysis of Woolf's writing and found that she does not use subordinate clauses frequently. Her writing can be characterized by the use of co-ordination, primarily 'and'. This is quite interesting, since co-ordination is considered to be a less sophisticated way of organizing text.[8] Woolf defines the male sentence as a hierarchical sentence in terms of its structure, and as Leonardi says: 'The hierarchical sentence is a kind of metaphor for an ordered world, for ordered relationships in general' (Leonardi 1986: 151). Thus, the male sentence is seen as a sentence which contains subordinate clauses, but the explanation given for the effect of these clauses is one of hierarchizing and ordering. We might be able to find examples of the female sentence, full of subordination, where the subordination could be interpreted as refusing closure, endlessly deferring an authoritative statement, and therefore it is clearly not sentence structure which is really at issue here, but interpretative schemata.

Leonardi also asserts that in Woolf's prose there is a lack of completion which she takes to be a feature of the female sentence. Yet when we even discuss the notion of the sentence we are talking in terms of completion, which creates an immediate contradiction. There are perhaps other ways of classifying language which are not concerned with the notion of units being complete in this way.

Leonardi also alludes to a common assumption about women's writing: that there is a lack of rationality and authority. The female sentence is often seen to be one where the writer simply pours out her feelings into the text; women's writing is often characterized as the outpouring of the soul, without the mediation of a structure or plan (see Battersby 1989). Control is an important element in defining the male sentence, as one of its primary characteristics is that the writer chose to include a certain element and could have chosen to express himself in a different way. Thus, male modernist writers could also write critical 'masculine' essays about their 'feminine' writing, showing that their 'feminine' writing was a matter of conscious choice. Yet, this assumes that women do not write in a rational, controlled way and that their writing is not a matter of choice. Mary Ellman even criticizes Simone de Beauvoir for 'the authority of her prose' (Ellman 1968: 212). However much we attempt to 'deconstruct' the rational, and logic, it seems rather counterproductive to suggest that the rational is allied to maleness and hence out of bounds for females. The male sentence is therefore seen to be one which is clear and rational, where the author appears to have control. This type of sentence is typically seen as an assertion, appealing to authority. Yet, are these in fact characteristics of sentences, or are they rather elements of the ideological stereotype of males in our society?

A further point which Leonardi points to is subject-matter; many critics have been led slightly astray into defining the female sentence as that which describes female experience, and thus the male sentence would, in this perspective, be one which described male experience. Since a great deal of western literature is concerned with a description of women's experience, by men, this cannot be the case.[9] Furthermore, from a poststructuralist point of view, we might also question the notion that writing is about experience in the real world. Any man who has learned the conventions of *écriture féminine* or of women's writing, can write a 'woman's' book. Similarly, any woman can write a male sentence.

When I asked a group of students in Strathclyde University to give typical male and female sentences they came up with sentences which were different in terms of content on stereotypical grounds.[10] For example, they produced the following opposing pairs:

1 I came I saw I conquered. *Male*
   Shelia felt as if her whole being was conquered by this man whom she hardly knew. *Female*

2 I'm hungry and I want something to eat. *Male*
   I wonder if there's something to eat. *Female*

These sentences can be categorized as male and female according to their stereotypical subject-matter, but also interestingly in terms of some of their linguistic features. In example 1, the aggression of the first statement is characterized as male together with its brevity – context might also have some bearing here. The female sentence is far more grammatically complex than the male sentence which is linked only by hypotaxis, that is, by that fact that the clauses are placed side by side; but it is classified as female because it is concerned with emotion and dominance. The second set of sentences is largely to be distinguished, not by subject-matter, but by indirectness of expression. Thus subject-matter can be seen to be a factor which may lead people to assume that sentences are gendered in some way, but it cannot be considered in isolation from other factors.

A number of feminist theorists have suggested that the use of metaphor is crucial to describing the distinction between women's and men's writing. For example, Ellen Moers suggests that women tend to use bird metaphors when they describe women characters; she cites lines from Christina Rossetti's poetry; for example, 'My heart is like a singing bird / Whose nest is in a watered shoot' (Moers in M. Eagleton 1986: 209) and also 'Me, poor dove that must not coo – eagle that must not soar' (ibid.). Moers says: 'Is the bird merely a species of the littleness metaphor? Or are birds chosen because they are tortured, as little girls are tortured by boys ... or because bird-victims can be ministered to by girl victims ... or is it because birds are beautiful and exotic creatures, symbols of half-promised, half-forbidden sensual delights ... because birds are soft and round and sensuous, because they palpitate and flutter when held in the hands and especially because they sing? (ibid.: 209). This analysis of the use of bird metaphors in women's writing has a number of problematic assumptions about women themselves: that women are always weak, are victims and are sensual. Moers goes on to say: 'From Mary Wollstonecraft's *Maria* – to Brontë's *Jane Eyre* – to Anne Frank's *Diary of a Young Girl* – I find that the caged bird makes a metaphor that truly deserves the adjective female' (ibid.: 210). Horner and Zlosnick argue in a similar way that women's writing is characterized by a preponderance of certain types of metaphor. They suggest that 'many novels by women writers of the late nineteenth and early twentieth centuries have certain configurations of metaphor in common. What are these configurations? We noticed repeated use of a dynamic relationship between room, house, land and sea and we began to realise that this relationship carried a significance which went beyond plot' (Horner and Zlosnick 1990: 6). For them, women writers in this period tend to concentrate on descriptions of enclosed and open spaces and this entails a metaphorical pattern throughout their work. However, whilst it may be the case that certain women writers within a very specific period and style of writing may be characterized as drawing on certain metaphorical tendencies, it is clearly not the case for other women writers.

Rather than considering women's writing to be a question of content alone, some theorists like Cameron have suggested that many of the sentences we find in our everyday reading address us not as people but as males, and these we might perhaps consider as examples of the male sentence. For example, she gives an extract from a newspaper: 'The lack of vitality is aggravated by the fact that there are so few able-bodied young adults about. They have all gone off to work or look for work, leaving behind the old, the disabled, the women and the children' (Cameron 1985: 85). Women here are excluded from a position of equal citizenship with the males referred to in the text, and the supposedly generic nouns like 'young adults' are seen to refer not to them but to males only. In a complex interpretative move, the female reader may feel herself implicated in this exclusion. The text uses nouns like 'adult' as if they referred only to males, constituting a world in which male is the norm and female is the marginal. The texts do not represent women as being equal citizens, and a female reader who registers this is likely to feel excluded. (For a full discussion of address, see Chapter 3.)

Finally, in addition to these elements, the gendered sentence is also defined as one where it is assumed that meaning is different for male- and female-authored texts. For the male sentence, meaning is a simple matter, where language is a transparent medium, not drawing attention to itself, a medium which simply carries thought. The thought which is carried is rational, assertive, clear. These adjectives which we are using to describe the male sentence bear a striking resemblance to the ideologically formulated notion of the male character. The female sentence, in contrast, is presented as opaque and difficult to understand.

In order to challenge some of these assumptions, we should analyse some sentences which would, according to these theorists, normally be classed as male or female. The following two passages might well be considered as being made up of 'male' sentences:

> 1) This incident, which might be said to have added to his undoing, did not arise out of Mr Stone's passion for gardens. Gardening as he practised it was no more than a means, well suited to his age, which was 62, of exhausting the spare time and energy with which his undemanding duties in one of the departments of the Excal company, his status as a bachelor and his still excellent physique amply provided him.

> 2) I went to the cloakroom and put on my overcoat and cap. I could never bring myself to sport a trilby or a bowler; the cap provided some protection, even though it signally failed to cover the ears. I could not descend to the Arthur woolly beret level. I set off down the stairs. I always used the lift to come up, the stairs to come down. The lift carried the hazards of social life. It was a concession to old age that I no longer walked up.

According to the criteria outlined above, we could classify these two texts as containing examples of the male sentence: both texts are made up of sentences which have subordinate clauses; the sentences used are complete; they are rational and straightforward (neither text has any foregrounded language items); both texts are about male characters. Because of these facts, we should be led to assume that the authors are male; however, whilst text 1 is indeed by a male, V. S. Naipaul (1964), text 2 was written by Iris Murdoch (1971).

Let us then consider the following examples of the 'female' sentence:

3)   O
                        tell me about
                 Anna Livia! I want to hear all

about Anna Livia. Well, you know Anna Livia? Yes, of course, we all know Anna Livia. Tell me all. Tell me now. You'll die when you hear. Well, you know when the old cheb went futt and did what you know. Yes I know go on. Wash quit and don't be dabbling. Tuck up your sleeves and loosen your talktapes. And don't butt me – hike! – when you bend. Or whatever it was they threed to make out when he thried in the Fiendish park.

4) She is giving birth. With the strength of a lioness. Of a plant. Of a cosmogony. Of a woman. . . . A desire for text! Confusion! What possesses her? A child! Paper! Intoxications! I'm overflowing! My breasts overflow! Milk. Ink. The moment of suckling. And I? I too am hungry. The taste of milk, of ink.

Both texts could be classified as being made up of 'female' sentences, since they do not use subordinate clauses (most of the clauses are non-co-ordinated); some of the clauses are incomplete; neither of these texts could be defined as particularly rational or authoritarian (there does not appear to be in either text one 'voice' which is dominant); both are about women's experience, both draw attention to themselves in terms of their language use and they are quite difficult to read. Yet, although text 4 is by a woman, Hélène Cixous (1986), text 3 is by James Joyce (1922 [1960]). It would seem that these definitions of sentences according to gender are clearly inadequate, and perhaps they are eliding avant-garde or experimental writing with feminine/female writing.

CHALLENGES TO THE GENDERED SENTENCE

To attempt to escape from this critical impasse, let us look briefly at the work of Monique Wittig whose position is in contrast to the work of other French feminists. One noticeable point of divergence is in her aim to 'deconstruct' the difference between male and female sentences.

That there is no feminine writing must be said at the outset, and one makes a mistake in using and giving currency to this expression. What is this 'feminine' in feminine writing? It stands for Woman, thus merging a practice with a myth, the myth of Woman. 'Woman' cannot be associated with writing because 'Woman' is an imaginary formation and not a concrete reality; it is that old branding by the enemy now flourished like a tattered flag refound and won in battle.

(Wittig 1983: 2)

Thus, for Wittig, it is important to dispense with a monolithic notion of 'woman'. She goes on to say: '"Feminine writing" is the naturalising metaphor of the brutal political fact of the domination of women, and as such it enlarges the apparatus under which "femininity" presents itself' (Wittig 1983: 2). She shows how this metaphor of the feminine is used to undermine the fact that women's writing is work, a production process, like men's writing. She notes that *écriture féminine* seems to refer to an almost biological process, what she terms a 'secretion' (Wittig 1983: 2).

Thus, as with everything which is labelled masculine/male or feminine/female, these terms have very little to do with biological sex difference, but a great deal to do with assertions of power. In defining the female sentence we are not in fact defining a sentence at all, but defining females; this is just part of an ideological enterprise; we do not define males to anything like the same extent. As Cameron says: 'Stereotypes, however false, tend to persist for as long as they reinforce important social inequalities' (Cameron 1985: 33). Defining the feminine sentence as lacking rationality, coherence, assertiveness and so on, is an attempt to set up a particular subject-position for females in the real world.

To sum up, I would like to question the notion of a simple binary gendered sentence for three reasons: first, both anti-feminists and French feminists seem to have encountered the same theoretical problems through arguing by sexual analogy; the anti-feminists state that the male sentence is better, as it has all the qualities that men supposedly have; the feminists state that feminine writing is better for the same reasons. This is pure essentialism, and is dangerous because it leaves feminists with no room for change or effective political action. (See Butler 1990; Fuss 1990.)

Second, Woolf and the French feminists assume that there is a radical, easily identifiable difference between the male sentence and the female sentence. They assume that a male sentence *can* assert, that it *can* be clear and that there is a clear difference between those which do and those which do not. Once we reject notions of language as a tool and adopt a post-Saussurean model, surely such notions of assertion, clarity and rationality must be brought into question. Are we, for example, to assume that the male sentence has one homogeneous voice? Or are we to admit that in the very act of asserting, the writer is calling into existence a host of other negations or questions, what Macherey calls the 'unsaid' of the text (Macherey 1978)? Given this more complex view of language, we simply cannot propose these types of writing as binary oppositions. Rather, there is a range of discursive positions which the writer can adopt and these are not gender-neutral (see Mills 1991). However, rather than simply assuming that women write in a particular way because they are female, we can see women writers adopting a range of different positions, depending on their locating of themselves within a predominantly male or female tradition.

Third, Wittig challenges not only the distinction between male and female sentences but also the notion of a 'natural' distinction between men and women. She states that 'a lesbian society pragmatically reveals that the division from men of which women have been the object is a political one and shows how we have been ideologically rebuilt into a "natural group"' (Wittig 1981: 41). She says that there are dangers in accepting sex differences as natural: 'by admitting that there is a "natural" division between women and men, we naturalise history, we assume that men and women have always existed and will always exist. Not only do we naturalise history, but also consequently we naturalise the social phenomena which express our oppression, making change impossible' (Wittig 1981: 42).

If we are entertaining the notion of a sex-specific sentence, it is worth considering the anecdote of the publication problems experienced by 'Rahla Kahn', who was in fact a white British vicar who wrote an account of life as a Pakistani woman; he wrote this as an autobiography, signing himself Rahla Kahn, and he sent it to Virago Press, where the manuscript was accepted and negotiations started to take place through an agent. When it was discovered that 'Rahla Kahn' was a man, the manuscript was shelved and has not been published. There is no reason whatsoever that writing which is posed as women's writing should be written by a woman (except that in this case there were problems of duplicity); anyone is capable of using any form of sentence structure given the necessary education and exposure to different language styles. We are engaging here with questions of authenticity and not with questions of distinctive styles. If women did write differently, the Rahla Kahn incident would not have been possible.

A more productive way of examining the question of gender and sentence structure is that put forward by Sandra Gilbert and Susan Gubar, who have considered that there might be what they call, drawing on Edward Said's work, a female affiliation complex (Gilbert and Gubar 1988). This they state consists of a textual signalling to the reader that the writer or the persona is affiliating with a particular literary tradition, either a mainstream one dominated by male writers and hence displaying predominantly value-systems which foreground maleness and masculinities, or, in a much more problematic way, a female tradition. Since females often write under the conditions of what Deleuze and Guattari term 'minority' writing, they have a range of choices which they have to make because of the pressures which are enacted on their work. Knowing that one's work is categorized as 'minor' leads the writer to react in a range of different ways (see P. Williams 1989, for a discussion of Black women writers and minor literature). Gilbert and Gubar give very little detail of the way in which this affiliation can be tracked down, but it would seem that we could use Lynne Pearce's work on textual cues here to suggest that there are means by which a text signals to the reader which way it is affiliating (Pearce 1991b). Within the affiliative process there are three possibilities; that is, first, for women to write they can adopt a supposedly masculine voice and align themselves with a male tradition; or, second, they can adopt a stereotypically feminine voice and align themselves with the same set of values, since they are not challenging the status quo. The third position is one where women writers, mainly feminists, signal their alignment with a female tradition, by a range of cues within the text.

An example of male affiliation of the first kind would be Iris Murdoch in example 2 cited on p. 55. This is writing which explicitly aligns itself with a mainstream novelistic tradition; it poses itself, both in its language and its content, as an unexceptional and non-foregrounded realist text. Feminine writing within this grouping would be exemplified by the following example, taken from Anita Brookner's novel *Hotel du Lac* (1984).

From the window all that could be seen was a receding area of grey. It was to be supposed that beyond the grey garden, which seemed to sprout nothing but the stiffish leaves of some unfamiliar plant, lay the vast grey lake, spreading like an anaesthetic towards the invisible further shore, and beyond that, in imagination only, yet verified by the brochure, the peak of the Dent d'Oche, on which snow might already be slightly and silently falling. For it was late September, out of season; the tourists had gone, the rates were reduced, and there were few inducements for visitors in this small town at the water's edge, whose inhabitants, uncommunicative to begin with, were frequently rendered taciturn by the dense cloud that descended for days at a time and then vanished without warning to reveal a new landscape, full of colour and incident: boats skimming on the lake, passengers at the landing stage, an open air market, the outline of the gaunt remains of a thirteenth-century castle, seams of white on the far mountains, and on the cheerful uplands to the south a rising backdrop of apple trees, the fruit sparkling with emblematic significance.

Here, the writing style is distinctly feminine in the conventional sense, and it is here that we need to make a useful distinction between that which is stereotypical and that which is consciously affiliating itself to a female tradition and aiming at a female audience. In terms of the language used, it is conventionally feminine in that there is a large number of clauses which display epistemic modality (that is, which have some form of modification or which contain verbs or abverbials which seem to mediate the force of a statement); for example:

> From the window all that *could* be seen was a receding area of grey.

> *It was to be supposed* that beyond the grey garden, which *seemed* to sprout nothing but the stiff*ish* leaves of *some* unfamiliar plant . . .

The grammatical construction of the second sentence is very complex and meandering, and there is a constant insertion of clauses in apposition, for example:

> there were few inducements for visitors in this small town at the water's edge, whose inhabitants, *uncommunicative to begin with*, were frequently rendered taciturn by the dense cloud.

Rather than a simple description of the landscape, what is given is the point of view of the central character who describes the landscape in a very impressionistic way. For a contrasting masculine description of landscape see the following passage, taken from *Under the Volcano* by Malcolm Lowry (1984).

Two mountain chains traverse the republic roughly from north to south, forming between them a number of valleys and plateaux. Overlooking one of these valleys, which is dominated by two volcanoes, lies, six thousand feet above sea-level, the town of Quauhnahuac. It is situated well south of the Tropic of Cancer, to be exact, on the nineteenth parallel, in about the same latitude as the Revillagigedo Islands to the west in the Pacific, or very much farther west, the southernmost tip of Hawaii – and as the port of Tzucox to the east on the Atlantic seaboard of Yucatan near the border of British Honduras, or very much farther east, the town of Juggernaut, in India, on the Bay of Bengal.

The walls of the town, which is built on a hill, are high, the streets and lanes tortuous and broken, the roads winding. A fine American-style highway leads in from the north but is lost in its narrow streets and comes out a goat track. Quauhnahuac possesses eighteen churches and fifty-seven *cantinas*. It also boasts a golf course and no fewer than four hundred swimming-pools, public and private, filled with the water that ceaselessly pours down from the mountains, and many splendid hotels.

The Hotel Casion de la Selva stands on a slightly higher hill just outside the town, near the railway station. It is built far back from the main highway and surrounded by gardens and terraces which command a spacious view in every direction. Palatial, a certain air of desolate splendour pervades it. For it is no longer a Casino. You may not even dice for drinks in the bar. The ghosts of ruined gamblers haunt it. No one ever seems to swim in the magnificent Olympic pool. The springboards stand empty and mournful. Its jai-alai courts are grass-grown and deserted. Two tennis courts only are kept up in the season.

This text poses itself very much within the tradition of factual writing, in this case guidebook writing. Rather than describing the landscape in an emotional way, the narrator takes a position that is almost that of an automaton dispensing information. It is difficult to sense the presence of a narrator, unlike the Brookner passage. For example, Lowry's narrator states: 'The walls of the town, which is built on a hill, are high, the streets and lanes tortuous and broken, the roads winding.' The narrator's opinions or feelings about the walls, the streets and the roads are not given – the description is lifeless and seemingly objective. The town is described as if it were not populated, since the amenities are remarked upon – the pools, the churches, the golf-course – but not the inhabitants. The first two paragraphs are geographical in tone and might be characterized as masculinist and aligning with a masculine form of writing. These two texts are stereotypically feminine and masculine.

The third position available to female writers is that of female affiliation where the writer signals to her readers that she is not writing within the mainstream tradition and is drawing attention to the fact that she is a woman writing to women. This positioning can be traced through textual cues. If we consider a passage from *Moll Cutpurse* (1993) by Ellen Galford, it is clearly a text which signals to the reader that the persona is attempting to reclaim/rewrite the history of this seventeenth-century figure, who has appeared in a number of male-authored texts such as *The Roaring Girl* by Thomas Dekker and Thomas Middleton.

> Whoever first named her the Roaring Girl was no liar. She had a voice like a bellowing ox and a laugh like a love-sick lion – and when she strutted through the streets the crowds parted and stood goggling . . . Moll loved an audience; she'd have been a player if they'd let her.
>
> (Galford 1993: 3)

Moll, the central character, displays qualities which traditionally are viewed as unfeminine, but the text does not offer a judgement on her behaviour. The narrator takes up a position of slightly ironical detachment, signalled by such terms as 'strutted' with its potentially critical implication of excessive self-confidence. The text does not reproduce ideological messages about the way that women should behave, at the same time as coding Moll's behaviour as exceptional. Even though the text does not pass an explicit value-judgement on her behaviour, such is the system within which texts are written and read that the very presence of a female character's pride which is not coupled with an implicit assessment of its inappropriacy, marks the text as belonging to a feminist tradition of female-affiliated texts. The similes used in this passage are clearly a departure from those traditionally used in literary texts in association with female protagonists (see Chapter 5). They are not feminine, but neither are they unambiguously heroic within a tradition of male characters.[11] But what we are analysing here is less the content of the text but rather the text's subversive address to the reader, where she is called upon to agree with certain judgements on characters and certain positions.

To summarize, female writers have a variety of options when they write to produce their texts within a conventional mainstream; they can either mimic masculine writing styles or feminine writing styles, or decide to try to challenge these traditions by consciously drawing on and subverting them and addressing a female audience. Cues in the text can be used to differentiate one style of writing from another; for example, syntactic style, such as the mimicking of a formal style as in official documents, legal writing, or canonical literature, can signal to the reader that the writer is affiliating with a 'male' tradition. Prose where the syntactic structure is closer to the patterns of informal speech, or which uses conflicting registers to subvert such formality, places itself in opposition to the literary tradition and by default suggests an affiliation to a female tradition. Lexis is also an important cue to a text's affiliation. Terms which are associated with gender stereotypes may be used predictably or against the grain

(e.g. Moll Cutpurse has a voice 'like a bellowing ox'). Such cues cannot be interpreted in isolation from their context, since they may be used with irony, or as
either positive or negative character assessments. They are, however, moments
in the text where the writer's position regarding affiliation can be seen to be
explicit. The content of the text also contains cues – obviously a central female
character and a focus on her relationship with other female characters is one
feature which may indicate a female-affiliated text. The notion of female affiliation means that it is not necessary to simply categorize writing as female- or
male-authored and assume that there are stylistic differences in the texts because
of that biological difference.

PHALLOCENTRISM AND JUDGEMENT OF WOMEN'S TEXTS

I would like to move finally to a discussion of the way that women's writing is
treated and most notably how it is judged in a different way from men's writing.
Phallocentrism can be seen to operate when we look at discussions of gender
and literature, since we talk about women's writing in opposition not to male
writing, but to human writing; there are histories of British or American literature, but not histories of male writing. There *are* histories of women's writing. As
Christiane Rochefort says: 'A man's book is a book. A woman's book is a woman's
book' (Rochefort in Marks and Decourtivron 1981: 183). Yet there are just as
many differences between women writers as there are similarities.

A further way in which phallocentrism manifests itself in the analysis of writing
is the judgement of women's writing in terms of a male norm. For example,
William Gass states: 'until women can find an openly lustful, quick, impatient,
feral hunger in themselves, they will never be liberated and their writing . . . in
pallid imitation of the master, will lack that blood-congested drive which energizes
every great style' (Gass cited in Hiatt 1977: 2). Here Gass takes a sexual metaphor
which is based on a stereotype of male sexuality; women if they are to write well
must in fact write as if they were sexually male; there is an assumption here that
women at the moment do not write in this way, and that they can only imitate
male writing. Once they have attained male sexuality, they will be able, paradoxically, to write in a truly 'liberated' way. This quotation is an extreme but
fairly typical example of the type of presuppositions which some phallocentric
critics have about women's writing. (For a full discussion of the way that women's
writing is judged, see Battersby 1989.)

Many feminists have criticized the injustice of phallocentrism which has
restricted women writers in certain styles of writing which are deemed appropriate for them, and which has generally described certain types of women's
writing in negative terms. Some women have accepted this classification; for
example, when Joyce Carol Oates states: 'how am I to feel when discussed in
the *Harvard Guide to Contemporary American Literature* under the great lump "Women
Writers" the only works of mine analysed being those that deal explicitly with

women's problems – the rest of my books . . . ignored?' she protests about being classified as a 'mere' woman writer, as if this were self-evidently a negative term (Oates 1986: 208). What is necessary is not to complain when you as a writer are classified as female, but to complain about the fact that being classified as female is a negative trait.

Some feminists have paradoxically gone on to celebrate the traits or behaviour that we have been assigned, as if these traits were in some sense inherent, rather than socially constructed. I would prefer to question the very basis of phallocentrism's construction and show that it is part of a much wider strategy of devaluing that which is classified as female. Mary Ellman in *Thinking about Women* describes the strategy whereby women's views/attributes/writing are not valued, as 'arguing by sexual analogy' (Ellman 1968). She states that these differences which we describe as male and female, in fact have nothing to do with sexual or even gender differences; we argue simply using the terms of difference which we think are most basic.[12] Hélène Cixous makes exactly this point in 'Sorties': that the terms 'male' and 'female' are seen as the basic binary opposition to which all other oppositions refer. She says:

> *Where is she?*
> Activity/passivity,
> Sun/Moon,
> Culture/Nature,
> Day/Night,
> Father/Mother,
> Head/heart,
> Intelligible/sensitive,
> Logos/Pathos,
>
> Man/Woman
>
> (Cixous 1981b: 90)

By listing these elements in this way, Cixous demonstrates that binary oppositions such as these are not neutral and are predicated on a basic sexual difference, which is itself a hierarchical division: all of the terms on the 'male' side are positioned as superior to the 'female' side.

There is a long tradition of critics judging women's writing in a different way from men's writing; for example, corralling the reviews of women's writing into a separate compound, where several women's books are reviewed together, as if they necessarily had something in common, because of the simple fact of having been written by women. Male texts are certainly not treated in this way.

Joanna Russ describes wittily and irreverently the way that women's writing has been treated so that it has not been accorded literary status (Russ 1984). She catalogues the various strategies which have been employed to downgrade women's creative writing; she states: 'What to do when a woman has written something? The first line of defence is to deny that she wrote it. Since women cannot write, someone else (a man) must have written it' (ibid.: 20). Russ documents the way that this accusation was levelled at Margaret Cavendish, Elisabeth Vigée-LeBrun, Margareta Havermann, Adelaide Labille-Guiard and many others: all of whom were accused of having their husbands write work which they presented as their own. A more subtle form of downgrading women's writing is to suggest, as Russ puts it, that 'It wrote itself' (ibid.: 21). For example, Ellen Moers describes Mary Shelley as a 'transparent medium through which passed the ideas of those around her' rather than 'an author in her own right' (cited in Russ 1984: 21). A further strategy employed to discredit women's writing is termed by Russ 'The man inside her wrote it' (ibid.: 22); that is, she wrote the book with the masculine side of her nature. She cites Robert Lowell's foreword to Sylvia Plath's *Ariel* where he states 'Sylvia Plath becomes . . . something imaginary, newly, wildly created – hardly a person at all or a woman, certainly not a poetess' (cited in Russ 1984: 23). It is hard to imagine a similar strategy being used to describe writing by a male writer.

If we consider cases where books have been mistakenly assumed to be by male writers, only later to be discovered to have been written by female authors, it is possible to examine the differences in response to the gender of the author. Elaine Showalter examines the way that this was the case with Charlotte Brontë who wrote *Jane Eyre* as Currer Bell, a gender-neutral name (Moi 1985). Initially, Bell was considered to be a male and 'his' novel praised as strong and forceful. However, once it was discovered that it was Brontë in fact who had written the novel, reviews began to appear which described the style in strongly negative terms. Showalter comments: 'many critics bluntly admitted that they thought the book was a masterpiece if written by a man, shocking or disgusting if written by a woman' (Showalter 1978: 32). Toril Moi describes a similar process at work in the judgement of the poetry of Cecil Bodtker, whose name again is gender-neutral. Her work was well reviewed whilst it was thought that she was a male; once her sex was discovered her work began to be less well reviewed. Alicia Ostriker has also drawn attention to the way in which women writers, particularly poets, tend to be described in terms of their supposed feminine qualities. Thus she remarks that Marianne Moore's poetry is described by a large number of critics as 'modest' and her modesty is seen to be a positive quality. The question of phallocentrism is obviously the key element in the way that sentences are judged to be male or female: it is not a neutral judgement but rather a judgement which classifies male sentences and writing in positive ways and female writing and sentences in negative ways. Consider the following comment from Cynthia Ozick who was teaching students Flannery O'Connor's *Wise Blood*. After three weeks of teaching, her students were surprised when she referred to O'Connor as 'she' since they had all assumed that the author was male. Only one student was not surprised: she said: '"But I could *tell* she was a woman . . . her sentences are a woman's sentences." I asked her what she meant and how she could tell, "Because they're sentimental," she said, "they're not concrete like a man's." I pointed out whole paragraphs, pages even, of unsentimental, so-called tough prose. "But she *sounds* like a woman – she has to sound that way because she is"' (Ozick cited in Russ 1984: 92).

To sum up, it is clear that it is extremely difficult to define a sentence as simply male or female, since most of the accounts of the linguistic differences between male- and female-authored sentences seem to be based on overgeneralized and false interpretations of the data. It is a simplification of gender difference to assume that all women will write in a similar way or that all men will. However, that is not to say that there are no differences between texts which are due at least in part to gender, and I have tried therefore to examine the differences that there might be in texts which signal their affiliation on gendered lines. The notion of affiliation allows us to analyse the differences amongst female writers, in the same way that male texts have been assumed to be relatively heterogeneous. It is clear that female and male sentences do not exist except in stereotypical forms or as ideal representations of gender difference; however, because of different value-systems operating on women's writing, it is quite evident that women's writing is read differently from male writing.

Chapter 3

Gender and Reading

As I noted in Chapter 1, in feminist stylistic analysis, it is necessary to analyse the text using a model of meaning and reference quite different from that which is conventionally used in traditional stylistics. In feminist stylistics, stress is laid on the interaction between the text and the reader in the production of interpretations, and there is an emphasis on the factors beyond the conscious control of both writer and reader in the analysis. For example, the author is seen as someone who is writing within a set of discursive parameters which are not of her own making or of which she is not even necessarily consciously aware. Similarly, the reader is subject to many discursive pressures which lead her to read in particular ways. Furthermore, the notion of linguistic features being 'in' the text, a staple claim of stylistics, is finally laid to rest, since it is impossible in this more complex view of the text simply to assume that every reader will be able to understand the same message from the same set of linguistic signals.[1]

Michel Pecheux's work is particularly interesting in this context (Pecheux 1982). In an experiment, Pecheux presented two groups of students with the same economics text, but told one of the groups that it was a left-wing text and the other that it was a moderate text. The two groups interpreted the same text in radically different ways, because they were reading with different conceptual frameworks and different expectations. In the light of this work, it is clear that readers will come to different conclusions about the meaning of a text, depending on the framework and expectations that they bring to the text. It is important to remember that we never come to a text without some hypothesis and some conceptual framework into which we fit the text; thus we do not simply interpret the text according to our own personal concerns, but we share ideological frameworks which will mean that we are more likely to interpret the signals or traces in the text in similar ways. This does not mean that the text itself is a blank space upon which we as readers impose ideological frameworks of interpretation. As well as there being certain ideologically constructed frameworks within which we interpret the text, it is also clear that the text itself influences the way that we read. It addresses the reader either in a direct or an indirect way, and presents certain ways of interpretation as the most likely to make sense of the text, what I shall be calling the 'dominant reading' (see S. Mills 1994 and S. Mills 1992c). In this chapter I shall be tracing linguistic elements which attempt to position you as a particular type of reader. The focus of this chapter is on the gendered positioning of the reader, that is, the way that the reader in a wide range of texts is positioned as predominantly male. Drawing on the work of Judith Fetterley on literature and Judith Williamson on advertisements, and adding a linguistic analysis, this chapter will examine the way that a range of texts (literary, advertising and newspaper) address the reader as if that person were self-evidently male; I also discuss the consequences of this positioning for female and feminist readers and for those male readers who are not comfortable with this form of address. Elements such as generic pronouns and nouns, the cultural code, shared knowledge/members' resources attempt to force the reader to accept gendered information as natural or commonsense. I shall also analyse the cases where the reader is positioned as female. In many of the examples it will be seen that, in fact, although there is an attempt to position the reader as female, the address is destined for a male as voyeur. Finally, I will analyse the way that readers negotiate and interact with that gendered positioning, since it is clear that readers are far from passive and do not simply accept the way that a text addresses them. Readers are also 'hailed' by a range of conflicting and contradictory messages which they may attempt to resolve, or in reaction to which they may develop a position of critique.

ADDRESS

Theories of reader-response and reception have concerned themselves with the role of the reader in the process of interpretation, but primarily with examining a consensus of interpretation through the notion of the implied or ideal reader, that is, an idealized figure whom the text is presumed to be in dialogue with (Suleiman *et al.* 1980; see also T. Eagleton 1991). Even those critics who do consider reader positioning, that is, the way that a text seems to construct certain roles for the reader, pay little attention to the formal features in the text which signal the dominant reading to the reader. In order to formulate a mode of analysis which considers formal features and the way they relate to context and reader address, I will draw on the work of Louis Althusser on interpellation and obviousness.

Louis Althusser's work on Ideological State Apparatuses is an interesting combination of Marxist theory and psychoanalysis with a strong concern with language and its role in shaping subjectivity (Althusser 1984). The basis of his argument is that Ideological State Apparatuses are those institutions and elements whose indirect effect is to reproduce the conditions of production within a society. He considers these institutions to be primarily the educational system, the media, the Church and the family. ISAs, as he terms them, achieve this aim through a constant barrage of images and information which maps out the role of the subject.[2] He describes the way in which individuals are called into a position of subjecthood: when you recognize your role/s in society, you become a subject in both senses of the word: you are a subject in that you are an individual psyche, and you are also subject to the state and authority. In this way, you are forced to mis/recognize the imaginary (i.e. ideological) conditions of your relation to the means of production. Althusser states that interpellation or hailing is one of the mechanisms whereby this is achieved; he gives the much-cited example of a police officer in the street calling 'Hey you'. In the process of turning round, the individual has recognized not only herself as an individual who may be guilty of something, but also herself as a subject in relation to a position of authority. Thus, for Althusser, interpellation constructs the subject into a role or position in the act of hailing.

This model has been rightly criticized for being too simplistic an account of the way that interpellation works, because the construction of subjecthood is obviously a much more complicated process than the simple responding to a name or call. With Althusser's model of hailing there is a one-to-one fit between the calling and the recognition. However, when interpellated by a text, the reader can adopt either the position of the supposed speaker or the role of the supposed addressee, or can be positioned as an overhearer of the interaction. Furthermore, there are clearly other elements in the text which position the reader, but which are more indirect than this model suggests. There is an unending series of hailings, both direct and indirect, to which the reader responds or does not respond. Thus, although certain texts attempt to address themselves to the reader, she may be critical of them and may decide not to take them at face value. However, despite these misgivings about the notion of a direct and unproblematic hailing by the text, it is clear that there are indirect effects of such interpellation. Even the hailings which are not intended for the reader, or which are intended for her and not received, nevertheless do have an effect on her and it is this effect of indirect interpellation which I will describe in this chapter.

A second point of interest from Althusser's ISAs article is the notion of commonsense or 'obviousness' which, along with interpellation, is a strong element in the positioning of the reader. In each text, there are elements which are posed as self-evidently true and Althusser asserts that these are the most truly ideological:

> It is indeed a peculiarity of ideology that it imposes (without appearing to do so, since these are 'obviousnesses') obviousnesses as obviousnesses, which we cannot *fail to recognize* and before which we have the inevitable and natural reaction of crying out (aloud or in the 'still, small voice of conscience'): 'That's obvious! That's right! That's true.'
>
> (Althusser 1984: 46; italics in original)

Each text contains an ideological message which we accept (or reject) as true or obvious, and it is in this way that the reader is positioned by what I would like to class as the dominant reading. This is a seemingly coherent message which the text carries, and which the reader is supposed to find as 'obviously' what the text is about, even if s/he would like to disagree with or take issue with that message.[3] These two elements, interpellation and obviousness, will be of central importance in the following sections.

Direct address

Martin Montgomery's work on radio disc-jockey talk is one of the few examples of an attempt to deal with reader address using linguistics (Montgomery 1986b; Montgomery 1988). He concentrates on the analysis of direct address to the reader in the form principally of deixis, that is, the way that the text situates the reader in relation to a textual world through the use of forms such as this/that, here/there and now/then. He also examines the use of vocatives ('you', or a name) and selectors ('all of you in Edinburgh'). Montgomery shows that an audience is addressed by a text as 'you', or a subsection of that 'you', and he notes: 'The audience is not uniformly implicated all in the same way the whole of the time . . . while the use of selectors has the effect of singling out sometimes quite specific addressees, the talk is always available for others than those directly named as addressees' (1986b: 13). He draws attention to the fact that there are various sections of the audience who will be overhearing elements of the talk by DJs at various times. He also notes that in DJ talk, 'as listeners we are made constantly aware of other (invisible) elements in the audience of which we form a part' (Montgomery 1988). This is particularly interesting for the purposes of this chapter, where gender is seen as a crucial element in determining whether readers consider that they are being directly addressed or whether in fact they are in the position of overhearing or resisting the address.

Alan Durant draws on Montgomery's work on address, but uses it for the analysis of pop music lyrics (Durant forthcoming). He distinguishes between the various positions which a listener can adopt when listening to a pop song: for him, there is the position of the singer or the singer's persona, the role of the addressee, or the role of someone who is overhearing this interaction. For Durant, the reader chooses which position to adopt. Whilst this is clearly an advance in that it maps out several alternative positions of the reader if applied to literary texts, the notion of a willed positioning by the reader eliminates any of the ideological positioning described by Althusser. Furthermore, these positions which the reader takes up are not necessarily critical positions, and it is this notion of critique or resistance which I find it most necessary to retain. What I am trying to maintain is a judicious balance between the text addressing the reader as a member of a group and the reader's negotiation of that process of address. It is quite clear that it is important to maintain that the reader is an active agent in relation to the text, but this does not mean that the reader is free to choose whatever reading s/he wants from the text; in this sense, the text determines the positions which the reader can take up. In addition, in Althusser's work, the reader is, in the main, unaware of the processes at work in the inter-pellation; in fact it is the very obviousness of the messages received which prevents the subject's becoming aware of their ideological nature. Thus, although Durant's work on the varying positions available to the reader is insightful, especially given the fact that most reader-response work suggests that there is only one place of coherence for the text, the notion of reader choice is one which will be treated with some caution. There are clearly texts which suggest what the reader's position is: for example, it is unlikely (but not impossible) that a female listener will position herself in the role of the singer in the Rolling Stones song 'I can't get no satisfaction'. Whilst not impossible, it is likely that certain of the lyrics actively discourage her from taking up this position. Thus, the female listener may sing along with the lyrics whilst feeling at a distance from them, knowing that she is 'miming' them, rather than being able to 'say' them. This notion of a gendered difference is crucial, and since few critics speak of gender in their analyses of reader positioning, I would like to reinscribe that political edge and argue for a gendered reading process.[4] This does not mean, however, that the reader is positioned as female in a simple homogenous way; nor that she responds to the text in a simple way as a woman; it means that gender always makes a difference.

Indirect Address

One of the major problems with Althusser's concept of interpellation, as has been noted on p. 67, is the concentration on *direct* addressing of the subject. It is clear that the reader is also addressed in an *indirect* way. Unless readers analyse texts for the way that they are being positioned, this type of address goes largely unnoticed, because it is more difficult to locate. There are, however, several markers of indirect address which I now describe. I will concentrate on two, obviousness and background knowledge, before going on to discuss the way that indirect address helps to constitute a dominant reading.[5]

Althusser's notion of obviousness consists of a range of statements which the reader is supposed to nod his/her head at sagely or simply to accept as self-evidently 'true' within that culture. Normally, this group of statements does not even require such a response from the reader, since they pose themselves as information that 'everyone knows'. Roland Barthes, whose work follows Althusser in this respect, suggests that we can detect these elements of the obvious, since these statements can be prefaced by 'we all know that' or 'it is evident that'. Thus, texts contain a substantial amount of information to which we agree indirectly, and which, in that process, constitutes a role for us as readers: we become the type of people to whom this information would appear to be self-evident (Barthes 1977).

Norman Fairclough describes background knowledge or what he terms 'members' resources' (Fairclough 1989). These resources are knowledges which the text assumes that the reader has. This is slightly different from obviousness since rather than being information which is presented as being that which *everybody* has, this information may well be more specialized; thus this information is the province of only certain readers and the text thereby delimits its audience. Members' resources can be traced by mapping out explicitly the presuppositions and implicatures that exist in statements (see Chapter 6 for a more detailed analysis of these terms). For example, in the advertisement for Femme hair-remover shown overleaf, there is a range of traceable ideological assumptions about women. The first can be located in the headline 'Get to the root of your hair (growth) problem'.

Some of the implicit assumptions are:

1 that you, the reader, have a hair problem
2 more specifically, that the problem is one of growth
3 that hair growth is necessarily a problem (for women).

The text characterizes hair growth as 'unsightly, embarrassing' and 'ugly' and 'unwanted' and assumes that hair on a woman's body must be 'superfluous'. The text sets up the 'problem' of facial and body hair for women by the use of the chart on the right which lists the places where hair self-evidently should not grow. The text does not explicitly state that hair growth should not occur in these places, but it does so indirectly by saying that Femme will remove hair from them. Thus, the reader is encouraged to agree implicitly with the 'fact' that hair on the upper lip and full arm is unsightly and needs to be removed. The display of this information in a chart form enables the markers of the product to deny their own agency in the making of claims about where women should and should not have hair. Here the information is presented as if everyone knows that these places should be without hair.

There is a range of other assumptions contained within the text; one is that women spend a great deal of their time trying out unsuccessful products to remove their body hair; as the text states: 'New FEMME makes shaving, waxing, plucking and all other methods of hair removal outdated and obsolete' (col. 1) and in the order box it states: 'YES – I'm finished with old-fashioned hair removal methods.' We are to assume that the reader will recognize these as methods which she has already tried to get rid of her body hair, and that she will also recognize that these methods involve 'hard stubble, skin irritation, smelly creams, and painful plucking' (box on right). Second, the text assumes that the perfect state for women's skin should be not only hairless but 'silky smooth to the touch' (col. 1). If there is to be any hair (since inevitably there will be some regrowth) after the use of Femme it will be 'soft and downy like a baby's hair' (col. 2). This information is presented as if the reader will self-evidently recognize this as good. Skin is not necessarily good if it feels so to the woman herself, but implicitly only if it is good for someone else to touch, and adult hair on women is not to be tolerated. Hidden in these statements is a characterization of the perfect female who does not have visible body hair (that is, she is not masculine or man-like) and who is not fully adult (babies and children have soft hair). The text backs up its assertions about Femme by using pseudo-scientific statements about research, and by presenting informa-tion in diagrammatic form. It is significant that graphs in adverts are rarely read

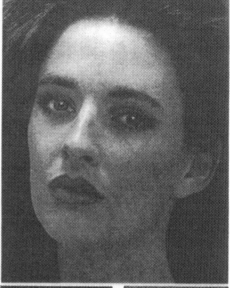

but rather serve as a signification of scientificity and authority. The text uses the language of medicine: Femme *treats* (box on right) and it is referred to as a 'treatment'. Medical terms are used, such as 'papilla', 'formulation', 'growth inhibitor' and 'compounded' (the use of the passive 'has been compounded' is also an indicator of scientificity). At the same time the language of beauty and cosmetics is also used. For example, the name of the product, Femme, is French, and many cosmetics have French names to denote femininity, glamour and perhaps otherness (L'Air du Temps, Cacharel, Paris; and also many advertisements on television for perfume are entirely in French). This name 'Femme' also delimits this product to females, since it is considered 'obvious' that whilst males have body hair, theirs is not problematic.

Many texts for and about women set up a problem which the female reader should recognize and in that moment of recognition also realize that the solution to the problem is contained within the purchase of the hair removal cream; indeed Femme is explicitly labelled 'The PERMANENT solution'. Michael Hoey has suggested that many texts are formulated around the basic structure: problem–solution (Hoey 1983). Advertisers sell their products by addressing the female reader as if she had constant problems which only their products could repair; this refrain is taken up in articles in women's magazines where there are advice columns, on how to improve or solve the problems which the reader assumes she is supposed to have (see Chapter 6). And even when the reader in this case does not have facial and body hair, she may implicitly assume because of this and other interpellations that such hair is necessarily and obviously negative. In this way, texts construct a notion of what cultures consider is commonsense or natural.

DOMINANT READING

The notion of a dominant reading has been much debated in literary theory. Yet it would seem that most readers can recognize the 'obvious' roles, positions and interpretations which the text maps out for them. This dominant reading is not the writer's intention (which is unrecoverable), but a position (or positions) which the text offers or proffers to the reader within a particular historical moment, because of the range of ideological positions available which make that text understandable. This reading will be one which is reinforced by various ideologies circulating within the culture of the time; thus, for example, a text which constructs femininity in a particular way will be made understandable because it is reinforced by a range of other texts and discourses on femininity. Without these other discourses, the text would be difficult to understand or might be incomprehensible. The link between indirect address and dominant readings is therefore that unmediated, seemingly obvious information – ideological information reinforced by other discourses – which is one of the factors in the constitution of a dominant reading.

Judith Williamson has discussed these ideas of dominant readings to some extent in her work on advertisements. She has analysed the ways in which advertisements address the reader, and the way that the reader is in fact a key element in making sense of seemingly incoherent texts (Williamson 1978). She gives the example of juxtapositions in advertisements: in an advertisement for Chanel No. 5, Catherine Deneuve holds a bottle of Chanel perfume: these are the only images in the advertisement. The reader makes a cognitive leap to make sense of these juxtaposed images by adopting the message of the advertisement: i.e. that if you want to be as beautiful, rich and famous as Deneuve, you should use Chanel perfume. It is an interesting form of advertisement, because it does not seem to address the reader directly, (there is no 'hailing' the reader as 'you') and yet indirectly it is positioning the reader into a discourse of upward aspiration through consumerism. In making that cognitive leap to make sense of the advertisement, Williamson asserts, the reader has in fact made herself into a subject, i.e. a consuming subject. The notion that texts are necessarily incomplete and incoherent and require the reader to resolve that incoherence is suggestive, and it is one which I will be drawing on later in this chapter.

To sum up, address is, in the main, partial and indirect rather than the successful and complete hailing which Althusser described, and for this reason it is possible to track it down when it is unsuccessful and to construct positions for reading other than the dominant. Because texts are always overdetermined, there are always other elements intermingled with the dominant reading. It is these elements which lead to a different oppositional reading, which I would now like to consider.

GENDER AND READER POSITION

One of the factors which critics have generally omitted in their discussion of address and positioning is gender. Judith Fetterley considers the importance of gender in reading: she has described the way that most texts in American literature appear to address a general audience, whilst in fact they are addressing the reader as a male: 'One of the main things that keeps the design of our literature unavailable to the consciousness of the woman reader, and hence impalpable, is the very posture of the apolitical, the pretense that literature speaks universal truths through forms from which all the merely personal, the purely subjective, has been burned away or at least transformed through the medium of art into the representative' (Fetterley 1978: xi). Her work is primarily a content analysis, that is, she examines various depictions of female characters which it is difficult for females to read easily unless they adopt the position of a male reader. She states: 'To read the canon of what is currently considered classic American literature is perforce to identify as male' (ibid.: xii). She suggests, and Elaine Showalter's work in this area would seem to reinforce her point, that it is standard reading practice for women students at university studying literature to position themselves as male in order to make sense of the text (Showalter 1971).[6] Fetterley states: 'While women obviously cannot rewrite literary works so that they become ours by virtue of reflecting our reality, we can accurately name the reality that they do reflect and so change literary criticism from a closed conversation to an active dialogue' (1978: xxiii). By describing the position that these texts are addressing and constructing, we can then go on to challenge literary criticism's avoidance of gender issues in the analysis of address, and we can also map out a position for ourselves as female or feminist readers in the process of doing so. It is this notion of a 'resisting reader' – a space from which female readers can read against the grain – which is most suggestive for this chapter. Thus, although texts may address us as males, we as female readers can construct a space of reading which resists the dominant reading.

Some theorists go so far as to suggest that gender itself might be considered a 'schema', that is, a framework for making sense of a text: Mary Crawford and Roger Chaffin describe schemata in this sense as 'a heterogeneous network of associations representing general knowledge rather than specific incidents' (Crawford and Chaffin 1986: 17 and see the discussion of schemata in Chapter 6). In this way, a gendered reading is one whereby the reader comes to the process of reading with a framework of expectations which are determined by her gender, and she interacts with elements in the text which are addressing her in a gendered way. These two sets of elements may not enmesh in any easy way: in fact they may often clash because the text may address the reader in a stereo-typical way which does not constitute 'being female' for her.

For example, in the accompanying advertisement for Toyota Corolla GT the reader is addressed as male.

What every young executive worth his GTi should know.

The Corolla GT has a faster top speed than the Golf GTi (122 mph v 119 mph).*

It develops considerably more brake horse power (119 Bhp v 112Bhp).*

And it is every bit as quick from 0-60mph.

The outstanding performance of the new front wheel drive Corolla GT is courtesy of its revolutionary 1600cc, 16 valve twin cam fuel injected engine.

The additional 2 valves per cylinder give you not merely extra power, but extra smooth power.

In fact, smooth is the word for everything about the Corolla.

You can go through its 5 gears like a hot knife through butter. And the clutch is light and very forgiving in stop-start conditions.

All this can be yours for only £7296 (£1068 less than the Golf GTi).

So come and test drive one.

Preferably after you've driven a Golf GTi.

The generic pronoun 'he' is used in 'What every young executive worth his GTi should know'. The reader could assume that this is a true generic and female executives might well continue to read it as addressed to them. However, the information contained within the text is stereotypically male: the car is described in terms of its top speed, compared to a Golf GTi, its braking horse-power, and its ability to go from 0 to 60 mph. There is a great deal of technical description (16 valve twin cam fuel injected engine) which signals that the text is assuming that the reader will understand this information. It should be stressed that this is a stereotyped view, and it is also a very narrowly targeted advertisement, since it assumes that the person who reads the advert will be someone who has or wants to have a GTi and who will be very concerned about driving at great speed. It does, however, assume that all male readers will know what a twin cam engine is and that women will not, and it is in the presentation of this information that the text maps out a position for its readers, which they then have to negotiate with. There will be many men (older men, men who do not drive, men who drive more expensive cars, men who know nothing about cars) who will not feel that their set of expectations maps on to the information which hails them in this text. Thus, readers are not hailed in simple ways by texts, nor do they bring to the text uniform frameworks of interpretation.

MULTIPLE POSITIONINGS

One of the primary problems for feminists when considering the notion of positioning the reader has been the notion that texts simply address us as male or female and that this is necessarily something to be avoided. Admittedly, there are a great number of problems for women in simply accepting the ideological messages which are contained in many texts; however, it is equally important not to assume that the process of criticizing these messages is a simple one of stating that a text is ideologically unsound or politically correct. Julie Rivkin, in an article on resisting readers, states that even in the process of resisting a text which provides certain information about women with which she, the reader, does not agree, she is nevertheless drawn to the text because it contains other information with which she does agree or which she finds interesting (Rivkin 1986–7). She says:

> Any convincing account of reading as a woman would have to account for the process by which one comes to a certain critical stance. Moreover, the term 'stance' is misleading, because it implies a unity and stability that is utterly alien to the experience of reading. What I would wish to substitute for stance is a sense of the historical layering and complex and often conflicting cultural investments that condition any given act of reading.
>
> (Rivkin 1986–7: 15)

Rivkin is using a psychoanalytical model of analysis in this article, and for this reason she seems not to be concerned that this view undermines a feminist critique in some ways. However, it is possible to take on board the challenging of a simple feminist position and refine that position, since as Rivkin states: 'As long as the culture is patriarchal, women will have some investment in patriarchy, and their reading stance will therefore be at least double' (Rivkin 1986–7: 16). An illustrative example of this double stance might be the advertisement for Fendi perfume, where the feminist reader can easily mount a simple critique of the image and text.

Particularly when read in conjunction with other texts of the sort, this advertisement seems to be presenting an image of femininity and female passion which is in keeping with stereotypical views of women. Here a blank-faced, rather featureless, statue-like woman is about to kiss a male statue. Her closed eyes mirror the statue's empty eyes. Her nose and lips are the same shape as his and form an interesting pattern in the middle of the text, the centre of which is the line which unites his chin and hers. Her face resembles other representations such as advertisements for the perfume Anais, Anais, and these images reach back to the 1960s with the images associated with Biba. The woman is at once presented as passive and as an object; here her object status is emphasized since her skin is the same colour and quality/texture as the statue. There are numerous intertextual references to statues being brought to life by the kiss of a female who has fallen in love with them. The female reader will gain some pleasure in recognizing the references in this rather stark text, and she may also feel pleasure in the beauty of the woman's image: the soft modulations of colour, her classical features, her finely plaited hair. The female reader may also take a more difficult pleasure in this representation of yearning signified in the woman's closed eyes and partly open mouth in stark contrast to the closed features of the male statue. As many feminist theorists have shown, some women do gain pleasure in love from the difficult pleasures of masochism and yearning (Haugg 1988). In the written text which accompanies the images, passion is stressed (in Italian) and the fact that this perfume comes from Rome is emphasized. The exclusivity of this product is stressed; it is available only in select department stores or by telephoning a Freefone number for stockists. Thus, the product is presented as occasioning passion in you the purchaser, rather than in males, which is the usual advertising strategy. Whilst the image presented of female sexuality is easy to critique in many ways, the beauty of the image is also striking, and the detective work in making sense of the text is involving. The text therefore does not present us with a simple message which we can take a position on: there are elements in the text with which we as readers might feel uncomfortable at the same time as there are elements which might give us pleasure. Even more paradoxically, those elements which make us uncomfortable may be the very ones which occasion pleasure (as in this advertisement in the suggestions of masochism).

Tanya Modleski questions the notion that we take up the positions which a text offers us, since she says:

> psychoanalytically informed theory, concerned largely with describing the way subjects are inscribed or constructed . . . tended to ignore actual social

subjects who by virtue of their complex histories and multiple cultural affiliations . . . always it is argued exceed the subject implied by the text . . . the
manipulated consumer of mass culture and the actual consumer, who in
real life is always caught up in a network of discourses unharmoniously
clamouring for the subject's allegiance, an allegiance that the individual
. . . may choose either to grant or to withhold.

(Modleski 1991: 36–7)

In this view of ideological position, the reader is never interpellated in a simple
way as only a woman or as a man; there will be multiple positionings and
multiple negotiations with them. Modleski goes on to say: 'For feminism it is
not simply a question of affirming or denying the accuracy of patriarchal
representations but of understanding what texts . . . do, how they produce the
very resemblances they are then seen to reflect' (Modleski 1991: 51).

To summarize, address to the reader or interpellation is clearly more complex
than conventionally described, and it is therefore necessary to integrate into this
framework the notion of indirect address and its relation to the production of
a dominant reading. Furthermore, gender is an important element in the
construction of the reader's position, but gender cannot be considered as a unitary
element either in the construction of the reading position or in terms of the
reader's response to that positioning. However, this does not mean that gender
is not a significant factor in the process of reading; what is required is a more
complex notion of what 'reading as a woman/man' consists of, which would
take account of other factors which interact with gender.

Part II

Analysis

Chapter 4

Analysis at the Level of the Word

In this chapter, I deal with the question of gender bias at the level of the analysis of individual words. In the first section, I focus on the more general and theoretical aspects of sexism and give an account of generic usage; in the second section I examine specific types of sexist language-use. In both sections, I am concerned with the way that feminist critics have dealt with sexism in language, and the effects which they claim this type of language-usage has on readers, particularly females. By examining examples of usage such as the sex-specific pronoun use, the misuse of generics, address terms and the negative descriptions of females in a variety of texts, it is hoped to show that language-use can present and perpetuate a particular view of women. However, from this chapter, it is clear that although we may be encouraged by the norms of the language to speak in particular ways and reinforce certain visions of the potentialities of women and men in our society, there is a range of options open to speakers to resist sexist usage. I describe a gender-free use of language which avoids unnecessary gender-specific terms and uses generics to refer to both women and men. As well as giving examples of ways to use gender-free language, I also give examples of strategies which can be used to counter sexism in general.

SEXISM IN LANGUAGE

Sexism in language can be defined in a variety of different ways; Mary Vetterling-Braggin suggests one definition: '[a statement] is sexist if it contributes to, encourages or causes or results in the oppression of women' (Vetterling-Braggin 1981: 2). She shows that this is perhaps too limited a definition in that it restricts sexism to language about women and therefore she suggests the following definition: '[a statement] is sexist if its use constitutes, promotes or exploits an unfair or irrelevant or impertinent distinction between the sexes' (ibid.: 3).

When considering these issues, it is necessary to ask to what extent our perception of the world, and what we understand 'natural' sex roles to be, is in fact influenced by the language we speak. This last point is probably the most significant, and controversial, of all the questions relating to meaning which will be posed in this chapter. We need to consider whether language just 'reflects' the world (i.e. just 'puts names' on things which self-evidently exist without language), or whether there is a case to be made for language affecting the way we perceive the world (i.e. things which our language names become more 'evident' than things which our language does not name). The argument for the second position, linguistic determinism, was put forward by Sapir and Whorf. [1]

Linguistic Determinism

The theory of linguistic determinism suggests that differences in the structures of languages actually determine the different views societies have of the world. Furthermore, it is suggested that the language of a culture shapes the way its speakers see the world. It is possible to analyse this argument as consisting of two stages. The first stage – that people name the world differently, emphasizing different aspects, depending on what is most relevant to their way of life – is not too problematic. The example most commonly given of this is the many different words for snow used by Inuit people, in contrast to the limited number of words for snow available in the English language (see Whorf 1956; Montgomery 1986a: 171–97). Because snow is less a part of everyday life in Britain, we have developed fewer words for talking about it. However, certain communities of English speakers *do* need to be able to talk about the quality of snow as part of their normal activities – competitive skiers, British Rail, geographers and mountain climbers, for example. We assume that a language responds to the needs of a community, and the fact that some languages have a great number of ready-made ways of describing certain phenomena, and others do not, is seen to reflect what those cultures find relevant and important to their way of life.

Linguistic determinism takes this argument one stage further, however, and argues that language *produces* our perception of the world. According to this second stage of the argument, our thought-systems are influenced by the language of our community, so that our idea of 'reality' is constrained by the linguistic forms available to us as members of that community. 'The fact of the matter is that the "real world" is to a large extent unconsciously built upon the language habits of the group. No two languages are ever sufficiently similar to be considered as representing the same social reality. The worlds in which different societies live are distinct worlds, not merely the same world with different labels attached' (Sapir in Mandelbaum 1949: 162). Thus, according to the Sapir–Whorf hypothesis, if a speech community does not have a pre-formed way of expressing a certain concept, it follows that members of that community do not have that concept as part of their readily available knowledge about the world. There are of course infinite gradations in how strongly this view is held by its subscribers. Most people who concur with the theory of linguistic determinism do so to a greater or lesser degree (see G. Lakoff 1987). It has also been strongly criticized, because of its potentially racist applications. It would be possible, for example, to use the theory to argue that some cultures were, in some way, lesser because their languages were perceived as inadequate.

The argument about how language influences our perception of the world is important to feminists for a number of reasons. There have been many critical feminist surveys of English lexis (Nilsen *et al.* 1977; Schultz 1990; J. Mills 1989), which have argued that sexism is inherent in many of the labels which English speakers use. Other feminists have written about lexical gaps in the language – women's experiences which they find hard to talk about, because English provides them with no readily available term (Spender 1980). It is frequently argued that these usages, and others detailed below, reveal how sexist our society is. Feminists taking this position argue that language reforms are in essence pointless, because as long as society is sexist, sexist meanings will reappear, and to change language forms is to deal with the symptoms, not the cause. However, feminists who accept the linguistic determinism argument to any degree are in favour of language reform, because they claim that the circulation of these meanings produces and reinforces sexism in our society. There are good arguments on both sides of the debate. In support of the case for language merely being a mirror of patriarchal societies, there is evidence that where gender-free terms have been created they have often been contaminated with sexist meanings through their use. An example of this is the terms 'chairperson' and 'spokesperson'. What has happened is that the labels 'chairman' and 'spokesman' have continued to be used by the media when reporting about a male, and the gender-neutral terms are used when reporting about a female. Feminists tend to interpret this usage as indicating the higher status of male speakers, in a public world where it is still seen as anomalous for a woman to have a high-status position. Thus, a language reform has simply involved a temporary shifting of meanings, until the old hierarchy has been restored. Feminists who argue that how people view the world, and the relative position of the sexes within it, is influenced by language-use, have conducted empirical work in support of their claims. Wendy Martyna has researched the extent to which women feel excluded by the use of the male pronoun 'he' as a generic to refer to both women and men (Martyna 1983). Sandra Bem also reports studies where sex-unbiased job advertisements have been found to encourage more high-school females to apply for male-related jobs (Bem *et al.* 1973). Evidence of this kind suggests that language choices do have an impact on how we view the world, and therefore affect the material conditions of women's lives.

For many people, the issue of sexist language may at first seem rather trivial: first, because it appears to be a dispute which raged in the 1960s and 1970s, but which is of little relevance now in the seemingly more egalitarian 1990s. Many feminists believe that this is not the case (see, for example, Spender 1980; Cameron 1985; Miller and Swift 1980). The debate over gender-free language has indeed been rather swept aside, and has certainly been devalued as an attempt to impose 'political correctness'; however, the issue is still seen by many as a persistent problem. Language is used not simply for the communication of ideas, but also for the creation and maintenance of an environment for effective communication between people, either in face-to-face interaction, in mediated interaction (for example, on a phone or through an electronic medium), or through texts. As I have mentioned, sexist language is that language-use, conscious or unconscious on the part of the speaker, which may alienate females (and males), and which may lead to the establishment of an environment which is not conducive to communication and effective social interactions.

For many people, debates about what they see as 'politically correct' language are simply discussions of an academic linguistic nature; for them, the real struggles take place not around the use of a particular word in a text, but over questions of equal pay and discrimination in the workplace.[2] For feminists such as Robin Lakoff, sexism in language simply *reflects* sexism within society, and is a symptom rather than a cause (R. Lakoff 1975). They argue that only by changing that wider sexism will any change occur in language. Sarah Shute summarizes this claim by stating 'that people cannot help to eliminate sexism merely by "talk", by replacing terms with other terms, but only by *actions*' (Shute 1981: 25). However, this view fails to see language as also constituting action in itself; we not only communicate or give information in language, we also perform actions (see Brown and Yule 1983).

A further problem for many with the notion of sexist language is that accusing someone of sexism is a statement of moral superiority over that person. As Mike Bygrave states in his article on politically correct language, those who accuse others of sexism are speaking as if their own language-use was 'purified' and above reproach (Bygrave 1991: 14) and as Frye states, 'To accuse a person of being sexist is to accuse him of having certain false beliefs, and in some cases of having tendencies to certain reprehensible behaviour presumed to be related one way or another to such beliefs' (Frye 1981: 12). Thus, attempts to change someone's language-use can often be met with great resistance and ridicule. Consider, for example, the following passage from a cookery article from the *Sunday Times* where attempts to reform language are treated as ridiculous: 'Of course full justice to a steamed pudding can only be done by a true trencherman. The term is used advisedly, for I have never encountered a feminine trencher-person whose curves could easily expand to accommodate a second helping.' Here, not only are anti-sexist strategies parodied ('feminine trencherperson' is used whereas an anti-sexist would try to find an equivalent but non-sexist term), but also women are ridiculed as they are not 'man' enough to eat the full portion of the pudding referred to.

Some feminists, such as Casey Miller and Kate Swift, see sexist language as symptomatic of larger-scale discrimination, but propose that most sexism is unintentional and therefore reform is possible (Miller and Swift 1979). Simply to point out to someone that their language is sexist and to suggest more acceptable alternatives will lead to changes in language-usage in the long term. There is an alternative to these views, proposed by feminists such as Mary Daly and Dale Spender; they see sexist language as a *causal* factor in women's oppression (Daly 1981; Spender 1980). Basing their work on the theories of Sapir and Whorf, they propose that language is an extremely important element in the formation of our world-view and the way that we think (see Cameron 1990b). Language, here, rather than simply reflecting society, actually brings about and shapes changes in the way we see and think. The fact that, for example, there are few words for certain areas of women's experience means either that women do not apprehend their own experience or that they apprehend it only through male-oriented terms. The example Spender gives is the word 'motherhood' which she states cannot collocate with words like 'unhappy' or 'depressing'; she says that this leads women who do not experience motherhood in positive ways to feel that their experience is in some way aberrant. For Spender, language is controlled by men, and therefore women begin to see their experience from a male perspective (see Cameron 1985 for an account of the debate over whether sexist language is a symptom or a cause of larger-scale discrimination).[3]

Cameron states that in order to change sexist language it is not enough to reform the language-use of individuals whom you meet; the change has to be at an institutional level, at the level of what she calls the 'gatekeepers of language'. Feminists have thus attempted to influence institutions to adopt policies concerning sexism, often as part of an overall equal opportunities policy. Many institutions, such as educational establishments, publishing houses and organizations like the British Sociological Association, have developed gender-free or anti-sexist language policies, which advocate that care be taken to avoid sexist usage in documents. However, whilst changes have happened in the type of language which is used to describe women or the relative merits of either sex within these institutions, it is clear that such policies are not being adhered to in many documents and interactions. It is very difficult to attempt to formulate a policy which is sufficiently flexible and yet sufficiently limited in order to define sexist language, and it is also very difficult to impose a policy on language-use. I would like therefore to discuss several aspects of the gender-free language debate and provide strategies for avoiding gender-specific or sexist language.

In this section, I will concentrate on generic forms: that is, those elements in language which perpetuate a view of the male as a norm or universal and the female as deviant or individual. The linguistic forms present the male as an unmarked and the female as a marked form.

Generic Pronouns

The generic pronoun 'he' is perhaps the most well-known example of gender-specific or sexist language, and is frequently referred to as 'he-man' language. An example of a generic pronoun is: 'When an author has completed *his* manuscript, *he* can send it to the publishers.' The traditional argument is that the 'his' and 'he' are used here not sex-specifically, but generically; that is, although the pronouns refer grammatically to the singular male author, they should be taken to refer to both male and female authors in general. Many researchers have shown that, in fact, this is not the way that generic pronouns are understood (see, for example, Kidd 1971; Eberhardt 1976; Martyna 1978 and 1980; Brannon 1978; Mackay *et al.* 1979). In most of these research experiments, students were asked to complete fragmentary stories which contained the generic pronoun 'he', and in the majority of the cases, they completed the stories with the use of 'he' as a sex-specific pronoun or with a male named character. Robertson's research on visualization and generic pronouns also supports this notion that people tend to visualize male participants when the supposed generic pronoun 'he' is used (Robertson 1990).

In the media in general, the seeming generic 'he' is often disambiguated with a male image; for example, in an advertisement for Lufthansa, there is the following caption: 'What does today's business traveller expect of his airline?' A generic noun (business traveller) is followed by a generic pronoun (his), and one is to assume from analysis of the sentence in isolation that both male and female business travellers are being addressed; however, the accompanying picture depicts an aeroplane full of male business travellers reclining comfortably in their seats, the only female participant being the air-hostess serving them. Thus, the supposedly generic pronoun is in practice presented in a way in which it can only be understood as gender-specific, i.e. as referring to males.

Mackay (1983) has argued that the so-called generic 'he' is confusing for the reader, since, in some instances, it is not clear whether the reference is truly generic or in fact gender-specific; for example, 'The more education an individual attains, the better his occupation is likely to be.' Mackay asserts that, in this example, it is impossible to be sure whether the nouns and pronouns are being used generically, that is, that this is true of all individuals, or gender-specifically, that is, that this is true only of male individuals. Thus the so-called generic use may in fact confuse rather than clarify.

Gender-specific pronouns are often used in a sexist way to refer to people working in stereotypically male and female professions; for example: 'If a physics lecturer needs a lab. assistant, he should contact the secretary' and 'A secretary is permitted to smoke in her own office.' Professors, scientists and engineers tend to be labelled as necessarily male, and nurses, librarians, secretaries and models as female. Similarly, where the sex of a person referred to is not known, it is common practice to assume that the person is male; for example, in this situation where B does not know the sex of the director:

A: I'm going to complain to the director.
B: Do you think he'll be able to do anything?

There is an assumption here on B's part that all directors are male. Non-sex-specific pronouns, such as 'he or she' or 'they' are preferable, unless the speaker wishes to run the risk of seeming to align herself with stereotypical ideas of male and female work-roles.[4]

Generic Nouns

Sexist language is also that language which presents male-oriented experience as generic or as the norm: for example, in its clearest form, when discussing humanity as a whole, the terms 'mankind' and 'man' are often used. Research has shown that rather that these being understood as true generics, readers recognize them as terms which refer to males (Martyna 1983). For example, in a book entitled *Prehistoric Man*, where 'man' seems to be being used generically, in fact, the 'man' referred to is the male member of the species whose exploits are subsequently detailed in the book, with women's activities being described as only auxiliary. This can be further seen where, for example, prehistoric 'man' is represented as male. The representation below shows that the generic 'man' is not a term which refers to both men and women, since here only males of the species are shown to be involved in the process of evolution.

There are phrases which contain 'man' which are equally gender-specific; for example, 'to be man enough' and 'to be the right man for the job'. The gender-specific nature of this term can be seen when we try to use the term to refer to females, for example: '*Man is a mammal which breastfeeds his young.'[5] For many people, this sentence sounds strange, since, when the referent to the term 'man' is female, it cannot be used generically. This example makes it clear that 'man' is commonly used not as a true generic, but rather as a gender-specific term. It is difficult to try to change these to gender-free examples, by replacing

Source: Cover illustration from Stephen Jay Gould, *Ever Since Darwin*, London: Random House.

Salesman
(Male/Female)
Scotland

This is an outstanding opportunity to join one of the major UK conglomerates which can boast genuine profitable growth both organically and by acquisition.

After successful reconfiguration of the Housewares Division, we currently seek a self starting, highly motivated sales person to achieve our objectives for 1993

Reporting to the Northern Divisional Manager, the successful applicant, with a wide and varied product portfolio, will manage and develop a mixed range of customer types in the non-food market.

Aged 24–34, you will be able to demonstrate proven territory management skills along with a successful sales record on FMCG and be totally committed and hungry for continued success.

Ideal location is the Glasgow/ Edinburgh/Central Belt. In return we offer an attractive salary, bonus, lunch allowance, telephone allowance and Sierra 1.8 GL company car and real personal growth opportunities.

If you match our requirements, interested male or female applicants should send their CV to Mr C. Lochrie, Northern Divisional Manager, The Croydex Company Limited, Central Way, Andover, Hants SP10 5AW.

A Lionheart Company

Source: The Herald, 24 July 1992.

'man' with 'person', since 'to be person enough' does not have the same connotations as the term it replaces. There are also ready-made phrases which, because of their rather fixed nature, are difficult to alter to gender-free language; for example, 'men in white coats' to refer to scientists, and 'man in the street' to refer to ordinary people; as I will discuss later in this chapter in relation to proverbs, these phrases are usually taken whole, that is, there is a fixity about them which does not lend itself to alteration, and in some ways their overall meaning surpasses their surface meaning. It would be difficult to substitute 'women in white coats' or 'woman in the street', except if marked or ironic. This fixity of usage often leads to some strange uses of language; for instance, in the example from *The Herald* (24 July 1992) where the job description asks for 'Salesman (male/female)' as if salesman and female were not contradictory terms. It is clear here that the people who are advertising the position of sales-man are either uncomfortable with the connotations of the term 'salesperson' or simply have not realized in any real sense that 'salesman' can really refer only to men.

'Man' is also used as a prefix in such examples as 'man-power' or 'man-hours', or as an affix in such examples as 'craftsman', 'seaman', 'policeman', 'fireman', 'postman', 'dustman', 'fisherman', and in the verb 'to man' ('He manned the stall').[6] In all of these cases the seemingly generic nature of the term is often undercut by the context, and is usually understood as referring only to males. Some of them have truly generic alternatives; for example, 'craftworker', 'angler', 'police officer', 'firefighter', 'postie', 'refuse collector' and so on. These generic alternatives may be used in equal measure to the more sex-specific ones; for example, 'signalworker' was used as frequently as 'signalman' in reports of the 1994 strike. Other sex-specific terms have not as yet developed substitutes; for example, 'seaman', 'ombudsman' and 'workman'. Let us examine an example of this.

The Royal Mail leaflet features a picture of a postman, taking up most of the front cover, and a picture of a postwoman in a small section on the back. The text on the front of the leaflet is ambiguous as to whether the 'man' in 'postman' and the 'he' are generic or not; it is possible to interpret 'postman' as being generic since it is clearly not just this postman who 'has a message about the environment', but all of the 'postmen' who deliver mail. However, it seems that 'postman' here refers to all those 'postmen' who are in fact 'men' (although the word 'postie' has been suggested to refer generically to mail-deliverers, there is not as yet a generic term which has been used widely), because on the back of the leaflet next to the representation of the woman, the text states 'Postmen and postwomen deliver 60 million letters a day'. This usage leads the reader to assume that the original usage of 'postman' is generic only in so far as it refers to all males, and does not include females in its reference.

There are similar difficulties with the word 'gentlemen'; it would seem to be sex-specific in that it has a binary opposition of 'lady', but it is used in a seemingly generic way to refer to certain types of polite behaviour, speaking of behaving

'like a gentleman', and calling a verbal contract 'a gentleman's agreement'. It is unclear whether these words can be used to refer to verbal contracts between women or to polite behaviour by women. It is interesting that even new words are being developed within this framework, since a personal stereo is generally termed a 'walkman'.[7]

The seeming generic is not restricted to the word 'man'; there are many nouns and verbs which are also used in a similar way. For example, in a book by Ronald Hyams entitled *Empire and Sexuality* (1990), the author states: 'Circumcision lingered much longer in America, where it was estimated that at the beginning of the 1970s more that 90% of Americans were circumcised at birth' (Hyams 1990: 86) and 'Indians were accustomed to establish friendship bonds with strangers by the loan of women' (Hyams 1990: 95). In the first example, Hyams uses 'Americans', a generic noun, to refer, in fact, only to American males; we are to assume that only American males are circumcised. In the second example, he uses 'Indians' to refer only to Indian males and 'strangers' to refer to male strangers. Women here are characterized as objects since they are the object of a prepositional phrase, 'loan of', which normally takes only a non-animate object. A further example is a headline from an article on AIDS in the *Observer*, which clearly shows that generic nouns, even those which seem to be gender-free, are often used in a gender-specific way: 'TOP PEOPLE TOLD: TAKE A MISTRESS'; here top people are being advised to restrict their sexual indiscretions to one person when they go away on business (that is, one person other than their spouse). Here 'people' is generic, but the ensuing sentence 'take a mistress' and the accompanying story make clear the fact that the reference is to males only, since we are to assume that the *Observer* is not suggesting that female top people should also take a mistress.[8]

But generic nouns which refer in fact only to males can be found in other contexts as well; for example, in the TWA advertisement overleaf, the term 'transatlantic business travellers' is clearly generic in its usage. However, the images do disambiguate the text, since although the reference could be generic and refer to female business travellers as well as males, in the images which accompany the text females act as flight attendants and secretaries. There is one small image of a woman who is a business traveller, but the overall impression of the text and the image together is of business travellers being male rather than male and female.

There are a number of terms which originally were male-specific and which have evolved to refer to women as well, but here again, it is debatable whether women really are referred to in these terms. One example is the use of the term 'guy' which can be used, particularly in America, to refer to women as well as men. So 'you guys' can be used to refer to a group of young women and men. In a similar way, 'research fellow' was originally a male-specific term which is now used for males and females (Bachelor and Master of Arts/Science could also be classified in this category). Other terms such as 'sort' (as in 'he's a decent sort') and 'chap' can also be used generically. However, many women feel that because of their history, these terms do not include them within their reference and they resent being referred to by a term which was originally male-specific. As Hodge and Kress state: 'former meanings often survive to complicate the lexicon and gesture at history' (Hodge and Kress 1988: 187) as we will see in more detail in the next section.

Women as the Marked Form

The range of insult terms for women which relate to their sexual availability has been widely documented (see, for comprehensive surveys, Spender 1980; Kramarae and Treichler 1985), and I will discuss this in the next section. I would like to concentrate here on affixes used to refer to women, which lead to a view of women as a deviation from a male universal norm. The female form is seen as the marked term and the male as the unmarked term. There are a range of different affixes which are used to refer to women, such as 'lady' and '-ess', '-ette', '-enne', '-trix', and these have connotations which the male term does not; these connotations are generally derogatory and trivializing. Terms like 'lady poet', 'lady doctor' and so on generally lend an air of amateurism to the person whom they are describing. Lady poets rarely write for a living. It is interesting

that even with the more acceptable term 'woman' (as in 'woman writer'), it is still necessary to mark the gender of the female, but not the male, who is referred to simply as a 'writer'. The terms 'actress', 'authoress', 'hostess', 'stewardess', 'poetess', 'comedienne', 'aviatrix' and so on also have this sense of lack of seriousness about them, especially when they are compared with the male term (compare 'aviator' and 'aviatrix'). Many of them, etymologically speaking, are diminutive forms of the male term; that is, '-ette' can be seen to mean 'smaller than' or 'less than'. It is interesting to note that terms like 'usherette' (in the context of a cinema) have no male equivalent. These terms pose something of a dilemma for feminist analysis; for most theorists, these are terms which should be avoided because they have trivializing connotations.

In the animal 'kingdom', the generic noun which is used to refer to the animal grouping is often the same as that used to refer to the individual male, so that, for example, we talk about the lion as an animal and about the behaviour of the lion (the individual male); whereas if we wish to talk about female lions we use a marked term: 'lioness'. It would seem more logical to use the generic in all cases; however, since that generic is already coded as male, it seems as if women's presence in the language is being erased. For some theorists, these marked terms, although negatively coded, at least demonstrate the presence of women.

Effects of Sexist Language-Use

As mentioned earlier, the use of sexist language items may have three effects:

1 it may alienate female interlocutors and cause them to feel that they are not being addressed;
2 it may be one of the factors which may cause women to view themselves in a negative or stereotyped way. It may thus have an effect on the expectations women and men have of what women can do;
3 it may confuse listeners, both male and female (for example, as to whether a true generic noun or pronoun is being used or a gender-specific one).

Much research (Eberhardt 1976; Martyna 1980; Adamsky 1981) has shown that sexist language does have far-reaching effects not only in the short term on people's relation to others and their environment, but also in the long term on their self-image and confidence.

Gender-free or anti-sexist language is a conscious choice by speakers to assure readers and listeners that they do not view the world as the male domain that it may appear to be. By their language-use, writers and speakers can demonstrate an acceptance of the validity of women's experiences and contributions. The use of 'he or she' in sentences does not simply give information; rather it signals a certain orientation and attitude which is critical of stereotypical views of the roles of the sexes.

Gender-Free Language

In this section, I provide some guidelines as to what might constitute a gender-free language practice.[9] There are many possible strategies, and I list the most feasible for a writing practice.

Address terms should be truly generic unless a gender-specific term is necessary; for example, if someone wishes to refer only to the male or the female members of her group. In the case of addressing a chairperson, the terms 'chair', 'chairperson' (without 'Madam' or 'Mrs' before it), 'convenor', or the person's name should be used. This should be the case for all chairs and not simply those chairpersons who are female.[10] Official documents and forms should use 'Ms' or should leave a space for 'Ms' or for no title at all as options. In such documents, marital status should not be requested. When writing to someone whose sex or marital status is not known the following strategies are available.

1 Do not assume that all people who use initials rather than their first names are male (i.e. T. G. Brown could be male or female).
2 Use the name that is given to you rather than trying to guess someone's marital status (i.e. 'Dear T. G. Brown' or 'Dear Terry Brown').

If it is necessary to use a title, use 'Mr/s' which seems to include within it all eventualities; for example, 'Dear Mr/s Brown', which covers both females and males.

To avoid the problems of seemingly generic pronouns in the example cited on p. 87, 'When the author has finished his manuscript, he can send it to the publisher', there are the following choices.

1 *Use the plural pronoun.* The example becomes: 'When authors have finished their manuscripts, they can send them to the publishers.' This is the easiest option since it is the least cumbersome to continue reference throughout a paragraph.
2 *Use s/he.* The example becomes the slightly more unwieldy: 'When an author has finished his/her manuscript, s/he can send it to the publisher.' For many, this is an attractive option for isolated sentences, rather than for repeated reference in a paragraph. It does, however, signal to readers that a conscious effort is being made to include them.
3 *Passivize.* The example becomes: 'When manuscripts have been finished, they should be sent to the publisher.' This, like example 1, is better for extended use in paragraphs, since it is not as unwieldy as example 2; it can also be used in alternate sentences with the plural pronoun in a passage of extended pronoun reference.
4 *Use the female pronoun as generic.* The example becomes: 'When an author has finished her manuscript, she can send it to the publisher.' For some writers, this is an option to be chosen because 'she' can be seen to 'contain' 'he' within it. It can also foreground the effects of other types of so-called generic use. (See Cameron 1985 for a discussion, and an example of its extended use.)

5 *Use the male pronoun as generic with a proviso.* For example: 'When the author has finished his manuscript, he can send it to the publisher', is prefaced by the statement 'When I use the pronoun "he", this should be taken to refer to both females and males.' However, much research (see Martyna 1980 for a review) has shown that even with this proviso, the generic pronoun is still understood to refer to males.

6 *Use alternate pronouns.* Some authors use 'she' for the first occurrence of the pronoun, 'he' for the next, and so on. This has the disadvantage of being potentially confusing.

These changes make little alteration to the informational content of the sentence, but the address of the sentence has changed so that both males and females are equally addressed.[11]

One gender-free language-usage which often causes irritation is the use of the pronoun 'their' as a referent for 'everyone' or 'anyone'; for example: 'Everyone should complete *their* assignments on time.' It is argued that this should not be encouraged, since it is grammatically incorrect. However, it is used widely in spoken English and is beginning to be used extensively in written texts (see Coates 1987 who uses it consistently and elegantly throughout her work).

Generic nouns should be used appropriately, so that terms like 'people' should be followed by the pronoun 'they' or by generic reference. When gender-specific reference is necessary, generics should not be used; that is, 'people' should not be used to refer to males only; 'men' should be used instead. However, a problem which arises in this context is one which Deborah Cameron has noted; she says: 'What if the word astronaut . . . is used by most people as if it too were male-only' (Cameron 1985: 85). What she means by this is that we may try to reform language, but that reform may be ineffective if people still think in sexist ways and use language accordingly. Thus when referring to women who are astronauts, it would not make a great deal of difference if the term 'spacewoman' or 'woman-astronaut' were used; behind each usage is the notion that spaceman or astronaut is a male norm. A further problem that some feminists have encountered is that if you accept the generic noun rather than using gender-specific words, using 'flight attendant' rather than 'steward' and 'stewardess/air-hostess', the very specificity of the female is lost altogether, and woman are made 'invisible', as mentioned above, where it is still seen as anomalous for a woman to have a high-status position. However, in much the same way that most people avoid terms which are openly racist, or which refer to someone's colour where that is not a salient feature, terms which seem to be derogatory to women should be avoided. Terms which refer to a woman's sexual characteristics or body shape, or even which refer to her gender when this is not relevant, should be avoided, since these should not be seen as features which define her. When we are talking about a female actor, the most important feature about her is that she is an actor and not that she is female; only where her sex is the most important feature should it be included. Thus, 'actor', 'steward', 'writer' should be used for both males and females. Where it is necessary to mark for gender (and there are remarkably few cases where it is necessary to do so), 'female' and 'male' should be used; for example: 'Male stewards on British Airways wear ties, whereas female stewards do not.' Care should be taken that this usage of 'male' and 'female' to modify the generic is done equally; i.e. that 'male' is used in equal measures to 'female'. With terms such as the above, it is often objected that these changes cannot be implemented because the terms themselves are inelegant or too complex: 'Ms' is too difficult to pronounce, 'chair' does not sound as elegant as chairman, 'she or he' is unwieldy, and so on. However, in terms of phonetic structure and grammatical complexity, they are clearly not in essence any more complicated or inelegant than the terms they replace.

Apart from these fairly slight problems of which terms to use, there are more fundamental theoretical problems with the notion of sexism. For Cameron:

> There is a slippery heterogeneity about so-called sexist language; it is not just the case of certain words being offensive, but of sexism entering into many levels of language from morphology (for example, word endings) which is usually seen as part of a language's core, through to stylistic conventions in specific 'fields' or discourse, which are much less general, more conscious and more context-bound . . . 'sexist language' cannot be regarded as simply the 'naming' of the world from one, masculinist perspective; it is better conceptualised as a multifaceted phenomenon occurring in a number of quite complex systems of representation, all with their places in historical traditions.
>
> (Cameron 1990b: 14)

Thus, it is quite clear that it is not sufficient to restrict our analyses of sexism to lexical items, although these terms do need investigation; rather it is necessary to see the development of those terms as symptomatic of larger-scale problems at the level of discourse as I will show in later chapters.

Vetterling-Braggin feels that there are problems with restricting sexism to the usage of certain words, since as I show in the following section, words out of context do not mean in the way that they do in context; therefore we need to be very specific about the context in which these words appear in order to come to some evaluation of whether a word is sexist or not. Take, for example, the word 'girl'; it is not sexist when it is used to describe females of under 16 years old, but it is sexist when used of females over that age. Even here there are problems; consider, for example, the phrase 'We're just going for a girls-night-out', when used by women. If the same phrase is used by men in order to make fun of women's evenings together, then perhaps the phrase becomes sexist. This makes clear the importance of context, and emphasizes the need not to assume that sexism resides within individual language items. The term 'girl' has further problems since it is frequently used asymmetrically; it is used as one term in a binary opposition men:girls (rather than men:women), for example, when girl is used to refer to women athletes and man is used to refer to male athletes.

It should be noted that Suzanne Charlton who reads the weather forecast on television is referred to in the *Daily Mirror* as a 'weathergirl' whilst Michael Fish is referred to as a 'weatherman'.

Marilyn Frye feels that the conventional definitions of sexism are inadequate, since, for her, sexism is a question of attitude or belief and not a question of simple language-use; for her 'sexists are those who hold certain sorts of general beliefs about sexual differences and their consequences' (Frye 1981: 9). This is rather unspecific as to what sorts of effects these beliefs have, and therefore Sarah Shute suggests a further definition; sexists are those 'whose actions, practices and use of laws, rules and customs limit certain activities of people of one sex but . . . not the other' (Shute 1981: 27). Thus analysis of sexism in language is not simply concerned with objecting to differences in language concerning the difference between males and females but rather it is interested in those differences which have effects.

Vetterling-Braggin (1981: 2) says that it is extremely difficult to state once and for all that a sentence or phrase is sexist; however, she gives examples of sexist language which she claims we can all agree on:

1 Women make terrible drivers.
2 She's a foxy chick.
3 Some women drive badly.
4 She's attractive.

For her, example 1 is sexist as is example 2, since both of them make statements about women which are negative and demeaning. Example 1 assumes that all women behave in a similar way, and makes this appear to be part of the nature of being female. Example 2 demeans the woman by referring to her in terms of her sexual attractiveness as her most important attribute, and the metaphor which is used is an animal one, denying this woman's human qualities. Examples 3 and 4 she asserts are not sexist, because they are specific to individual females. It should be noted, however, that it is difficult to say categorically that these last statements are *not* sexist; they are clearly less sexist than the first two statements, but they are more likely to be used for women than they are for men, since they accord with stereotypes of female behaviour. The statement 'Some men drive badly' makes very different sense from example 3, since there is no stereotype of males that they, as a group, drive badly. Similarly, in example 4, it may not appear to be sexist to refer to a specific woman's attractiveness, but that ignores the fact that women as a whole are more frequently referred to in relation to their physical characteristics. 'Attractive' is also a term which is generally used more for women than for men. Where there is this sex-differential at the level of usage, these statements cannot be analysed simply as not being sexist.

Sexism in language is obviously an extremely complex issue, which is often simplified in discussions for the sake of clarity. However, although sexism is clearly more than simple language items, there is action which can be taken at the level of those language items. The conscious adoption of a gender-free language policy

GENDER-FREE LANGUAGE

Gender Studies Research Unit

GUIDELINES FOR THE USE OF GENDER-FREE LANGUAGE

What is sexist language?

Language is not simply used for the communication of ideas, but also for the creation and maintenance of an environment for effective communication between any group of people. Discrimination in language – whether conscious or unconscious – has direct implications for equal opportunities practice in all aspects of education, by alienating and offending certain members of a community. Just as we would seek to avoid terms which are discriminatory on the grounds of a person's race, class or disability, so an increasing amount of attention is being paid to terms which are described as sexist. Sexist language is any item of language which, through its structure or use, constitutes a male-as-norm view of society by trivialising, insulting or rendering women invisible. It can also be seen as language which makes an unnecessary and irrelevant reference to a person's sex or gender.

GENDER-FREE LANGUAGE

Sexist language tends to fall into the following groups:

ADDRESS:

There are a number of terms of address which may irritate women and which may signal that they are not being taken seriously by the addresser:

X *Mr/Mrs/Miss*: avoid using these three titles only as women may feel irritated by having to reveal marital status when the same is not expected of men.

• Unless a preference is stated, use parallel terms such as Mr and Ms or offer a choice of Ms as an option. e.g. Mr/Ms/Mrs/Miss.

X 'Virginia Woolf and Dickens', (when referring to Woolf and Dickens): avoid using first names for women and second names for men, this suggests that women are being treated in a discriminatory fashion.

• Use parallel terms when addressing women and men, whether for writers, students or colleagues; 'Virginia Woolf and Charles Dickens', 'Susan Coles and David Shepherd' or 'Ms Coles and Mr Shepherd'. Use a woman's first name rather than her husband's: i.e. Ms Gill Spencer, rather than Mrs David Spencer.

GENERICS:

The terms *he* and *man* are frequently used as so-called 'generic' terms, as in the following examples: "You must know your client's circumstances before you give him advice"; "Man is the most intelligent of the species"; and "TV Street paved with gold for admen". Empirical research shows that these 'generics' are generally understood as gender

GENDER-FREE LANGUAGE

specific terms, in that they trigger images of male referents alone. There is clearly a disparity between the way generics are intended to be used and the way in which they are commonly understood. In addition, since *he* and *man* have two meanings, it is often unclear whether the nouns and pronouns are being used generically or gender-specifically, as in the example "the more education an individual attains, the better his occupation is likely to be". This use may confuse rather than clarify.

X "You must know your client's circumstances before you give him advice." Avoid making assumptions about a person's gender. Use *he/him/his* for gender-specific reference only. For generic reference (as above) the following strategies are possible:

• Change the form of the sentence to plural or passive: "You must know your clients' circumstances before you give them advice" or "A client's circumstances must be known before advice is given."

• Use one of the following as a singular generic pronoun: *s/he, she or he, they,* or *she* (as a form of positive discrimination). "You must know your client's circumstances before you give him/her advice', or "You must know … before you give them advice."

X "Man is the most intelligent of the species": avoid the use of *man* to refer to people in general as it excludes women from the reference.

• Choose neutral alternatives such as *humanity, humans, people*: "Humans are the most intelligent of the species."

GENDER-FREE LANGUAGE

X "Give our policemen the officers they deserve"; avoid this use of *man* in compound nouns, as it implies that the group is exclusively male.

• Use a noun phrase without *man*; "Give our police the officers they deserve." Neutral alternatives can be found for most examples, such as 'fire-fighters', 'sales staff' and 'reporters' for 'firemen', 'salesmen' and 'newsmen'.

DEROGATORY/PATRONISING TERMS:

There are a number of terms frequently used to address groups of women, such as girls', which many people find patronising. Other terms, 'authoress' for example, which describe women in professional roles, suggest a lack of seriousness and carry the assumption that women are an exception to the male norm: "MacEnroe is one of the best tennis players in the world today and Navratilova is one of the best women players."

X 'Hostess', 'lady poet', 'female scientist' and 'madam chairman'; avoid affixes which mark for female gender as they may lend an air of amateurism. Even with the more acceptable affix of 'woman', it is often the case that the female gender is marked but not the male, as in 'woman doctor', not 'male doctor'.

• Use terms which do not make gender distinctions. Thus 'poet', 'doctor', 'chair/chairperson' and 'scientist' should be used as terms which include females and males. Where it is necessary to mark gender (and there are remarkably few cases where this is necessary) the affixes 'female' and 'male' should be used equally; "MacEnroe is one of the best male tennis players in the world today, Navratilova is one of the best female players."

GENDER-FREE LANGUAGE

STEREOTYPING:

Within the university setting there are many situations where sexist language may appear: in verbal interactions during meetings, lectures, or informal conversations between colleagues and students and in written form, such as formal university documents, memos and handouts. In any of these situations when an idea is being communicated, there is likely to be frequent use of examples and analogies. Some of these may draw on male oriented experience and stereotypical female and male roles.

X "John played football" (an example commonly given in linguistics): avoid the use of examples which exclusively draw on male-oriented experience or which present males as the norm. Also avoid making assumptions or selecting examples which draw on stereotypical roles for women and men: secretary as 'she' and engineer as 'he.'

• Use female names and females in roles as frequently as male names/roles; "Alice went to the cinema" should be used as frequently as "Paul went to the cinema".

• Where possible use generic examples, thus avoiding stereotypical roles: "Carla went to the cinema" not "Carla did the washing up".

WHY USE GENDER-FREE LANGUAGE?

The conscious adoption of a gender-free policy in all aspects of university life can bring positive results in the way that members of a community respond within any communicative situation. Far from being a form of censorship, gender-free language shows that a conscious choice has been made to include all potential addressees and acknowledge everyone on an equal basis through the language used.

GENDER-FREE LANGUAGE

Administrators, teaching staff and students can thus be assured that the university is not the male domain that it may appear to be.

CHECKLIST

• Use parallel terms when addressing females; 'Mr and Ms', 'Liz Lochhead and James Kelman'.

• Use *he/him/his* as gender-specific terms only; "When Bill eventually arrived, he was over an hour late".

• Use *s/he, he or she, she or they*, as generic pronouns; "You must know your client's circumstances before you give her/him advice".

• Use neutral terms in generic compound nouns; 'fire-fighter', 'homeworker', 'business person', 'spokesperson'.

• Use neutral terms for females and males, thus avoiding gender distinctions; 'writer', 'actor', 'chair'.

• Use marked terms equally (and only when absolutely necessary); 'female engineer/male engineer', 'female doctor/male doctor'.

• Draw on both female and male experience when citing examples; use generic examples thus avoiding stereotypical roles; "Alice drove to work," rather than "Alice washed the dishes."

For further information please contact
Sara Mills
Gender Studies Research Unit
Department of English and Drama
Loughborough University
Loughborough, Leics, LE11 3TU

in writing involves very little self-monitoring, as is often feared, and in fact it brings positive results. Rather than being a form of censorship on one's speech, it can be seen to be a positive step towards addressing and including all of one's correspondents or interlocutors. Adamsky (1981) notes that the changes she made in pronominal usage in her class led to a marked improvement in self-esteem in her female students. By changing sexist language, one is not changing the social system and attitudes which determine in large measure such language-usage; however, such minor changes may have a wider impact on both females and males than can presently be realized.

From this, it is clear that the types of changes which are required are not of the order suggested by the media, and characterized as 'pronoun-envy', i.e. that feminists would like to change 'manhole cover' to 'personhole cover' and 'manipulate' to 'personipulate'.[12] This trivializing of the gender-free language debate is regrettable. There have been a large number of changes mainly through the work of feminists who have tried to get policy changes at an institutional level; feminists have also invented new terms such as 'herstory', 'wimmin', 'chair'. However, as Deborah Cameron states: 'Conscious linguistic reform by feminists, or even "natural" change deriving from women's changing experience and consciousness, is not simply left to take its chance with other social forces affecting language in a free market competition for semantic supremacy.' (See the second section of this chapter for a full discussion of some of the factors which prevent changes taking place more rapidly.) However, it is worth considering the strategies that can be adopted when encountering sexist language. One of the most effective strategies but perhaps the most difficult is making open comments about the language used by someone and stating that it is sexist. This may lead to the person using the sexist term feeling threatened and becoming aggressive. A further way of dealing with such a situation in interaction is to provide them with an impersonal leaflet, such as the one illustrated.

In this way, the conflict is less at a personal level and locates the problems with someone's language at an institutional level. It is also possible to try to get a policy adopted in your place of work or institution. Again it is by institutionalizing this practice that change can take place. Change in language-use will obviously not alter most sexist practices, since sexism is, as I have mentioned, more than a question of choice of lexis; however, it is possible to make significant changes in language-use which do have effects on the way that people perceive their position in relation to their environment.

SEXISM AND MEANING

In this section, I raise some specific questions about meaning itself, particularly about the way in which meanings may be sex-specific. The previous section examined sexism in language particularly in the area of generic usage and proposed a gender-free language-usage. That section also recognized that sexism in language is not simply a matter of locating offensive lexical items and proposing alternatives. This section is concerned with the description of structures in language which seem to determine that terms associated with gender will take on particular types of meanings, in such a way that those terms associated with women will take on a range of clearly identifiable connotations. The structures whereby this process takes place are not always apparent to us as speakers of the language, and therefore the analysis in this chapter is concerned to foreground some of these less obvious forms of sexism in language. Meaning is conventionally seen as something neutral – it is just something which is *in* a word; however, the process whereby meanings are created is much more complex than this. This section is therefore concerned with the question of whether we simply have to accept the meanings which are available within our culture.[13]

This section reviews the examples of sexist meaning which have been documented by feminists, and catalogues some of the places in English where meanings seem to work in a different way for males and females. It is important to ask what we can deduce about our society from the meaning of certain words, and question who decides on the 'official' meanings of words. I am not suggesting that a word has one fixed and singular meaning – far from it – but there do tend to be meanings which are dominant in words, and these meanings seem to be the result of larger-scale processes which have to do with discrimination against women. These processes are coded in the language as a record of the history of such discrimination against women. It may be possible to argue that they are simply a record in the language and are not activated when the words are used, but I would argue that these types of language-usage can be seen to play an active part in the production of ways of thinking about gender roles. Language is clearly not simply a place where meanings are imposed, but rather a site where certain meanings are negotiated over, or struggled over. Language clearly changes and that change is often brought about through protest and complaint. I examine some of the strategies feminists have suggested for coping with sexist meanings in our language and raise the question of how much these words actually reproduce a patriarchal culture. I begin by examining some of the ways in which sexist meanings manifest themselves, by focusing on naming, the semantic derogation of women, gender-specific conventions, endearments, taboo, collocation and metaphor.

Naming and Androcentrism

Naming has always played a major role in feminist discussions of language. As Cameron notes: 'many strands in the feminist critique of language have specifically concerned themselves with representation. They have concluded, on the whole, that our languages are sexist; that is, they represent or "name" the world from a masculine viewpoint and in accordance with stereotypical beliefs about the sexes' (Cameron 1990a: 12). She goes on to say: 'many feminists have made the claim that the names we give our world are not mere reflections of reality, nor arbitrary labels with no relation to it. Rather, names are culture's way of fixing what will actually count as reality in a universe of overwhelming, chaotic sensations, all pregnant with a multitude of possible meanings' (ibid.: 12). Some feminists have held the extreme position that language is not only shaped in the interests of men but is in fact 'man-made', as I mentioned in the last section in this chapter. Thus women have had to see their experience through the filter of the male view and they do not themselves play a role in the creation of new meanings (Spender 1980). This extreme position has been discredited by later analyses, such as Black and Coward's review (1981) of Spender's work. It is not necessary to claim that 'men invented language' to perceive a strong androcentric bias in many areas of English. To illustrate this point, I will consider the vocabulary available for describing female genitalia, and the terms in which sexual activity is most frequently described.

Many feminists have argued that the non-correspondence between the range of terms available to describe male and female genitalia is evidence of attitudes towards women and women's sexuality influencing the linguistic resources of English speakers. As speakers of English, we find there is a lack of acceptable terminology to bridge the gap between the formal words for female genitalia associated with medicine and science, like 'vagina' and 'vulva', and the most colloquial, glossed in dictionaries as 'taboo' and 'offensive': 'cunt'. There is, as far as I know, no word to refer to the clitoris, in a non-medical way. An article in the *Guardian* suggested that there is a choice of abusive or clinical words, as given above, as well as whimsical terms ('tunnel of love', 'golden doughnut'), terms learned in childhood ('front bottom', 'fanny'), or those evasive terms 'down below', 'women's parts/bits' – 'but the general consensus is that women are loath to call their genitals anything at all' (Viner 1992). This is an issue faced particularly by parents who are having to teach their children words for their own sexual organs, and who do not want their daughters to grow up with the sense that their genitals are shameful. Boys, and parents in referring to boys' sexual organs, can use joking names such as 'willy', 'John Thomas' and other nonsense terms, and they can use the more tabooed words 'dick', 'cock' and 'prick' and any of an enormous range of familiar terms in the context of their peers. However, girls do not have the possibility of referring to their sexual organs even in this joking way. Girls and women do not have a familiar term that they can use in public and be assured that it will not cause offence. All of the words which refer to female genitalia do so as sexualized terms which are viewed from a male perspective; thus 'snatch', 'box', 'pussy', 'quim' and 'muff' are unlikely to be used by women about their own bodies, unless they are prepared to refer to them only in sexual terms. It is interesting also that these words can be used abusively to refer to the woman herself, so that sexual organs come to define the whole person. Furthermore, the most abusive term 'cunt' is viewed by many people as the most offensive in the English language; there certainly is not a male equivalent, and in a 1993 survey on Channel 4, it was found to be the only word which viewers agreed should not be allowed to be heard.

Solutions which have been proposed for this lexical gap in our language include 'ginny', but there is still no term which includes the clitoris or the labia. It does, however, avoid the coyness and imprecision of 'front bottom' which is not gender-specific, and of 'fanny' which seems to have negative connotations and to be less socially acceptable than 'willy' (it also has a certain vagueness about it and has quite different meanings in American English). 'Ginny' is derived from 'vagina' and in the etymology of this word, there is a profound case of androcentric naming. 'Vagina' is derived from the Latin for 'sheath' – a place to keep a sword. So, although the word does not retain for us the meaning 'a sword's sheath', this female organ was originally named in such a way as to suggest that its only purpose is penetrative sex with men. The implication of this is that a woman is not really in control of her own body – a suggestion reinforced by the fact that when a woman is in labour, the name of this part of the body changes to 'birth canal', so that attention is distracted from the sexual function and focused on the reproductive function. Both names suggest that this part of a woman's anatomy is primarily not for her own use, but for the use of a man or a baby. The term 'penis' (or any of the other available terms) does not change depending on whether a man is having sex with another person, masturbating, or urinating. In a similar way, 'clitoris; is glossed in the *Collins Concise Dictionary* as 'homologous with the penis', which leads us to assume that it has a dependent position in relation to the penis; whereas anatomically, the clitoris has no relation to the penis whatsoever and does not function in an analogical way.

Similarly, when describing sexual activity between women and men, there is a tendency to represent it from a male point of view so that females may have difficulty expressing their own experience of sex. If we consider some of the slang terms for sex, it is difficult for women to see themselves as other than passive. For example, 'screw', 'leg over' and even the more medical 'penetrate' present the sex act from the male perspective: terms like 'enclosure' which view the experience from the female's point of view are not used, and all sex which is based on forms of sexuality other than that centred around the penis is termed 'non-penetrative' or called 'foreplay' as if to suggest that it is just a precursor to the real sexual act.

Even pregnancy is conventionally described from a male perspective in slang terms; for example, 'to get someone pregnant', 'to get someone in the family way', 'to put someone in the pudding club', 'to put a bun in the oven', where impregnating someone is something which a male does to a female, rather than its being seen as a female activity. The female terms are more passive; for example, 'I'm expecting', 'I'm pregnant', 'I'm in the family way', where a state is referred to rather than an action. This may accord with stereotypical views of pregnancy and fertilization where the egg is seen as static and the sperm as the active element. The conventional ways of writing and talking about sex extend to human reproduction. 'Scientific discourse' habitually projects stereotypical feminine and masculine behaviour on to ova and sperm. The commentary of 'scientific' television programmes has been analysed by Rosalind Coward: 'We were treated to the sight of the "sperm armada" going into battle, and a display of male bonding as the lads helped the "successful" sperm make his conquest' (Coward 1984: 214). It is not only human reproduction which is written about from this perspective of gender stereotypes; as Barbara Crowther and Dick Leith have shown in their analysis of wild life programmes, animal sex is habitually written about in terms of human gender stereotypes (Crowther and Leith in S. Mills 1995). As Coward puts it: 'Here in the animal kingdom, a natural world of male dominance and aggression is revealed. Here are males defending their property (territory and wives). Here are females selecting their mates as "good" parents, either for their genetic endowments or their ability to provide' (Coward 1984: 212). This can be striking when animals which traditionally have female-only groups allow one male to enter their group for mating; for example, elephants and lionesses. Crowther and Leith have shown that these arrangements are generally described as 'harems' rather than as polygynous (ibid. 1994).

Emily Martin has compared accounts of reproduction to 'fairy-tale romances'; she suggests the egg is presented as a Sleeping Beauty: 'a dormant bride awaiting her mate's magic kiss which instils the spirit which brings her to life' (Martin cited in Crowther and Leith 1995). In all of the above cases, meaning has been created, imposed on events, in order to produce 'knowledge' which fits in with certain patriarchal myths. We make sense of the world by imposing meaning on it in the light of what we already know, and this process is frequently andro-centric, that is, oriented to a male perspective. Thus a system of knowledge is produced which denies that the role of the female in a given process is active, is important, or even exists at all.

Consider, for example, the diagram from a science textbook on sex in rats (opposite). The experiment is supposed to be concerned with the length of time rats spend on copulation. In this diagram the sex of the male rat is considered whereas the female rat is described only as being the recipient of 'mounts' and 'ejaculations'. The female rat is only a container and recipient of male sexual activity and this metaphor of male active/female passive runs through, in perhaps a less extreme form, many discourses about sexuality.

I have reviewed the semantic field of women's genitals and more broadly sex, reproduction and the representation of women in order to illustrate how a language can have lexical gaps (i.e. no informal non-offensive words for female genitals) and can name objects and actions (e.g. the vagina as a sheath or birth canal, sex as active for males and passive for females). This perspective makes other perspectives very difficult to talk about, and it is hard to create other meanings which express a different viewpoint.

Illustrations of this phenomenon can be found in other areas of life. Dale Spender gives the following example to show how androcentric the process of naming can be (Spender 1980). An experiment was conducted to investigate sex differences in perception. A stimulus situated in a surrounding background was shown to male and female experimental subjects, such that subjects could either perceive the stimulus (an embedded figure) as a part of the field in which it was

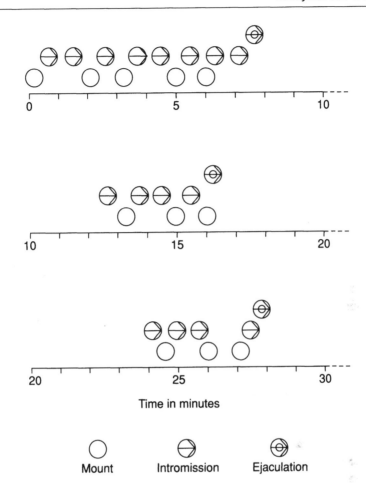

Time in minutes

Mount   Intromission   Ejaculation

Source: Dale Spender, *Man-made Language*, London: Routledge & Kegan Paul.

embedded, or as separate from the field. It was found that men were more likely to do the latter and women the former. In naming this phenomenon, the experimenter revealed his own bias regarding gender difference; Spender states: 'He named the behaviour of males as *field independence*, thereby perpetuating and strengthening the image of male supremacy; he named the female behaviour as *field dependence* and thereby perpetuated and strengthened the image of female inferiority' (Spender 1980: 164–5). Spender points out that alternative names for these choices were possible. For example, the female response could equally appropriately have been named 'context awareness' and the male response as 'context blindness'.

One very stark reminder of the way in which naming informs the lives of women is when we consider the fact that there are differential codes for naming men and women themselves. Women have to reveal their marital status through the use of such terms as Miss and Mrs when males are not marked in a similar way. Here again, we see the female as the marked form and the male as the unmarked. The expectation that a woman will change her name to her husband's on marriage is being challenged by some women; however, there are many organizations which insist in using the husband's name on documentation, which results in the woman's family name being lost entirely. Even more extreme is the example below in the *Daily Telegraph* where, in the 'Forthcoming Marriages' section, parents of the couples are referred to by the male's names only: for example, Mr and Mrs Andrew Garden, Mr and Mrs. P. Simcox, Colonel and Mrs James Capadose.

Mr J D Steele and
            Miss A S Baile
The engagement is announced between John David, younger son of Mr and Mrs Richard Steele, of Dorking, Surrey, and Annabel Sophie, second daughter of Lieutenant Colonel and Mrs G D Bailey, of Kingsland, Herefordshire.

Mr P G Hulett and
            Miss S L Garner
The engagement is announced between Peter, only son of Mr and Mrs Barry Hulett, of Little Poundsford Farm, Punnett's Town, East Sussex, and Sarah, elder daughter of Mr and Mrs Andrew Garner, of The Manor, Tansor, Peterborough.

Source: Daily Telegraph, 2 June 1990

    In these examples, not only does the woman lose her family name (her father's surname) but she also loses her first name. It should be noted that the campaign for women to retain their own family name has been in progress since Lucy Stoner in the nineteenth century began her fight to retain her family name on marriage. Since many more people do not find it necessary to marry, the practice of taking the male name on marriage is in decline, but only in certain class, age and ethnic groups. The problem arises when people have children; the system of naming is derived from the fact that the inheritance laws in western Europe are largely patrilineal, that is, the inheritance of wealth and property, and therefore the lineage, is passed through the male line, from father to son. Therefore when we construct a family tree, we are encouraged by the conventions of our society to concentrate on the father's line, and the women because of their status within a patrilineal system are counted only as relatives or wives.

    If women now decide not to take their husband's surname on marriage, or if they do not marry, they have the choice of maintaining their own name, or joining their name to their husband's/partner's in a double-barrelled name. The children may then be named with this double-barrelled name; however, when these children have children themselves, they have to make a difficult decision about their family names, because it is not possible to continue this process of doubling names. In addition, even with double-barrelled names it is generally the case that the woman's family name comes first and this is the one which is seen to be more like a middle name than a real surname.

    Whilst there has been substantial change in recent years in terms of the use of family names, change has been very gradual in the way marital status is denoted on forms. It is still customary to leave no space for an alternative to the terms Mrs and Miss. Some organizations have, however, begun to find it simpler to refer to all women as Ms, in the same way as men are referred to as Mr. However, whilst Ms is proposed as a neutral form, in fact it has picked up certain negative connotations, so that some people think that it can be used to refer only to young women, divorced women, or feminists.

The first names of women and men are also interesting: some names are shared by both sexes, for example, Hilary and Jocelyn, although usually similar names to these are marked by one letter as being different; for example, Leslie:Lesley; Lindsey:Lindsay; Francis:Frances. However, many women's names are derived from male names; for example, Stephen: Stephanie; Christopher:Christine; Peter:Petra; Antony:Antonia. Some of them show signs of diminutives, as I showed in the last section with the use of '-ette'; for example, Ginette, Suzette, Lynette, Janette. When women's names are shortened they can be identical to male shortened forms, although they may sometimes be spelt slightly differently; for example, Terry and Chris, or Stevie and Georgie. But this process is not reciprocal; women can use some men's names especially if they are in a diminutive form, but men cannot use females names – just think of the horror contained in the lyrics of Johnny Cash's song about 'A Boy named Sue'.

This process of androcentric naming can also be seen in the way that women are often called by their first names in contexts where that is not the appropriate form. In order to examine why this should happen we need to discuss the work of Brown and Gilman, who have investigated the way that power relations are manifested in European languages, such as German and French, by the use of what they call 'T' and 'V' forms of the pronoun: that is, '*tu*' and '*vous*' (Brown and Gilman, 1972). '*Tu*' is used is much the same way as 'thou' was used in English until the seventeenth century, that is, between intimates who are equal, and downwards in a power hierarchy to inferiors. '*Vous*' is used between intimates at a formal level or between strangers and upwards in a power hierarchy.

In Figure 4 it can be seen that pronouns can highlight asymmetrical power relations. In much the same way as these forms disappeared from the English language, they are undergoing change in languages where they are still at present retained. However, that is not to say that English does not have equivalent T

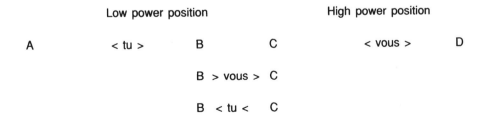

Figure 4 T/V relations

and V forms. One of the areas in which T and V forms exist in English is in the process of using names. If you use someone's first name, it generally means that you are on equal terms with them and that you are intimate. So, for example, friends of the same age group will use first names. However, those in an asymmetrical power relation will use differential naming patterns: in schools, teachers tend to use the first names of their students but they are themselves called by their title and surname. When we examine the way that women are frequently referred to by their first name, this may have some resonance: it is quite common, for example, in literary criticism for female authors to be referred to by their first name only ('Virginia' or 'Virginia Woolf' when referring to Woolf) and for male authors to be called by their surname only ('Dickens' when referring to Charles Dickens). This is most notable when there are female and male authors with the same surname, for example, Mary Shelley and Shelley; Elizabeth Barrett Browning and Browning.[14] Similarly, I have often been surprised by the way in which, in a work situation, strangers will change from calling me 'Dr Mills' or 'Ms Mills' to 'Sara' much more rapidly than they do my male colleagues.

An analogous situation can be found in the use of vocatives to strangers. When I need to hail someone that I do not know, I can use a hailing form such as 'excuse me' which is gender-neutral, or it is possible to refer to them differentially according to their sex. So, for example, males can call a stranger 'mate', which suggests a relationship of equality, whereas the way that women can be referred to as 'missus' or 'darling' seems to suggest other forms of intimacy than equality. Thus, the names which we use for ourselves and others can be seen to be part of a larger system which categorizes us implicitly into groupings which are distinguished in relation to power.

The Semantic Derogation of Women

I shall now consider how the terms in English that are gender-specific have a strong tendency to be derogatory towards women in contrast with available terms for men. There are a number of contrasting pair words in English, where one is male-specific and the other is female-specific. But the female term has acquired a connotative meaning distinctly different from that of its partner. As Cameron reports, feminists have discovered that 'many languages have an underlying semantic or grammatical rule where the male is positive and the female negative, so that the tenets of male chauvinism are encoded into language' (Cameron 1990a: 13).

Consider these examples:

Male	Female
courtier	courtesan
master	mistress
host	hostess
governor	governess
adventurer	adventuress

These are all terms which are etymologically connected, but the scope of the female-specific term is different from that of the male-specific term, being used to refer to someone of lower status and frequently having an overlaid sexual connotation. The terms 'courtesan' and 'courtier', for example, now have meanings which seem so far apart that the original connection will come as a surprise to many. The male term has retained its meaning of someone attached to court, but the female equivalent now has the meaning of a sexual servant or prostitute (albeit a term which is rarely used except in a historical sense). 'Adventurer' and 'adventuress' are similar in that adventuress has a sexual connotation, as do the other female terms. This pattern is repeated frequently in other pairs of gender-contrastive terms such as these:

Male	*Female*
master	mistress
sir	madam
bachelor	spinster
lord	lady
king	queen
priest	priestess
god	goddess

In the cases of the terms like 'master' and 'mistress' and 'sir' and 'madam', the male term has retained its associations of power and prestige, but while the female term can still have this core meaning, it has acquired a sexual and non-prestigious meaning. Regarding the terms 'spinster' and 'bachelor', 'spinster' is now rarely used since it seems to have acquired the insulting meaning of 'old maid' referring to someone who is unable to find a husband, by implication because they are too ugly or too 'sour'. 'Bachelor' by contrast has the positive connotations of freedom and independence and still having all your choices open to you. In the 1960s the term 'bachelor girl' was developed to try to capture some of the positive connotations of bachelor for single women – notice that the word 'girl' is used, presumably to convey youth and irresponsibility lacking from the word 'woman' (nowadays it appears more common to refer to women and men as 'single' rather than 'unmarried'). In the case of 'lord' and 'lady', 'lord' has retained all its status, while 'lady' can be used of any adult female in certain contexts. Therefore it is considered polite to refer to any adult female stranger as a 'lady' whereas it is not possible to use 'lord' for adult male strangers. 'Lady' can also be used to form compounds such as 'dinner lady', 'cleaning lady' and 'lollipop lady', whereas 'cleaning lord' is clearly an impossible item. This indicates not only the semantic deterioration of the term 'lady' in comparison with 'lord' but the even greater decline of the term 'woman' which is avoided in certain contexts, in case it sounds 'rude'. People do not find the term 'man' when used for adult males potentially insulting as they do 'woman' used for an adult female. The term 'woman' itself has acquired connotations of low status and sexuality. The negative connotations of 'woman' are evident from the way that people will try to avoid using it – hence the use of the word 'lady' to partner 'man', in expressions like 'I am your lady, and you are my man' in pop song lyrics. That the terms 'man' and 'woman' have very different connotations is also evident from their meaning in certain phrases as I showed in the previous section. Telling someone to 'be a man' is asking them to be brave and strong, and someone who is 'man enough' for a job is competent. In fact, the word 'man' and related terms are so positive that they can be used to sell all kinds of products – we buy man-sized tissues, we eat man-size portions, we use Mr Muscle and Mr Clean cleaning fluids, driving instructors use He-Man controls, and so on. In the above examples, 'man' actually means bigger, stronger and better, and not simply male. 'Woman', however, has a different range of associations. If you call a man a 'woman' as in 'Don't be such a woman', it is an insult, and means that he is weak, tearful, or fussy.

If we consider the two final pairs in the above list, priest:priestess and god:goddess, we find that although they are equivalent terms they do not have the same connotations. 'Priest' refers to someone who has power and status within the established Church, whereas 'priestess' refers to someone who organizes religious ceremonies in a cult outside the Christian faith. It has fairly negative connotations for most speakers. In the same way 'goddess' refers to a deity which belongs to a low-status cult and not to an established religion.

'Girl' is also clearly used to denote low status as in the following extract from an article on motor-bikes: 'Harleys are OK . . . if you're a *girl*. . . . That's the attraction of the classic British bike: they're for *men*. Riders sit taut and upright, not slumped in the low crouch of foreign imports. British bikes offer no protection from the elements; others have sissy fairings. And they're not for amateur riders or the mechanically inept' (Goldberg 1992; italics in the original). 'Girl' here is clearly being used as the antonym of everything the motor-bike rider would wish to be. The implication is that girls are amateurs, mechanically inept and the opposite of everything contained in the word 'man'. This example not only illustrates how negative the meaning of the word 'girl' can be in some contexts, it also clearly shows that 'girl' and 'man' are used as paired words in some contexts, rather than 'woman' and 'man'.[15]

Consider also these sentences:

Male	*Female*
He's a real pro.	She's a real pro.
He's a tramp.	She's a tramp.

In the first example, the male will either be considered to be a professional in the sense of a golf-pro or be seen to have behaved in a professional manner. The same sentence for a woman could also be interpreted in this way, or it could be interpreted to mean that she is either a prostitute or promiscuous. In the second example, for the male, tramp refers to someone who sleeps rough, whereas for the woman it can also mean that she is promiscuous (R. Lakoff 1975).

The order in which paired terms appear is another dimension of the unequal status of masculine and feminine terms. The fact that many binary terms are conventionally fronted by the male term prioritizes the male, since the elements which come first in English are generally seen to be the most important in terms of information-processing. Examples of the masculine term conventionally preceding the feminine are:

> masculine and feminine
> male and female
> Mr and Mrs
> son and daughter
> man and wife
> husband and wife
> brother and sister
> man and woman
> lads and lasses
> lords and ladies
> kings and queens
> guys and gals

There is clearly a strong tendency with some binaries for the masculine to come first – for example, 'feminine and masculine' sounds odd to the native speaker, and if the term 'man and wife' is reversed to 'wife and man' the cohesion of the phrase is lost. However, there are also cases in which this ordering is reversed; for example, in the paired terms 'bride and groom' and 'ladies and gentlemen'. These are both phrases which are used in contexts still influenced by notions of chivalry, where a feminine ideal holds an elevated position, which perhaps explains the reversal of the usual order.

In the above cases I considered how gender-specific terms which might be considered pairs in some abstract way are used as if they had very different meanings. Another way of identifying the inequality of gender-specific terms in English is to look at the quantity and type of words available to describe males and females in relation to sexual activity. Consider the available terms for men who have many sexual partners: 'Jack the lad', or just 'lad' (as in 'he's a bit of a lad'), 'Casanova', 'gigolo', or 'stud'; and compare these with 'slag', 'scrubber', 'tart', 'slut', 'nymphomaniac', 'whore', 'goer', 'easy lay'. Note that the terms available for men have an element of boastfulness about them, and improve the man's reputation rather than diminish it. Even a term like 'gigolo', which refers to a male who prostitutes himself, usually to older women, seems to have positive connotations. In contrast, the available terms for women are insults and intended to degrade whoever they are applied to. It is possible in some circles to use 'tart' for a male, but it is interesting that the female term is used, and it is not seen as negative as it is for females. The terms for women not only mean sexually active but some of them have connotations of dirtiness and slovenliness – for example, 'slag', 'scrubber', 'slut' – or they attribute sexual activity to some patho-logical defect as in the case of 'nymphomaniac'. Words which refer to the sexual availability of men tend to have positive connotations suggesting that they are successful rather than social outcasts. These terms do not have equivalents for women; terms used for women seem to refer to sexual availability rather than sexual activity only.

Words relating to men in fields other than sex also seem to be associated with more positive qualities than the equivalent terms for women. Take the example of 'hen-party' and 'stag-party'. The connotations of 'hen' are stupidity, fussiness and domesticity. The connotations of 'stag', however, are nobility, strength, wildness and leadership. Even when referring to couples, there is a distinct asymmetry; for example, it is possible to refer to 'the missus' and 'the wife' where it is not possible to refer to 'the mister' or 'the husband'. 'Her indoors' is also a gender-specific term which has no male equivalent.

There are no male equivalents of the following terms:

single mum
working mother
career woman
unmarried mother

nor is there a female equivalent of 'family man' since it is assumed that all women will orient themselves naturally towards the family. Even the term 'mum' has negative connotations which are not manifest in the equivalent term 'dad'; for example, 'mummy's boy' is used as a negative evaluation for someone who is close to his mother, and phrases like 'groups for young mums' are generally used in a slightly patronising way.

Words which insult men usually relate to their penis ('dickhead', 'prick') and not to their sexual activities, although there is a range of insult terms referring to masturbation, therefore implying heterosexual inadequacy ('wanker', 'tosser'). It is interesting that these words generally mean 'stupid'. Other insult terms for heterosexual men generally focus around suggestions of homosexual orientation; for example, 'queer', 'poof' and 'nancy boy'. Many of these homosexual insults seem to operate by suggesting that the male is in fact 'feminine'. Women can be insulted in relation to their genitalia – 'cunt' – but cannot be called 'pricks'; whereas the worst insult for a man is to be called a 'cunt' or less extremely a 'prat'. In a similar way it is possible to use the phrase 'he has balls' to mean that he is strong and courageous, whereas no equivalent term exists for women (no part of the woman's body is seen to contain these qualities). There are many words which refer to female stupidity; for example, 'bimbo', 'dumb blonde', 'doll', 'bird', 'scatty' and 'babe' (as in 'dudes and babes'). Another wide field of insults for women are terms which refer to their lack of attractiveness to men ('cow', 'bag', 'crone', 'frump', 'hag', 'dog'). Women can also be insulted for having opinions and voicing them ('nag', 'shrew', 'battleaxe', 'warhorse', 'harridan' and adjectives like 'feisty', 'strident', 'shrill'). 'Nag' is particularly interesting as it is used to insult a woman who continually has to tell a male to do things, for example, to do his fair share of the housework – interestingly, there is no word for a man who does not do his fair share of the housework.

There are other words which refer to women alone ('skinny', 'bubbly', 'vivacious', 'pretty', 'voluptuous', 'tom boy') which seem to have no male equivalent. They seem to have a derogatory effect simply because they are generally used to refer to women. Consider this advertisement for Capri, an American cigarette which is explicitly marketed targeting women. In the advertisement, rather than the tough masculine cowboys of Marlboro country, here we encounter the question 'How can such a skinny little thing taste so fantastic?'

No other cigarettes are described as skinny, and the use of the diminutive 'little' is quite unusual in marketing strategies where 'king-size' is usually the term which is used. Although 'slim' is used for cigarettes which are targeted at males, this is 'the slimmest slim' which suggests that the manufacturers believe that women will respond to advertising which emphasizes smallness and thinness rather than the rugged qualities which are used for marketing other cigarettes.

Furthermore, if we consider the earlier examples of insult words referring to males and we compare them with those referring to women, it is harder to think of any which mean 'a man unattractive to women' or 'a man who has unwelcome opinions and voices them'. Thus whole semantic fields are available to describe women, which are totally lacking from our linguistic resources when it comes to men. For example, the activity known as 'wife-swapping' clearly demonstrates a male point of view: it is not 'husband-swapping'. That does not mean that language is 'man-made' in any simple sense, but it does seem to suggest that the same resources used in describing males are not available to describe females.

Feminists have addressed this issue of gender-specific terms in English having androcentric or even misogynous meanings. Schultz (in Cameron 1990a) has listed the number of negative and insult words that refer to women within dictionaries. She describes a process which she calls the semantic derogation of women: that is, that once a word becomes associated with women, it will begin to lose any positive quality that it originally had. Schultz gives the example of 'hussy', which derives from 'housewife', meaning the female head of the household, and 'spinster', referring to someone who uses a spinning wheel. She notes that many terms which originally referred to a female position within a household, such as spinster, laundress and nurse, eventually began to have sexual connotations, and she states that words like 'glamour' which originally meant having great magical power gradually began to mean being sexually attractive. Many words referring to women have at one time in their history been used as euphemisms for prostitutes. Jane Mills argues that the meanings associated with words for women have to be viewed as part of society's perception of the role of women:

> When, for example, such ordinary words as woman or girl acquire the additional meaning of 'mistress' or 'prostitute', as they once did, an attitude towards women held by some members of society becomes part of the experience of all that society's members. Language is at once the expression of a culture and a part of it. Just as changes in language may be understood by an examination of the social and historical context in which it is used, so may social attitudes be illuminated by a study of language change.
>
> (J. Mills 1989: xi)

According to this approach, an androcentric language reveals a correspondingly androcentric society.

However, androcentric meanings in gender-specific words are in evidence in English in other ways, as well as semantic derogation as described above, and this will be the focus of the rest of this section.

Endearments and Diminutives

Of course it is obvious that terms that we can classify as insults will be demeaning. It is often harder to explain why certain endearment terms, which may well be used with affection, can also be used to demean. There is a category of words which some men use to refer to their female partners; for example, 'my bird', 'my chick', which appear to be endearments, but which imply an equivalence between women and cute small animals. Similarly, there is a wide range of vocatives frequently used by men to and about women – 'doll', 'baby', 'babe', 'chuck', 'chick', 'duck', 'ducky', 'hen', 'pet', 'flower', 'petal' and so on. These terms can be used by women and can be used about men, but less frequently and only in particular contexts, such as an older woman to a younger man, where a parent–child relationship seems to be invoked (i.e. the relationship involves unequal status). These terms seem to be like the use of surnames and first names which I mentioned earlier as examples of a T/V distinction in English. That is, endearments are an intimate form which can be used between equals to signal solidarity and affection, but they can also be used between those who may perceive themselves to be in a hierarchical relationship.[16]

There is also a range of words such as 'honey', 'sweety', 'sweetheart', 'sugar', 'cheesecake' used to refer to women more frequently than men, which imply the referent is something good to eat, available for consumption. The history of the word 'tart' supports this as Jane Mills shows:

> Tart entered English c. 1400 from the Old French *tarte*, the name of a type of pastry or pie with a sweet filling. . . . In the mid-nineteenth century tart was applied to a young woman as a term of endearment. It may have been a contraction of, or rhyming slang for, 'sweetheart'. Like honeybun, sweetie-pie, cupcake and other terms employing a similar image, tart presumably derives from the notion of the supposed – and required – sweetness in a woman and perhaps from a male view that women are small, quick-to-consume, edible morsels.
>
> (J. Mills 1989: 234–5)

There are therefore terms which are apparently endearments but which are applied more frequently to women than to men and which in fact reproduce asymmetric patriarchal power relations.

Female Experience: Euphemism and Taboo

I have already discussed the idea that some common experiences in women's lives may be difficult to talk about, except in androcentric terms that present the experience from a male point of view. In this section I consider euphemism and the way that many areas of women's lives are surrounded by linguistic taboos. Euphemism is described by Fowler as the use of 'a mild or vague or periphrastic expression as a substitute for blunt precision or disagreeable truth' (cited in Holder 1989: vii). One area of women's lives over which very powerful taboos operate and which has generated many euphemisms, is menstruation.

Menstruation in many cultures is a tabooed subject, surrounded with special rituals and language-use, and sometimes involving a menstruating woman in physically distancing herself from the rest of the community whilst her period lasts. In Britain, there is a range of linguistic strategies which are employed to

make menstruation 'safe' although reference to it is still generally avoided altogether in mixed company. When menstruation is discussed, Holder shows that
there are a full range of euphemistic terms to avoid mentioning directly (Holder
1989). In *The Faber Dictionary of Euphemisms* he lists the euphemisms used and
then tries to group them under headings as follows:

Euphemism	Group
– a friend has come	an unwelcome visitor
– road is up for repair – manhole cover	unavailable for sex
– under the weather – indisposed, poorly	illness
– red flag is up	danger

Euphemism tends to describe menstruation negatively: 'the curse', 'the wrong
time of the month'. In advertisements for sanitary towels and tampons ('sanitary'
itself being a euphemism) there is a very consistent avoidance of the terms 'blood'
and 'bleeding'; instead some other less specific words are used such as 'flow' or
'moisture'.

In television adverts, as in the advertisement for Always, even when blood is
represented, it is shown as blue in colour, as if menstrual blood could only be
represented in this displaced way. Women who are represented in these advertisements show no sign that they are menstruating – they do not have swollen
stomachs, or appear tired – in fact quite the opposite, they are pictured roller-
skating in tight-fitting clothes, pushing a car in shorts, or sky-diving. In the
advertisement for Always, the woman is represented as smiling and relaxed and
she is dressed in a white towelling bathrobe. It is almost as if in an effort not to
refer to menstruation, the advertisers are forced to invert the representative
practices and present the exact opposite of the reality of menstruation.

> *Permission to reproduce an advertisement
> for Always sanitary towels was refused
> after lengthy negotiations. Rather than
> omitting reference to the advertisement and
> finding another advertisement, it was
> decided to leave this space blank as a
> critique of such measures by advertisers.*

Even the term 'period' refers to a passage of time, rather than using an item which refers to blood flow. Our culture assumes that reference to menstruation should be restricted to the private sphere (although there are increasingly advertisements which challenge that); when menstruation needs to be referred to in the public sphere, for example, in women's toilets, euphemism is again employed, often extending to reference to tampons or towels themselves. In several institutions they are referred to as 'feminine requisites' (Loughborough University). In other places, it is feminine qualities which are stressed. The disposal bag for sanitary towels is interesting since it does not say what it is a disposal bag for; the picture on the bag has a crinolined woman which symbolizes a particularly extreme form of stereotypical femininity, presumably in order to avoid any reference to menstruation. The woman is distanced from the present reality because she represents past time and she is also distanced by social class, since she represents a member of the aristocracy.

Another metaphorical framework often used in reference to menstruation which is more worrying is that of disease and injury. Several companies dealing with the disposal of sanitary towels refer to them as 'sanitary dressings'. It is not merely coincidental that one of the disposal companies is Rentokil, a company which normally deals with the extermination of rats and mice (see Laws 1990; Treneman

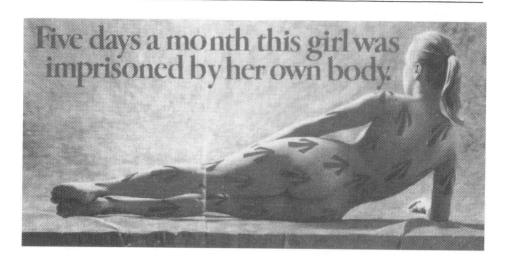

Five days a month this girl was imprisoned by her own body.

1988; S. Mills 1994). Even the Always advertisement stresses the 'cleaner' feeling of Always, as if menstruation normally induces a feeling of dirtiness.

Many of the advertisements on menstruation characterize it as imprisonment and sanitary towels as a release from that prison. In the Tampax advert this imprisonment is quite explicitly referred to and the woman's naked body is marked with arrows to indicate imprisonment. Implicitly there is an assumption that every woman will recognize the imprisonment which is entailed through having to wear towels during a period. This is made explicit in advertisements for Lillets where the tampon is shaped in the form of a key.

This is not only euphemistic but seems to be viewing menstruation from a male point of view. Whilst it is not necessary to celebrate menstruation, as Shuttle and Redgrove have (1980), it is not necessary either to portray it using such negative metaphorical structures. Many advertisements on television attempt to characterize menstruation as a form of confinement, or a form of stasis. Most of them employ euphemism: for example, in phrases like 'At this time of the month does everything seem to stand still?', where even the word 'period' is absent. Very often the product itself is not represented, or it is represented in a context for which it was not designed; for example, where tampons are shown in clinical jars of water or where ink is poured on to towels. The taboos around menstruation are still remarkably well enforced despite the fact that there has been some change in the way that it is represented (see Laws 1990). It is worth noting that there is no male bodily experience which is treated in the same way and no male products which are marked in this euphemistic fashion.

Lexical Gaps: Male Point of View

Additionally, some feminists have pursued the idea that there might be fields of experience which are not lexicalized at all – aspects of women's lives which are

commonplace, but have no words to describe them (Spender 1980). There are some obvious examples of concepts which had been 'invisible' before being lexicalized, because there was no single term to represent them and no socially agreed place for that concept because it was not socially recognized within the system of available words. One such example is the term 'sexism' which entered the language in the 1960s from the USA. Other examples are the areas which I have discussed so far in this section – words for women to describe themselves and their experiences, and words for sexual activity which do not imply a male point of view. The science fiction novelist Suzette Haden-Elgin invents in her novel *Native Tongue* a world where women create their own language to lexicalize aspects of their experience not named in the available male-dominated language. Some examples of words and definitions are:

radiidin: non-holiday, a time allegedly a holiday but actually so much a burden because of work and preparations that it is a dreaded occasion; especially when there are too many guests and none of them help
rahom: to non-teach, to deliberately fill students' minds with empty data or false information; can be used only of persons in a teacher/student relationship
wonewith: to be socially dyslexic; uncomprehending of social signals of others.

(Haden-Elgin 1985)

Feminism contains within its history notable instances of women who find themselves unable to express their meanings in the language available. At the centre of Second Wave feminism in the 1960s was the concept of the 'problem without a name' as Betty Freidan termed it – the experience of living as a woman in patriarchal society, where individual women assumed that the problems that they were experiencing were specific to themselves, since there were no terms in the language which demonstrated that this was a wider problem. The problem of lexical gaps in the language is part of a greater linguistic problem – the problem of not being able to express yourself within the discourse structures available to you. An example of this is described in a review of Paul Chilton's book *Language and the Nuclear Debate* (1985) in the *Guardian*. The review describes the experience of Carol Cohn, whose research is published by the Center for Psychological Studies in the Nuclear Age in Cambridge, Massachusetts. When Cohn went to spend a year at an American university centre of defence technology for research purposes she initially perceived herself as 'a feminist spy in the house of death'. However, she found that the vocabulary and discourses she was required to use in order to convince the men working there that she was technologically informed did not permit her to express her political point of view:

Though Cohn learned nukespeak, she vowed to speak only plain English. Yet she found that when she spoke English rather than jargon, the men responded to her as if she were ignorant. So she adopted their vocabulary to question them: she talked of 'escalation dominance', 'preemptive strikes' and 'subholocaust engagements'. But the better she became at using this discourse, the more impossible it became for her to express her own ideas and values. 'I could not use the language to express my concerns, because it was conceptually impossible. This language does not allow certain questions to be asked, certain values to be expressed.' She found that the language she had acquired to talk about nuclear war actually seemed to affect her own perception of the threat: 'The longer I stayed [in the centre of defence technology] the more conversations I participated in, the less frightened I was of nuclear war. How can learning a language have such a powerful effect?'

(Karpf 1985)

This is one example of a woman taking on the dominant (male) discourse in order to be taken seriously and then finding that she can no longer express her own concerns.

In this section I have so far considered the areas of meaning which relate to women and their experiences, and the ways in which meanings codified in the English language which have a bearing on gender are often sexist. The next consideration must be the origin of those meanings and how they are maintained.

Dictionaries and Gatekeepers

'Dictionaries like the Bible are treated as absolutes, yet are full of prejudice; more space is given to male items, sex-stereotyped examples are used to illustrate sentences, the masculine is presented first in a sequence where the feminine is also present, more insulting terms are included for women than men, prejudicial comments are included and there are more drawings of men and male animals' (Pace Nilsen quoted in J. Mills 1989: xiii). Definitions of existing words are not fixed or finite. Looking up many commonplace words in a good etymological dictionary will prove how much a word's meaning can change over time. As Ricks and Michaels state: 'the meaning of a word is not a matter of fact (which is why an argument about it cannot be settled by recourse to the dictionary) and it is not a matter of opinion (which is why it must not be unsettled by a refusal to have recourse to a dictionary). The meaning of a word is a human agreement, created within a society, but incapable of having meaning except to and through individuals' (Ricks and Michaels 1980). Perhaps a feminist would add to this quotation that words have meaning with recourse to groups of individuals and institutions rather than simply through individuals alone.

The meanings words have had in the past, their etymological derivations and the range of their current meanings can usually be found by turning to a dictionary. Dictionaries are created by people compiling information about how words are used and have been used in the past – that is, they are primarily descriptive. However, because of attitudes towards dictionaries, they are often treated not as descriptions but as prescriptions for what words should mean. Many people use dictionaries to check for the 'correct' meaning of a word; dictionaries are often used as arbiters in arguments about word-meaning. Some dictionaries abet this perception: they see their task as preserving certain standards in language-use, as gatekeepers of the language. For example, if a word has recently started to be used in a new context, that meaning will not be included in the dictionary if the editor thinks that it is too ephemeral, or if it is used by too small a group of people. A new meaning or new word has to prove it can stand the test of time before many dictionary editors will include it. It is important to stress that it is fallible human beings with limited access to the language of the wider community (and communities) who decide what should go into the dictionary and what can be left out, and no decision can be ideologically neutral.

One of the false ideas about word-meanings that dictionaries perpetuate is that words are fairly stable through time and context and that there is a finite and therefore listable set of meanings for each term. Only certain dictionaries such as the *Oxford English Dictionary* list etymologies in any detail; most present a simple definition. Paradoxically, most dictionaries also give credence to the belief that the etymology of a word is important for evidence of how a word should be used. In fact some words have so many meanings that it seems impossible to list them all (look up 'let', 'get', or 'put' in the dictionary, for example). Some words are continually developing new meanings. The myth that what a word used to mean fifty or a hundred years ago is a yardstick for how it should be used today is easily disproved by checking the etymology of the word 'nice', for example.

Because as I have mentioned it is human beings (nowadays with the aid of computers) who compile dictionaries, it is evident that the words which are assembled in dictionaries are likely to reflect the prejudices and preferences of lexicographers who compose them, or the prejudices of the range of texts which constitutes the database.[17] Lexicographers have been, in the main, white, male, middle-aged and middle-class. This bias is reflected not only in the words which are included in dictionaries, but in whether a form is marked or unmarked. The meanings which are associated with the language-use of the elite are usually the unmarked form and those which are not associated with this usage are marked as deviant. We have only to consider the debates that Burchfield describes about entries in the *Oxford English* and the *Concise Oxford* dictionaries (Burchfield 1980). Dictionaries often present a conservative view. For many years 'jew' was listed in dictionaries as having pejorative meanings, that is, as referring to miserliness, etc., and these meanings were not marked as offensive. Similarly Palestine was described as part of Israel for many years, and Pakistan was described as part of India even long after Partition. Only after substantial protest were these definitions changed. Even in more modern dictionaries like the *Collins Cobuild* 'Mohammedan' is listed as a synonym for Muslim, without its being coded as offensive. In these examples, it is not simply the definition which is incorrect but the fact that the coding used by the dictionary was not used accurately. These codes are where the male point of view may be seen to be foregrounded in many dictionary definitions, usually when lexical items are not coded as offensive or as obsolete.

Words which insult those in low status positions are often not marked as insulting. So, for example, the *Collins Pocket Dictionary* can give as the possible meaning of 'girl': 'informal: a woman of any age' without marking this as a potentially offensive term when used in this way. Although the possible meaning of 'bag' as 'an ugly or bad-tempered woman' is marked as offensive slang, the dictionary can also include 'girlie' as 'informal, featuring nude or scantily dressed women', without having to mark it as offensive to a sector of the population. Consider this listing from the Macquarie *Australian Dictionary* for the term 'woman' where none of the definitions is coded:

Woman: 1 female human being (distinguished from man)
         2 An adult female person (dist. for girl)
         3 A mistress or paramour
         4 A female servant, esp. one who does domestic chores, such as cleaning, cooking, etc.
         5 (formerly) A female personal maid
         6 Feminine nature, characteristic of feelings
         7 A wife
         8 A kept woman, a girl maintained as a mistress
         9 Old woman, a man who is pedantic or tends to fuss, gossip, etc.
        10 Scarlet woman; a prostitute, a woman whose sexual relations with a man are considered scandalous

                                                    (cited in Morgan 1989: 61)

Here the reader is obliged to supply the background knowledge for the text; for example, when the definition states 'etc.' as if the definitions were self-evident.

However, whilst it must be acknowledged that dictionaries are important determinants of meaning since people refer to them in the last instance to find out what a word 'really' means, words are defined more by their context than through recourse to dictionaries. Thus meaning is a much more complicated and transient business than most dictionaries could begin to suggest.

To summarize, in this section I have considered how certain terms for women are used in different ways from terms for males and how dictionaries may affirm that difference. I would now like to examine some proposed strategies for dealing with these linguistic problems.

STRATEGIES

Some feminists have decided to intervene in the construction of meaning. Some of them have tried to alter the way that words about women mean, and others have tried to chart the new words which have been developed in feminist theory, but which have not appeared in dictionaries. For example, Mary Daly suggests that one of the ways to combat this trend of pejorative words referring to females is to use those words and disrupt their meanings. She takes words such as 'dyke', 'virago', or 'crone' and she suggests that we capitalize them, making them into words with the same magnitude of importance as God and the Queen. This she suggests will subvert the meaning of the words and allow us to reclaim them. She states that by referring to herself as a Dyke rather than as a lesbian, a woman will rewrite the negative sense which is implicit in the term. Some homosexuals and lesbians have used this strategy to reclaim words such as 'queer', 'dyke' and 'bent' so that words originally used as insults are positive definitional terms. However, it is unclear whether feminist interventions are enough to change the meanings of terms. If someone used the word 'dyke' and intends to insult you, then there is little that reclaiming that term will have done. As Jane Mills states:

> There are many problems about the attempt to reform language. I might for example wish to impart a positive sense when using the word 'cunt' but if this meaning is not understood by my reader then we're back to square one: in the minds of sexists, language can always be sexist. But this is not to believe that there can be no change in either language or society. For me, one of the reasons for studying the history of word-meaning, as well as to analyse the way in which patriarchal society defines and thus controls women, was to draw attention to the past and present masculinist bias of conventional usage. Definitions are not static and closed, they are subjects for rational discourse. With almost every word we utter, we have a choice.
>
> (J. Mills 1989: xvi)

Thus, the very process of taking insult terms and 'turning them round' can have a subversive effect and may lead to a general change in the usage. As I have mentioned, Cameron suggests that it is more important to try to challenge the gatekeepers of language, those institutions which have the power to give authority to certain meanings. Educational institutions, television, publishing and so on all constitute gatekeepers, in that for a term to be generally adopted it is necessary to have it accepted by these institutions. This is why feminist meanings are not generally listed in conventional dictionaries.

Feminists have themselves constructed dictionaries; for example, Jane Mills traces the etymologies of words associated with women in *Womanwords* (1989) to investigate how definitions of women have changed over time. Maggie Humm has compiled *A Dictionary of Feminist Thought* in which she lists many of the terms which are omitted from conventional dictionaries. Kramarae and Treichler have also produced *A Feminist Dictionary* which attempts to provide a witty world-view countering that proposed by conventional dictionaries. Simply by their existence, these feminist dictionaries contribute to expanding awareness of how meaning works and what the implications of word meanings are. The process of change in language is relatively slow; however, it is clear that because of feminist pressure and general changes within society as a whole, changes within gender-specific word-meaning are beginning to be made.

When discussing meaning there is one question which must inevitably be returned to. This is whether the fact that English is a sexist language produces a sexist society, with androcentric patterns of thought – or whether society is intrinsically sexist somewhere outside of language and language merely reflects the sexism of the system. According to the first viewpoint, if you could reform language, you should be able to eliminate sexism. According to the second, language reform would serve no purpose, since the new words would be contaminated with the old meanings as soon as they were put into use. The examples of semantic derogation earlier in this section, where words which are associated with women automatically decline in status, bear out the view that language reform cannot be achieved as long as the society as a whole remains sexist. However, the semantic resources available to speakers are part of the system which produces sexism; thinking about meaning and making others aware of the implications of their language-use are ways of undermining the continual reproduction of sexist meanings. Meanings are not fixed for all time in dictionaries – language responds to new demands placed on it by its speakers. Increased awareness has resulted in institutionalized changes in usage – many sexist and racist terms no longer appear, or appear less frequently, in the national press, for example. Even if the change in usage does not achieve a total change in attitude, people are forced to confront their own attitudes when they use these terms. As Jane Mills states: 'With almost every word we utter, we have a choice.'

Chapter 5

Analysis at the Level of the Phrase/Sentence

This chapter is concerned with the way that we can analyse language-use beyond the level of the word. When we concentrate on words in isolation, it can sometimes appear that we have a particular view of meaning, i.e. that meaning is located within that word.[1] In the last chapter, I tried to show that some words do indeed have a history of usage which leads the hearer to interpret them in particular ways; however, words make sense only in relation to their context. As I showed in the last chapter, the word 'girl' can be a neutral word when it is used in a specific context, such as 'She goes to a girls' school', but may take on sexist connotations when it is used in another context; for example, when someone says to a little boy who is crying, 'Don't be such a girl', or when someone states, 'The school she goes to isn't very good: it's only a girls' school.' In these latter phrases, the word 'girl' begins to acquire negative connotations. In much the same way that words themselves make sense in relation to their co-text (that is, the words with which they co-occur) and their context, in this chapter I will be concerned with the way that phrases and sentences make sense in relation to their co-text, their context, the history of their usage and also the background knowledge which is needed for their making sense. I shall be arguing that the way that meaning takes place often involves the process of meaning-production not being accessible at the literal level of the individual words of which the sentence is composed. In that sense, in order to do a feminist analysis of sentences, some archaeological work is needed to excavate the places where ideological knowledge informs meaning.

I would like to analyse the following areas in turn in this chapter: ready-made phrases, that is, phrases which seem preconstructed and the patterns of background knowledge which give them meaning; jokes and humour; and transitivity choices.

READY-MADE PHRASES

There are words which seem to be sexist for most of their usage; for example, words which demean and degrade women and which seem to portray women

as a negative Other to a male norm. There are also phrases which are preconstructed and which convey sexist meanings. This is the case with proverbs which
have sexist messages underlying them. Proverbs and set phrases are curious
elements because they are posed as commonsense knowledge which is uncon-
testable. For example, in the phrase 'A woman's work is never done', there is a
sense in which the message seems to be that this is a natural state of affairs.
When it is used, it is very difficult to counter, because it is presented in a form
which is not personal: the person using the phrase does not claim responsibility
for inventing it, but is simply calling upon pre-existing knowledge, which it is to
be assumed is self-evidently true. Thus, if a specific woman complains of having
too much work to do, this phrase can be used to suggest that the specificity of
the difficulty of the conditions of her working life is not as important as the
general 'fact' that women always have too much work to do.

In a similar way the phrase 'Behind every successful man is a woman' can be
used to patronize women and to naturalize the role of the male's helper as the
nearest that women can get to holding power themselves. A further proverb,
'The way to a man's heart is through his stomach', naturalizes a range of different
ideological messages. As I will discuss in more detail later in the section on
inferences and background knowledge, the statement has a number of presuppositions: that women would like to get to a man's heart, i.e. that relationships
with men are an important element in women's lives (implicitly more important
for women than they are for men); that in order to get an emotional response
from a man, some subterfuge will need to be used, i.e. his heart cannot simply
be appealed to; and that women can cook in order to lure a man into a
relationship. Another phrase which seems to contain within it ideological
messages about women is 'old wives' tale' which is used to refer negatively to
any knowledge or practice which is developed outside the sphere of (implicitly
male) expertise.

As I mentioned above, many proverbs are difficult to deal with when used
in conversation, since they have ideological messages embedded in them for
which the speaker/writer will probably not take responsibility; in this sense it
is very difficult to say, for example, 'That's not true' or 'I don't agree'; they
simply are not posed as the type of knowledge about which it is possible
to disagree. If someone uses the phrase 'mutton dressed as lamb' they cannot
claim to have invented the sentiments; this phrase is used only to refer to older
women who are presumed to be dressing in a way which is more suitable for
younger women. It is not used to refer to men who are behaving in a similar
way. This phrase is complex since it works on a metaphorical level, in the
following way:

- mutton needs to be cooked in a way appropriate for older meat since it
  is tougher
- mutton cannot be treated as lamb, since lamb is young, tender meat
- mutton is older meat and therefore is a metaphor for older women

– dress can relate the metaphor to its ground because it can mean both 'to be clothed in' and also 'to be treated (for meat)'.

Therefore just as it would be absurd to cook old meat in the way you would cook young meat, it is absurd for older women to behave in the same way as younger women. This analogical structure is quite interesting, as I will show in more detail later, as, like many preconstructed structures, it is more difficult to argue with, without doing this type of laboured dismantling work.

Other phrases or proverbs which work in a similar way are listed in Fidelis Morgan's excellent *Misogynist's Source Book* (1989). For example, she cites the infamous saying by Samuel Johnson, 'Sir, a woman preaching is like a dog walking on his hinder legs. It is not done well; but you are surprised to find it done at all' (cited in Morgan 1989: 69). This phrase has been used on innumerable occasions as a supposedly witty view of women's capacities, and the most recent occasion that I have found is in a 1994 *New Statesman* article by Sean French when he uses it to refer to women comedians. The phrase is therefore a preconstruction which is infinitely flexible in that it can refer to a wide range of circumstances, that is, women doing anything which is considered not to be within their conventional sphere. The sexism is supposedly displaced from the speaker simply because the quotation originates in the eighteenth century and the listener is expected both to appreciate its witty construction and to recognize that it is a quotation (and appreciate the speaker's erudition). Most of the proverbs listed by Morgan have an interesting parallel grammatical structure which makes them memorable, such as the one cited above which works on the basis of a seeming paradox.

Rhyming slang also has this aura of being preconstructed and therefore immune to criticism at a specific level. Consider the phrase 'trouble and strife' to mean 'wife'; as I will show in a later section (pp. 137–42), humour here is used to neutralize the sexism contained within the phrase and because the phrase does not originate with the person who utters it, the responsibility for the sexism is located elsewhere. It is also as if the individual items which compose the message should not be analysed – that women here are being referred to in negative terms as the trouble that they bring to men – but rather it is 'simply' a rhyme for 'wife'.

It should be noted, however, that many feminists have been aware of the difficulty of phrases such as these and rather than engaging with them have proceeded to invent proverbs of their own. The phrase 'A woman's place is in the home' naturalizes the exploitation of women, but because of their formulaic nature, these phrases do open themselves up to the possibility of being subverted. So, for example, this phrase has been subverted in a number of badges within the Women's Movement, to generate new slogans such as 'A woman's place is in her union' and 'A woman's place is in the struggle'. Thus, although these phrases are preconstructed, and are therefore more difficult to tackle, we should not necessarily see them as impossible to subvert. Feminists have also invented phrases which sound like proverbs; for example, 'A woman needs a man like a fish needs a bicycle.' This has the same air of commonsense knowledge and is equally difficult to counter.

Although these phrases can be analysed as embodying sexist meanings which it is difficult to contest, perhaps they should be seen as a 'limit-case'. It should be noted that there are very few phrases which make sense in themselves in this way; the process whereby sentences have meaning is usually much more complex as I show in the next section.

PRESUPPOSITION AND INFERENCE

Brown and Yule state:

> One of the pervasive illusions which persists in the analysis of language is that we understand the meaning of a linguistic message solely on the basis of the words and structures of the sentence(s) used to convey that message. We certainly rely on the syntactic structure and lexical items used in a linguistic message to arrive at an interpretation, but it is a mistake to think that we operate only with this literal input to our understanding. We can recognise, for example, when a writer has produced a perfectly grammatical sentence from which we can derive a literal interpretation, but which we would not claim to have understood, simply because we need more information. ... At the opposite extreme, we can point to linguistic messages which are not presented in sentences and consequently can't be discussed in terms of well-formedness, but which are readily interpreted.
>
> (Brown and Yule 1983: 223)

What Brown and Yule are stressing here is that the meaning of phrases must be interpreted by drawing on factors other than the simple literal meaning of the words of which they consist. They state that there are 'three aspects of the process of interpreting a speaker's/writer's intended meaning in producing discourse' (ibid.: 225); these are, first, trying to work out what the intention of the speaker/writer is; second, using general knowledge, at the level both of facts about the world and knowledge which you assume you will be expected to know in the situation; and third, determining the inferences which need to be made. As I mentioned in Chapter 3 concerning the reader, there is an assumption that the audience of a text will share certain information or knowledge with the producer of the text. Some of this information will be of a fairly simple kind, that is, about the nature of the universe, i.e. that rooms have walls and doors, for example. Other information is of a more ideological nature and it is with this type of information that I will be concerned in this section. It is the contention of this section that there are patterns of background knowledge which are presupposed when texts address a female audience or when gender issues are discussed.

In the following letter to the *Leicester Mail* I would like to analyse the first two sentences to demonstrate the way that they make sense only in relation to a body of knowledge which is presupposed.

Give jobs back to our menfolk

SIR, Where have all the male shop assistants gone?

In most of the stores and supermarkets nowadays it seems shop assistants are usually women. I realise a lot of women do need to work for financial reasons, but as the mother of an unemployed boy, is it necessary that so many women need to work?

I heard one lady at a checkout complain that she was hot and tired, and she admitted she only went out to work for the company as her neighbours all worked.

And I've even seen a lady shop assistant in a menswear department.

Annoyed

I know some women get annoyed if you say there are too many women working, but how would they feel if they had a son who has been unable to find work for six months.

Our sons need to find work too you know.

I've read in the papers about courses which supply creches for women so they can train for work. My son would like to train for work too, so he could do something worthwhile instead of going to the job centre everyday and coming back frustrated.

I gave up my job, when the children were grown up, so it could go to an unemployed youngster. Now my own son cannot get a job.

Name and address supplied.

Source: The *Leicester Mail*, 2 September 1993

Let us consider the initial question which this letter poses: 'Give jobs back to our menfolk.' In order to be able to understand the sentence, it is necessary to locate certain assumptions. The word 'give' presupposes two things: that someone has the power to give jobs to people (alternatively it could be argued that the letter-writer is asking women to give the jobs back); that jobs can be taken from people and they can be given in a fairly easy way. This runs counter to any notion of people 'having' jobs in their own right. But the verb phrase is not just 'give' but 'give back', which assumes that men had the jobs initially and that the jobs were somehow taken by women (to whom of course they did not really belong). In order to make sense of this statement, therefore, we have to assume that women's access to jobs is very different from men's, and that men have jobs, whereas women only take jobs from them on a temporary basis. 'Our menfolk' is a curious phrase locating the speaker and her audience together as women ('our'), in viewing men in a rather outdated and traditional way as 'menfolk': a phrase which is redolent with connotations of traditional family life where men go out to work and women stay at home to look after the children. The next sentence is 'Where have all the male shop assistants gone?' a rhetorical question which the text itself answers in the following sentence. The presuppositions for the sentence are:

1 male shop assistants have disappeared;
2 we have all noticed that this is the case.

Because this knowledge is embedded within the background knowledge necessary to make sense of the phrase, it is more difficult to contest. It is almost as if in order to argue with the sentiments expressed by the letter, it is necessary to unpack the background knowledge and presuppositions, and take issue with them. Because the phrases work on the basis of assumed background knowledge, they can have a strong ideological impact in persuading people that they are in fact an accurate version of reality. If someone asks 'Where have all the male shop assistants gone?', it is difficult to take issue with the phrase as it stands, if you do not think that male shop assistants have disappeared.

The following advertisements also work with complex presuppositions that posit a particular view of women as necessarily having problems. Furthermore, the advertisements function on the inference that the products which are being advertised are the solution for that problem. First, let us consider the advertisement for the Surgical Advisory Service. The question heading this advertisement, 'Are you happy with your looks?', is a rhetorical one with the assumed answer 'No'. It draws on a body of ideological knowledge about women in assuming that their beauty is one element which is always in need of improvement. There is no reason why this sentence in itself should presuppose the answer 'No'

ARE YOU HAPPY WITH YOUR LOOKS?

In the right hands, cosmetic surgery can benefit you for life.
The Surgical Advisory Service offers you the best, fully-accredited surgeons and an affordable, all-inclusive fee.
For confidential advice on all aspects of cosmetic surgery, phone or write to our qualified Medical Advisor, now.

071-388 1839
THE SURGICAL ADVISORY SERVICE
108 Whitfield Street, London W1P 6BE
CS 49   Access & Visa accepted

and therefore we can only locate this knowledge at the level of ideology. The presuppositions to this text are that the woman who is pictured is happy with her looks (she is classically good-looking, dressed in elegant clothes and jewellery, smiling in an assured way and looking confident) and the inference is that she has already had surgery to improve her looks and therefore make her happy.

The presuppositions are:

1 that you are not happy with your looks;
2 that this woman is happy with her looks;
3 that this woman has had surgery.

The inference is:

1 if you want to be happy with your looks you will need surgery.

It is interesting that at no stage does the advertisement state that you will be happy with your looks if you have cosmetic surgery; instead the advertisement makes a general statement, 'In the right hands, cosmetic surgery can benefit you for life', which is fairly difficult to disagree with. The following phrase moves directly on to the Surgical Advisory Service and its surgeons and the inference to be made is that 'the right hands' referred to earlier are in fact the Surgical Advisory Service.

The second advertisement I would like to consider is for the Ambrose Wilson catalogue. Here again, there is a body of knowledge which this advertisement presupposes. The text states 'styled to make you look slimmer'; this presupposes:

1 that you want to look slimmer than you are;
2 that clothes which are styled in a particular way can make you look slimmer;
3 that Ambrose Wilson clothes are styled in this way.

The inference is that Ambrose Wilson clothes will make you look slimmer and therefore you will want to buy them. The curious element about this advertisement is that it is not necessarily aimed at readers who are seriously overweight, since the dresses start at size 12. It simply trades on the assumption that all women are conditioned by ideology to consider themselves overweight whatever their actual weight or size. Consider some of the other phrases in this advertisement; the fashions in the catalogue will in fact 'flatter', on the assumption that the clothes will be used to hide the truth of the actual size of the woman's body: clever details are needed to disguise a woman's body, so that her shoulders are emphasized and her hips are skimmed over by the fabric. There are further presuppositions in the phrase 'Forget all about dull dressing, you can wear bright bold colours and still look slim': the presuppositions are:

1 that wearing bright colours is good;
2 that wearing dark/dull colours is bad;

STYLED TO MAKE YOU LOOK SLIMMER

SIZES 12 RIGHT UP TO 30

You'll find all the fashions that really flatter in the new Autumn Collection from Ambrose Wilson. Slimming styles like drop-waist dresses, hip skimming tops and long line coats. Clever details such as dolman sleeves and padded shoulders. Forget all about dull dressing, you can wear bright bold colours and still look slim. A terrific choice for every occasion, in size 12 to 30.

Send for your free copy today.

3 that people who are overweight should dress in drab colours in order not to draw attention to their bodies;

4 that people who are overweight should not wear bright colours because these will attract attention to their bodies.

The inference is that if you wear Ambrose Wilson clothes you, who are necessarily overweight, will be able to wear bright colours without difficulty because the way that the clothes are styled will mean that you will not look the weight that you are.

These advertisements have demonstrated the way in which phrases can be interpreted only in their ideological context. By making explicit the presuppositions and inferences necessary to make the phrases make sense, it is possible to think through the implications of what is being asserted. Because many advertisements work precisely by posing material which is unproblematic as if it were material which could be presupposed unproblematically, it is important to perform an archaeological exercise in order to foreground this ideological work.

METAPHOR

Metaphor might appear at first sight to be a phenomenon which occurs at the level of the word, but I will be arguing that metaphor conventionally works at the level of the phrase rather than at the level of words in isolation; as Black states, 'metaphors are better regarded as systems of belief than as individual things' (Black in Ortony 1979: 33). I will be following Lakoff and Johnson's work here in their concern with metaphor as a fundamental element in the way that we structure our thoughts and words. Metaphor, in this view, is seen not as a literary form or as a deviation from some supposedly literal language, but rather as one of the building blocks of our thinking, at both the level of language acquisition and language-use (Lakoff and Johnson 1980). As Max Black states, metaphor is 'an instrument for drawing implications grounded in perceived analogies of structure between two subjects belonging to different domains' (Black in Ortony 1979: 32). In this sense, when you use a metaphor, you are drawing on a body of thought or background knowledge which might in fact skew your analysis or thinking of that particular object. Particularly if the metaphors which are being used are so-called 'dead' metaphors, i.e. those metaphors which are preconstructed, then the thought-processes which are involved in the use of those metaphors may not be as open to analysis as if a less preconstructed phrase were used. Let us consider two metaphors cited by Roger Tourangeau in his 'Metaphor and cognitive structure', one referring to males and one to females:

That man is a wolf.
Sally is a block of ice.

(cited in Miall 1982: 23)

Both of these metaphors can be interpreted as referring to male and female sexuality (although they can also be interpreted on other levels as well). The first one may be used to refer to a man who is promiscuous, and who is, on a metaphorical level, seen to hunt women in the same way as a wolf stalks its prey. Male sexuality is often described in terms of metaphors of animal behaviour, so that it is seen to be at the same level of instinctual behaviour as an animal's, and as little under control. The describing of sexuality in these terms means that extreme male behaviour such as rape may be understood to be only 'natural'.

Sexuality is often described at a metaphorical level in terms of heat and lack of heat. People may be said to be hot, or fiery when they are good lovers. But it is noticeable that women who are not interested in sex or at least not interested in the particular form of sexual activity offered by men, for example, penetration, are said to be cold. There are many metaphors which work within this metaphorical structure; for example, if we want to describe a woman as uninterested in penetrative sex and incapable of having an orgasm by penetration, we say that she is frigid, i.e. frozen. In the second example, we call upon this stereotypical 'knowledge' about sexuality, which states that if women are unresponsive to men sexually, then they may be described in terms of lack of heat. Thus, Sally is like a block of ice because of this pre-existing metaphorical system of meaning. We could also understand this phrase as meaning that emotionally Sally was not responsive, since we also describe people's emotions in terms of heat and lack of heat (she's a warm person; she was so cold to me the other day; I had a cool reception; she gave me a frosty look; and so on). But I would argue that although this double meaning is possible, if it were used to describe a man, it would be interpreted only at an emotional level and not at a sexual level. It is assumed at some level that men cannot in fact be sexually unresponsive and therefore the metaphorical structure does not exist.

Roger Tourangeau asserts that metaphor often works in this very conservative way to reinforce stereotypical knowledge; he says, 'Beliefs come in packages and the packaging is partly determined by the domains we see as relevant ... the beliefs we project on to the principal subject may be more or less in agreement with our prior beliefs about it' (Tourangeau in Miall 1982: 30). Take, for example, the phrase 'the battle of the sexes': in assuming at a metaphorical level that the relations between the sexes can be considered only as if they were always antagonistic, the user of this phrase will be led to consider males and females in terms of battles and warfare, rather than considering other forms of thinking. Therefore, in foregrounding the notion of conflict, other more productive ways of thinking will sink into the background. Metaphors may influence us to think about certain scenarios in particularly stereotyped ways.

JOKES AND HUMOUR

The area of humour is complex, because once again it is not possible to locate sexism at the level of the individual words used. As I have shown elsewhere, in an analysis of a poem by John Fuller called 'Valentine' the sexist nature of the sentiments expressed in the poem can be disguised through the use of wit and playfulness (S. Mills 1992c). Because the sexism may be disguised under the cover of humour, the reader may unwittingly participate in the perpetuation of the sexism embedded in the text when s/he laughs at the wit. Similarly, in this text by Ben Jonson, sexist statements are justified by critics because of the stylishness and cleverness of the poem.

> Follow a shadow, it still flies you;
> Seem to fly it, it will pursue:
> So court a mistress, she denies you;
> Let her alone, she will court you.
> Say, are not women truly, then,
> Styled but the shadows of us men?
> At morn, at even, shades are longest;
> At noon, they are or short, or none;
> So men at weakest, they are strongest,
> But grant us perfect, they're not known,
> Say, are not women truly, then,
> Styled but the shadows of us men?
>
> (Ben Jonson, 'That women are but men's shadows')

The poem plays on the phrase 'to be a shadow of' as in, for example, 'She's a shadow of her former self', asserting that females are lesser beings in relation to men, whilst at the same time making a metaphorical link between women's and shadows' behaviour in relation to men. Women are presented only in relation to men, either chasing them or fleeing them; the first four lines show women's fickleness, since if a man chases them, they will run away, but the moment the man runs away, they begin to chase him. Thus women do not have any volition of their own, but like shadows are 'tied' to men. The poem also shows that women gain stature only through their caring for men who are very young or very old (metaphorically at men's morn, or birth, and evening, or death; that is, when 'shadows' are at their strongest); when men are at their prime (at noon) women are seen to be non-existent. Thus there is a complex analogy being made here between women and shadows, which proposes that women are lesser beings than men and that they are tied to men.

Tom Gibbons writes that this poem's 'tone and intention could easily be mistaken by a too-serious reader . . . Jonson is not here writing a male-chauvinist polemic, but directing our attention to his skill in developing an ingenious argument in verse which is both highly-wrought and deceptively simple. The poem is primarily an elegant *performance* in short and Jonson's tone is witty, playful and good-humoured. To take this poem seriously would certainly be to mistake its author's intention' (Gibbons 1980). Here Gibbons seems to be asserting that feminists who have found this poem offensive are in fact simply missing the most important part of the poem: the skilful use of language and poetic structure. Jonson is in fact simply being playful, and this playfulness is stressed to deflect the charge of sexism.

The same strategy is at work in sexist jokes where the retort 'It's only a joke' or 'I was only joking' is frequently used when complaints are made about sexism. It is conventional to assume that women do not or cannot tell jokes; women are usually seen as the butt of jokes rather than as active agents in their construction, even though there are a large number of female comics now and women seem to have little problem telling jokes in reality (especially if they are in a single-sex environment). The problem may in fact be with format jokes, where the jokes have to be memorized; this is a particularly difficult strategy to employ in conversation since you are claiming an extended turn at talk, something which may at times be difficult for women in mixed-sex environments. Generally, this type of humour is seen as a male domain and humour has often been portrayed as a form of bonding and solidarity display. Consider, for example, the recent number of Essex girl jokes which focus around the supposed stupidity, vulgarity and/or sexual availability (for heterosexual sex) of women from Essex.

> Q: How do you get an Essex girl to laugh on Sunday?
> A: Tell her a joke on Friday.

These jokes take the form of a straightforward inversion of expectations through the simple two-line format. A question is asked and the response is a tangentially related statement which demonstrates Essex women's stupidity.

> Q: What's the difference between an Essex girl's tights and a window-cleaner?
> A: A window-cleaner has fewer ladders.
>
> Q: What's an Essex girl's favourite book?
> A: Don't be stupid.
>
> Q: What does an Essex girl put behind her ears to make herself attractive?
> A: Her knees.
>
> Q: What's the difference between an Essex girl and the man from Del Monte?
> A: The man from Del Monte sometimes says No.

(Leigh and Wood 1991)

These jokes, although superficially simple in format terms, rely on the audience providing the necessary logic to complete their meaning. In this way, the audience/reader is implicated in the sexism of the joke, even if they would not necessarily agree with this view of women from Essex (or women in general).

Reactions to these jokes are interesting. One reaction might be not to see any humour in them at all, and to perceive them purely as evidence of how misogynistic is the society that generates them. Another reaction might be to find them amusing and, if challenged, to make replies on the lines of 'It's only a joke, it doesn't mean that I think all females from Essex are like that, or that there's something wrong with coming from Essex; nor that I have a problem with female sexuality.' This means that it is possible to laugh at the joke and yet deny any involvement in the joke's message – a perfect example of having your cake and eating it. Another frequent method of obscuring the debate commonly produced in response to criticism is 'Feminists have no sense of humour'. There are of course other reactions to these jokes: you might laugh at them in the company of some people and not in other contexts. It is probable that hearing jokes like this in a social setting will involve you in having to decide on your reaction, since not laughing at jokes risks your social ostracization from the group and laughing seems to implicate you in the joke. If you laugh, you have somehow taken a position which aligns you with the presuppositions of the joke.[2]

Let us consider another joke from a rag-mag circulated by students of Imperial College, London in 1990:

> Frank comes out of a sex-change operation. A friend asks him: 'Was it painful, changing into a woman?' Frank replies: 'The only disturbing part was having a hole drilled into my head and half of my brain being scooped out.'

The jokes in this rag-mag seem to work by setting up an out-group; all of which can be classified as falling into one of the following groups: women and their sexuality/stupidity; Irish people and their stupidity; foreigners and their stupidity; and tabooed subjects like death and excretion. A further joke included in this rag-mag is:

> Q: What's the difference between a rottweiler and a woman with PMT?
> A: Lipstick.

Here a condition which affects only women is made to seem ridiculous, by making a comparison between women and rottweilers where the only difference is seen to be the trivial one of lipstick.

A joke which works in the same way, told to me by a student, is:

> Q: Why did the woman cross the road?
> A: That's the wrong question! What was she doing out of the kitchen?

Thus jokes seem to function as a way of affirming sexist views within society without allowing for a challenge to be made to them. Female comedians, such as Jo Brand, have in recent years begun to develop very critical jokes about the way that women are treated; but these comedians are still in the minority and the number of jokes where women are the butts of the humour are in the majority.

Doubles entendres are particularly interesting in this context, since women as sexual objects are often the recipient of this type of humour. Interestingly enough when *doubles entendres* are used in seaside postcards they are often concerned to depict sexual relations as being the only relationship possible between men and women, but they do this in a way which does not state that a sexual statement is being made. This is part of the supposed innocence and naivety of the seaside postcard, since they do not openly state that they are referring to sex. As I have showed elsewhere (S. Mills 1992c), *double entendre* can often have the effect of reifying women and their sexuality, that is, turning women into objects for male consumption. So, for example, in a poem which states 'I'd like all your particulars in folders marked Confidential', we can interpret this on one level as referring to the putting of confidential information about the woman into folders; at the same time, we have to interpret it at another level where the meaning is rather opaque but seems to mean that the persona would like to have the woman to himself ('particulars' works in a similar way to 'vital statistics', a phrase which refers only to women's body shape).

If we consider two of these postcards, this will become apparent. In the first, A, there are two partly clad people, the male sweating and, we presume, feeling sexually excited by the sight of the younger provocative woman. We are to assume that she is his secretary since she has a pen in one hand, she is leaning on a secretary's notepad and there is a file marked 'urgent'; the boss also has a letter in his hand. In some sense, her statement that 'I feel that any minute you will ask me to take a letter' is quite appropriate, since although they are on a beach and they are wearing swimsuits, she at least has the equipment necessary for 'taking a letter'. The humour resides in the fact that the male is looking at her in a sexual way and that she is displayed in a provocative way. We can either interpret this as a *double entendre*, that is, 'take a letter' can be read to mean 'sex' (a play on the phrase 'French letter'), or find the joke residing in the fact that the woman is naive and does not see the incongruity of her remark. The exaggerated body shape and posture of the woman mark her as the sexual being.

In the second cartoon, B, the *double entendre* works in the following way. A couple on a desert island are surrounded by broken coconuts and on one level the man can be seen to be saying: I thought I would never tire of coconuts, but the fact that he says 'one thing' makes us assume that he is referring to sex, since generally in *double entendre* if the reference is vague, referring to 'it' or 'thing', it is enough to evoke a sexual reference. Interestingly enough, many of the cartoons work on the basis of an assumption of male sexual incompetence. In the third postcard, C, the *double entendre* works on the possibility of interpreting 'take you' in two different ways, either as 'interpret you' or 'have sex with you' (particularly of a woman). What is interesting with all of these examples is that they view the sexual act as being something which is central to relations between men and women and which is fraught with difficulties (see C). Other postcards portray women as monstrously large in relation to small husbands who are nagged and henpecked mercilessly. Thus humour is an arena where difficulties and tensions about relations between women and men are displayed, but the humour which finds its way into the public sphere – in joke books, in format jokes, in postcards – is conventionally male-oriented. That is, the view of these difficulties is conventionally one which works in the interests of males. Women and other outgroups are the objects of this worried laughter.

(A)

12031 " I feel that any minute now you will ask me to take a letter!"

(B)

"FUNNY ISN'T IT? A MONTH
AGO, I'D HAVE SAID THERE WAS
ONE THING I'D NEVER TIRE OF."

(C)

He: "You're a funny girl. I never
know quite how to take you!"
She: "You've never really tried!"

TRANSITIVITY CHOICES

'The different patterns of transitivity are the prime means of expressing our internal and external experiences, which is part of the ideational function of language' (Wales 1989: 466). The concept of transitivity is associated with Michael Halliday's work in systemic linguistics from the late 1960s onwards. Systemic grammar foregrounds the idea of language as a system, or network, of choices, according to which 'Each major aspect of grammar can be analysed as a set of options, each option dependent upon the context or environment' (ibid.).

Halliday himself conducted a linguistic analysis of transitivity choices in William Golding's novel *The Inheritors* (Halliday 1971). In this analysis, he tries to link the systematic choices which Golding makes for his characters with the creation of a world-view. Transitivity for Halliday is 'the set of options whereby the speaker encodes his [*sic*] experience of the process of the external world, and of the internal world of his consciousness, together with the participants in these processes and their attendant circumstances; and it embodies a very basic distinction of processes into two types, those that are required as due to an external cause, an agency other than the person or object involved, and those that are not' (ibid.: 359). Thus, Halliday is concerned with the representation of *who acts* (who is an agent) and who is *acted upon* (who is affected by the actions of others). This view of transitivity forming a coherent world-view can quite easily be translated into concerns about the ways that language and ideology are interrelated.

In discussions of transitivity, there is a range of choices which are available and these revolve around three sets of choices: material, mental and relational.[3] In this system, processes can be categorized into those elements which are actions which can be observed in the real world and which have consequences (material), for example, 'She *swam* across the river'; those which take place largely in the mind (mental), for example, 'She *thought* about the situation'; and those which simply relate two elements together (relational), for example, 'It *is* rather cold'. Within material action processes, there are two further choices, between 'material action intention' and 'material action supervention': with material action intention, there is a clear will to do something, for example, 'I broke the window, in order to get into the house'; but with supervention there is an attempt to capture for analysis those verbal processes where things are not done intentionally, for example, 'I broke my favourite glasses'.

The study of transitivity is concerned with how actions are represented: what kind of actions appear in a text, who does them and to whom they are done. When we make choices between different types of process and different participants, between the different roles participants might take, these decisions are shown syntactically through transitivity choices. This system of analysing linguistic options in texts is primarily concerned with the roles of human participants. Therefore a broad distinction is made to differentiate conscious actors, who are perceived as beings capable of thought, communication, plans and actions, from everything else in the world, organic and inorganic, animate and inanimate, which is presumed not to be capable of conscious thought and planned action.

Verbs in English can be divided into categories, depending on the kind of activity they refer to, and the participants involved can be identified by terms which indicate the process and whether they are performing it, or having it done to them.

So in a schematic form, material processes can be shown as in Figure 5.

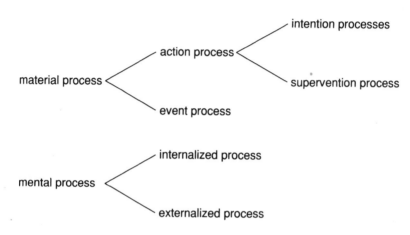

Figure 5 Material and mental processes

An analysis of transitivity consists of counting the ratios of choice of types of process; therefore, if an author or a speaker consistently chooses mental processes, a particular t ype of text will be produced. The main emphasis in this type of analysis is that in producing text, there is a range of choices to be made, and every text which has been produced could have been produced differently. In his 1971 essay, Halliday demonstrates that systematic use of certain types of transitivity choice can help us as readers to distinguish between world-views; in this case, the world-views of characters in Golding's novel. Halliday shows how one group of characters in the novel uses a form of language whereby agency is attributed to inanimate objects rather than people. Halliday argues that these choices about agency embody a view of the world whereby these characters operate within but not on nature, where they are in some senses the recipients of actions rather than the instigators. Thus, by analysing patterns in transitivity choice it is possible to make more general statements about the way that characters view their position in the world and their relation to others.

The significance of these divisions is that choices made on a syntactic level are part of the representation of character. The extent to which a character is the passive 'victim' of circumstance, or is actively in control of the environment, making decisions and taking action, is one of the concerns of feminist stylistics. If a character is very active in a text, in control of their own decisions and actions, an analysis of text describing them might be expected to show a range of processes, and a relatively high number of material–action–intention processes – where the character is performing an action which they have voluntarily chosen as a course of behaviour. A character whose behaviour consists of many internalized mental processes might be expected to appear as very introspective; similarly a character whose processes consist disproportionately of externalized mental processes may seem incomplete in some way. A character who is written in terms of supervention processes might appear somehow out of control of themselves. This is the claim Burton makes in her analysis of Plath's novel *The Bell Jar*. Burton writes of Plath: 'Her texts abound in disenabling metaphors, disenabling lexis, and . . . disenabling syntactic structures' (Burton 1982: 201). Burton analyses an extract from *The Bell Jar* in which the narrator is in a hospital being prepared for electric shock treatment. An analysis of the clause structure supports the reading that the narrator is positioned as a passive 'victim', and the hospital staff have control over their environment and the narrator's, and the narrator does not. This is one way to explore transitivity – to show how a character who on a first reading seems to be a victim, not actively engaged in controlling its environment, is disenabled by syntactic choices in a text. The character can be compared with other characters who have more control over their environment, realized in a higher proportion of material–action–intention processes: Burton compares Plath's narrator with the nurse in the same extract. Another use of this method of analysis is to question the construction of a character who is apparently assertive, in control of her life, and to monitor 1) whether the content of the text is supported or undermined by syntactic choices, 2) whether her behaviour reflects these characteristics in every aspect of her life. One aspect of texts which is very fertile for transitivity analyses is romance scenes (see Wareing 1990 and 1994). Even when gender roles are disrupted in a novel, stereotyping in romantic encounters has a strong hold in popular fiction. To illustrate how a text may be broken down into its transitivity choices – and to give some impression of what typical choices might be in a description of a heterosexual romance – consider the following extract from Helen McInnes's novel, *The Hidden Target*:

> 'I know more about myself than I ever did, I know that I – ' She raised her head, let her eyes meet his. 'I know that I love you,' she ended silently. 'Oh, Bob – ' She held out her hand.
>
> He grasped it, took both her hands, held them tightly, felt her draw him near. His arms went around her, and he kissed her mouth, her eyes, her cheeks, her slender neck, her mouth again – long kisses lingering on yielding lips. Her arms encircled him pressing him closer.
>
> (McInnes 1982: 314–15)

In order to analyse the transitivity choices in the passage, the actors in each process are extracted, with the lexical realization of each process associated with them, as below:

1 She raised her head	7 [he] held them tightly
2 [she] let her eyes	8 [he] felt her draw him near
3 she ended silently	9 His arms went around her
4 She held out her hand	10 he kissed her mouth . . .
5 He grasped it	11 Her arms encircled him
6 [he] took both her hands	

Five of these processes have the female character, or parts of her body, as the actor (i.e. the person who 'does' the verb or process); six have the male, or his body parts, as the actor. If the process is a material one, the actor will be called the agent; if the process is a mental one, the actor is referred to as the sensor.

Having identified the actors and processes, we can label the processes. The processes with the female as actor are:

1 She raised her head	= material action intention (affected = female body part)
2 [she] let her eyes meet his	= material action supervention (affected = female body part)
3 she ended silently	= mental action internal
4 She held out her hand	= material action intention (affected = female body part)
11 Her arms encircled him	= material action intention/supervention (affected = male) (actor = female body part)

Those processes which have the male in the role of actor are:

5 He grasped it	= material process intention (affected = female body part)
6 [he] took both her hands	= material process intention (affected = female body part)
7 [he] held them tightly	= material process intention (affected = female body part)
8 [he] felt her draw him near	= mental process internal
9 His arms went around her	= material process intention/supervention (affected = female) (actor = male body part)
10 he kissed her mouth	= material process intention (affected = female body part)

Now that we have a scheme of the transitivity choices in the text, we can compare the representations of the male and female characters, in terms of 'who does what to whom'. The female does slightly fewer material intention processes than the male (3:5), and while they both do one internal mental process, only the female does a material–supervention–action (she let her eyes meet his – as if she were not quite in control of them). However, what in this text is most disproportionate in the representation of the male and female characters is with respect to who (or what) are the affected entities. When the male does a process, he does four out of six to a part of the female's body (her hands, her mouth), and one to her as a whole (His arms went around her). Yet when the female does a process, who or what is the affected entity? Not the male, or parts of his body as might be expected – only one out of the five processes done by the female is done to the male, and then to the whole person, rather than to his body parts (Her arms encircled him). On the contrary, for three of the five processes done by the female, the affected entity is a part of her own body: her head, her eyes, her hand. So in this text, although there is not a great discrepancy regarding which character does what kind of process, there is a paradoxical relation between who/what they are done to.

A further text to illustrate the workings of transitivity is taken from Barbara Taylor Bradford's *A Woman of Substance*. This best-selling novel is the history of a kitchen maid, Emma Harte, who on the strength of her intelligence, determination and hard work, becomes the owner of an international business corporation, a multi-millionaire. She has four children each of whom has a different father, but she has no enduring, successful heterosexual relationship. In achieving financial success, but not monogamous domesticity, she differs radically from the stereotypical heroine of the popular romance genre:

> 'Take your robe off, my love,' he said softly as he came towards her. He covered her body with his own and cradled her in his arms, smiling down into her expectant face. 'It's such a pity to ruin this exotic hairdo,' he murmured as he began to pull the pins from her hair. The russet tresses spilled around her shoulders, porcelain fragile and pink in the warm glow of the lamp, and he gasped at her loveliness now so perfectly revealed to him. He ran his hand through the heavy lengths and held her by the nape of her neck, bringing her face up to his own. His lips met hers, savouring their warmth and sweetness, and they were both engulfed by their longing and the emotions which had been denied release for weeks. He moved his mouth into the hollow of her neck, kissing her shoulders, her breasts and the deep valley between, and his strong hands smoothed over her firm skin and he caressed every part of her until he knew her fervour matched his own. Emma was suffused by an unfamiliar warmth, a burning heat that flooded her whole being. Her whole body arched up, cleaved to him. She ached to be joined to him, to become one with him, and she marvelled at her pleasure in his body and in her own.
>
> (Taylor Bradford 1981: 666–8)

If the processes and the associated actors are abstracted from the text, the result is:

1 he said	11 His lips met hers
2 he came towards her	12 they were both engulfed
3 He covered her body	13 He moved his mouth
4 [he] cradled her	14 [his] hands smoothed over her skin

> 5 he murmured
> 6 he began to pull
> 7 [Her hair] spilled
> 8 he gasped
> 9 he ran his hand [through her hair]
> 10 [he] held her
> 15 he caressed [her]
> 16 he knew
> 17 Emma was suffused
> 18 Her whole body arched
> 19 She ached
> 20 she marvelled

If now we add up the number of processes the male is actor in, and compare it with the number in which the female is actor, the results have a strong bias.

Male (or male body part) as actor:

1	he said	= mental internalized process
2	he came towards her	= material process intention
3	He covered her body	= material process intention
4	[he] cradled her	= material process intention
5	he murmured	= mental process externalized
6	he began to pull	= material process intention
8	he gasped	= mental process externalized
9	he ran his hand [through her hair]	= material process intention
10	[he] held her	= material process intention
11	His lips met hers	= material process intention (actor = male body part)
13	He moved his mouth	= material process intention
14	[his] hands smoothed over her skin	= material process intention (actor = male body part)
15	he caressed [her]	= material process intention
16	he knew	= mental process internalized

Out of the twenty processes in the text, the male (or male body part) is the actor in fourteen. If this is compared with the processes in which the female (or female body part) appears as actor, the difference is striking.

Female (or female body part as actor)

7	[Her hair] spilled	= material process supervention (actor = female body part)
17	Emma was suffused	= relational process
18	Her whole body arched	= material process supervention (actor = female body part)
19	She ached	= mental process internalized
20	she marvelled	= mental process internalized

There are five processes in which the female appears in the position of actor, in comparison with the fourteen processes in which the male is actor. Furthermore, the processes performed by the female are of a different quality from those performed by the male. In contrast to the ten material–intention–processes in which the male is agent, the female is agent in none. In the two material processes, parts of her body move, not of her own volition (her hair spills, her body arches). The three remaining processes are mental and relational, more passive by contrast. There is a strong correlation between the transitivity choices in the above text, and the representation of the female as passive recipient of the male's actions, not as sexually active in her own right. While the male experience is represented in terms of the actions he does to her body, the female's experience is given as her thoughts and feelings, and her body's independent responses to physical pleasure (see Wareing 1994).

Thus, this type of analysis of transitivity choices can tell us a great deal about the ideological messages which circulate in texts where there are strong heroines and where there are passive victims. However, in the following section, I would like to consider some of the difficulties which this type of work engenders, and propose a model of feminist analysis which is prepared to acknowledge some of the problems in attributing straightforward meanings to sets of language items. In order to explore these general questions about feminist analysis, I will focus my analysis on the lyrics of a pop song, 'Hit' by the Sugar Cubes, to demonstrate that transitivity analysis can yield complex insights into reading a text.[4] Rather than simply assuming that we can interpret transitivity choices as having particular meanings, I argue in the analysis that transitivity choices, like other linguistic choices, have a range of meanings dependent on the context in which they occur and the presuppositions which the reader brings to bear on the interpretative process.

FEMINISM AND IDEOLOGY

For many feminists, women are particularly subjected to the effects of ideology. In many ways, it is clear that there is a range of belief systems about women which do not 'fit' with the reality of women's lives. These systems of belief are not simply imposed upon women, but women themselves actively take part in them and appropriate and reject them according to their investments and interests in them. In this way, it is possible to see ideology as something which is not unitary, but which is negotiated by individual agents. An ideology, in this view, is a sequence or set of statements which have certain conceptual links, but which individual subjects will negotiate, affirm, and/or resist. This point is quite important in relation to the analysis of language in texts, because it is essential that we do not see particular language items or statements necessarily having one undisputed meaning which is recognized by all readers. Similarly, language items do not 'make sense' in isolation, but only when they are set in the context of larger-scale ideological frameworks and frameworks of critique.

The set of myths or ideologies around romantic love and emotions is just one area where ideology affects women's lives in a way in which the effect is not so great on men. The ideology of romantic love, in Mills & Boon romances, for example, whereby romance is seen as the most important element in a woman's life and where women are literally taken over by passionate feelings, has been naturalized within our culture, so that it is sometimes difficult to 'see around' it. A great number of pop songs portray romantic love as a form of pain and suffering which women should take pleasure in. Women are constructed in different ways from men within pop songs and in culture in general, and the notion of who is in control is central to this ideological gender difference, since generally women are represented as passive 'recipients' of love and men are represented as 'agents'. In many pop songs, women are portrayed as out of control, where emotions take over and they 'fall' in love, without there being any active control over the process. But like all ideologies, romantic love has at its heart a fundamental contradiction: it is about pleasure and enjoyment at the same time that it is based on suffering and despair. In the analysis which follows I would like to focus on this contradictory ideological position and consider what this means for an analysis of transitivity.

The pop song which I would like to analyse is one which was issued in 1992 by the Sugar Cubes and which is entitled 'Hit'. Here is a sample of the lyrics (I have set it out in lines which correspond to pauses within the song):

1 This wasn't supposed to happen
2 I was happy by myself
3 Accidentally
4 You seduced me
5 I'm in love again.

Chorus

6 I lie in my bed
7 Totally still
8 My eyes wide open
9 I'm in rapture
10 I don't believe this
11 I'm in love
12 Again.
13 This wasn't supposed to happen
14 I've been hit by your charm
15 How could you do this to me
16 I'm in love
17 Again.

The rest of the song is similar in sentiments and expression, except that a hard-edged male voice with a different voice quality interrupts the reverie in a different key, stating:

1 I said ouch
2 This really hurts
3 This has been practised for millions of years

4 Therefore we are . . . guess what?
5 I'm a boy
6 You're a girl.

There are a number of points to make before beginning the analysis of the song. First, it is important not to forget the fact that this is a song and that the voice quality and the key in which the song has been written are factors important to the way in which it will be interpreted. A full analysis would consider the musical qualities of the song itself.

However, for the purposes of brevity, I will concentrate on voice quality because that is the most important analytical factor in relation to transitivity. Second, in contemporary pop songs the meanings and status of the actual words are subject to some debate; there are critics who feel that it is possible to analyse the words as if they were poetry (see Day 1988) and there are others who insist that this is not in fact necessarily the way that they are interpreted by listeners. Listeners may perform a 'slack' reading of the words, and not feel that they have to understand or even hear some of them; the indistinctness of some words may in fact be part of the whole 'feel' and atmosphere of the song. In this song, some of the words are unclear and they are not included on the record sleeve, so whether the words are as significant as they are in the analysis of lyric poetry is debatable. Third, it must be remembered that there are a number of different readings available for any text – there has been much debate within cultural studies in particular about the meaning of artefacts: whether a critic can simply discover or uncover the real meaning of a particular text or whether in fact the meanings can only be found through consulting the people by whom that cultural artefact is used. This is of particular significance in the discussion of transitivity, where it has been asserted in many of the analyses I have mentioned above that linguistic choices result in particular meanings. Finally, it must be remembered that pop songs are used in very specific ways; listeners have emotional investments in pop songs and tend to listen to them repeatedly. Pop music is particularly important for adolescents who use it as a way of constructing a sense of self and community. It is difficult to simply analyse these texts therefore as artefacts, since they have very tangible effects on listeners in the real world.

'Hit' itself is a very modern production; it is not a conventional romantic song written in a major key and dominated by a strong melodic verse and chorus. Instead, it opens in a minor key with discordant guitars and a very full sound; this suggests to its listener that it takes a 'modern' and hard-edged view of love. Nevertheless, as I will show, the view of love which is propounded in the song seems to be seriously at odds with the style of the backing and the singing itself. The beat of the song is fairly fast in contrast to the slow, drawn-out singing style of the female vocalist, who sings in a very grainy and melancholic manner; the voice is produced in a highly emotional way, each syllable being stressed and stretched, even words like 'I' and 'this' being extended over several notes. The musical range of her singing is very restricted in the verses, ranging over only four notes, and the melody does not harmonize at all with the backing; furthermore, each phrase ends on a lower note, giving an overall melancholic feel to the song as a whole. The verse which is sung by the male singer is, by contrast, shouted or spoken in a very staccato style, rather than being sung. The voice quality of both singers has an effect on the way that the text is interpreted; it could be argued, for instance, that the female singer's voice quality sets up a framework within which we decide how to interpret the song; for example, we could decide either that the voice quality has a 'longing' feel to it, which the female is enjoying, or that it is 'yearning' in despair and suffering.

Let us first of all analyse the transitivity choices within the text. The first phrase, 'This wasn't supposed to happen' (line 1), is a clear use of a transitivity choice where there is no agent: rather than someone acting – someone deciding to fall in love with someone else – something has happened. This puts the protagonist in the position of being 'affected', that is, 'acted upon'; but it also means that her being in love has just 'happened' – it is not as if anyone has made a conscious decision. Romantic love is portrayed and experienced in this way in western cultures but it should be stressed that there is nothing 'natural' about this form of representation. Even this verb 'happen' is mediated through the use of 'supposed to', and because this is passivized, it is unclear whose emotions are being described. This initial clause seems very distanced and lacking in an agent. The protagonist could have stated: 'I didn't want this to happen', but here the transitivity choice distances this level of decision-making from her. Her choice of 'this' is also interesting as a description of the process of being in love; the protagonist could have chosen to describe it using a verb (falling in love) or nominalization, rather than the use of the objectifying 'this'. Thus, from the very beginning of the song, the protagonist is presented as not being in control. This view of the protagonist is affirmed by other verbal choices; for example, 'Accidentally you seduced me' (lines 3–4). Here the woman is seen as the 'affected' participant, and there is another actor, 'you', who seduces her. This verb is one which is traditionally reserved for male activity and it is a curious choice, since it seems to be quite an old-fashioned word with connotations of rakishness, where the male is the only one with sexual appetite and the female is simply the recipient of male sexual action. 'Seduce' also has connotations of unwillingness on the part of the female, which affirms the sense from line 1 that the protagonist does not want this involvement. However, the verb is mediated by the use of 'accidentally', which seems to conflict with the intentionality of the verb 'to seduce'. Here, what is, on an initial analysis, a material–action–intention process is modified, so that it acts as a supervention process. We can interpret this clause in two ways: either the process by which she is 'seduced' is one where the male character is not necessarily in direct control either; or the male is portrayed as interpreting the relationship as a one-night stand. The first verse thus seems to present a particular view of romantic love which is contradictory: we have a female character who is independent, since she was 'happy by myself' and she states clearly that she did not want or intend to fall in love again; the male character, although portrayed as 'seducing' her, does so in a way which might suggest that he too did not wish this to happen. It is also interesting to note that this first verse signals that she does not see this as a once-in-a-lifetime event since she states 'I'm in love again', in much the same way that one might state 'I've got the flu again'. The ideology of romantic love works on the notion that there is only one person with whom we will fall in love and that this will last for ever. The first verse seems to be challenging this myth and proposing that romantic love is something which needs to be resisted. The second verse also takes up this idea that falling in love is a nuisance, but suggests that it is something for which the male is responsible and which the woman resents. The second verse affirms the first in that here again the female actor takes the role of affected or recipient; she is the recipient of the passive clause 'I've been hit by your charm' (line 14). It is interesting that the verb 'hit' has been used here since this is an unusual collocative choice, being a much more violent verb that is generally used with 'charm'. It suggests that the protagonist had developed a certain protective barrier around herself when she was single which the male has broken down by seducing her. In line 15, she asks 'How could you do this to me?' where her role is again the 'affected participant'. The other verses in the song have similar clauses where the female is positioned as the recipient of actions only or is the focus of passive clauses where the male character is the agent. Thus, rather than romantic love being viewed as something to be welcomed, here it is seen as something which is imposed on the female and which she resents and resists.

However, there is a sense in which this slightly challenging view of romantic love is itself undercut by the chorus. There seems to be a clear break in meaning between the verses sung by the female character and the chorus, also sung by the female. This break is signalled to the listener by the move to a major key and a more upbeat tempo. The voice quality is less melancholic and seems to gain a certain clarity and strength. The transitivity choices are in line with those of the first and second verses, in that the protagonist does not act but experiences. However, 'I'm in rapture' (line 9), which describes a very positive, almost religious experience, creates a much more positive interpretative context. Because of this positive context we interpret 'I don't believe this' (line 10) to mean 'This is so good that I can hardly believe it is possible', rather than 'I don't believe this could happen to me because I was happy to be single'. We also interpret the statement 'I'm in love again' (lines 11–12) in a more positive way than when it occurred in the first and second verses. The chorus serves to present us with an image of the female character as passive, but enjoying that passivity; she does not act, she experiences; all of the clauses here are either mental processes ('I don't believe this') or material–action–processes which are intransitive, that is, they do not have an effect on another person or thing. Thus 'I lie in my bed' is intransitive in that it does not have an object; there is no affected participant. The verbs in other clauses in the chorus have been omitted, so that there are simple descriptive phrases like 'my eyes wide open' which describes the state of the female character without her acting.

Given that we have two contradictory views of romantic love here ('I don't want to be in love as I was happy to be single' and 'I enjoy being in love') it is surprising that listeners do in fact impose some coherence on the song as a whole. This is partly due to the fact that the clauses are not related by co-ordination or subordination, but are hypotactic, that is, they are related by contiguity, and the reader is forced to make some connection between them. Each of the clauses is free-standing. Hence, the logical and temporal relations between them have to be inferred by the reader. If the listener considers the ideology of romantic love to be self-evident or commonsense, she will make a logical connection between the potentially negative first verse and the chorus, that is, between a representation of anxiety about being in love, and a representation of pleasure in being in love. She will therefore reconcile the contradictions: that is, love is a nuisance and love is blissful. If the listener is critical of this ideology where suffering in being seduced and pleasure in being in love are the same, then she will find it difficult to make this transition. For those who are critical of romantic love, this pleasure in suffering can be seen only as a form of masochism, the pleasures of being acted upon and being passive.

The male verse is a further contradictory element in this song; as I mentioned earlier, the verse is marked off from the rest of the song by voice quality, singing style, tempo and key. It is in marked contrast to the female's views, since it seems to be proposing that the form of masochism entailed in romantic love is 'natural' because it 'has been practised for millions of years' (line 3) and is inevitable simply because there are 'boys' and 'girls'. The male does not comment on his 'accidental seduction' of the female, but seems here to be suffering in a similar manner to the female; he does not foreground his agency here, using instead a passive 'this has been practised' (line 3) and a seemingly intransitive verb 'this really hurts' (line 2), where the affected participant is understood to be him: 'this really hurts *me*'.

We might also consider the way that the text addresses listeners, since these transitivity choices do not take place in a vacuum but in relation to a listener who interprets them. So, for example, we need to consider the ways in which listeners are called upon or co-opted to align themselves with the statements which are made in the text. Some pop songs call on the listeners in quite explicit ways to agree to certain statements, through direct address, that is, through the use of pronouns such as 'you' and 'I', where the listener accepts these pronouns as referring to herself. Within this song, there is very little overt reader positioning, because 'you' is not used in a way in which it could be addressed to the reader. It is used exclusively for the fictional character who is the absent lover. 'I', however, is thematized, i.e. put in the position of the most important part of the clause, in very many of the sentences. Listeners have the option of merging the 'I' of themselves with the 'I' of the song, and seeing, indirectly, similarities or differences between the two. Most of the address in this song is of an indirect kind, where the listener has to actively work at generating meanings from the text.

As I mentioned above, Burton has developed ways of challenging the representation of women as passive, and one of them is to rewrite the text using different
transitivity choices; this has a dual function – it can serve to highlight the choices
which seem in some way self-evident, and it can lead the listener to think in
different ways about action and agency. Thus, a rewriting of the transitivity
choices, following Burton, in this song would highlight the fact that the female
character is essentially passive and can lead to an analysis whereby it is clear that
the ideology of romantic love has difficulty in accommodating the notion of
women as agents. This does not lead to a 'politically correct' view of love, that is,
one where women are not represented as the victims, but rather simply highlights
the fact that within representations of romantic love, there are often roles carved
out for women which seem natural and which result in women being viewed as
'naturally' passive and acted upon. In the process of rewriting this text, for
example, we would see the impossibility of making the actions of the female all
'material–action–intention' within this type of ideology; for example, statements
such as 'I hit you with my charm' or 'I seduced you' do not make sense within
the ideological framework in which the song is set. Similarly, representations of
romantic love function from the point of view of the female in general and the
male is not fleshed out in such detail or is, as here, almost completely absent: we
might consider rewriting some of the passive clauses so that the male's actions are
heightened by the active voice; for example, 'Accidentally I seduced you', 'I hit
you with my charm' and 'How could I do this to you?' We do not know from the
song whether the male character is similarly 'in rapture' and lying on his bed
thinking about her or whether he has simply seduced her and is now busy seducing
someone else, or has his mind on other things; for example, work or leisure.

One feminist interpretation of this song, following Burton, would see the
woman as a victim of male 'seduction' who is turned into a passive character
through the male actions; the male would be seen as a powerful figure whereas
the woman was the powerless figure. This type of analysis would count up the
number of choices within certain transitivity categories and show that there was
a clear correlation between the choice of the passive/affected role, the use of
intransitive verbs, the concentration on mental processes and a more general
position of lack of control and agency. Whilst this type of analysis would probably
form the basis for any interpretation, it is clearly not adequate to describe some
of the complexities of this song, as I have shown. The meaning of the song is
not a simple question of adding up the number of clause types. A more complex
analysis would see the song and these transitivity choices as a representation
which displays some of the contradictions around romantic love, and would note
that the song can also be seen to be demonstrating some of the tensions that
exist at present around love: this would acknowledge the pleasures associated
with passivity and with being the acted-upon rather than the agent, as well as
acknowledging the wish not to be passive and acted upon. It would also see
power as more a relation than an imposition, that is, it is difficult to see here
who is in control; from one reading position we can see the absent male as in

control, and the female as simply the acted-upon: she is dependent on his actions; but in another reading we can see the male as almost irrelevant: he seduced her (accidentally) but she is the one who is now in control since she has adopted the ideology of romantic love, and she is after all 'in rapture' although perhaps no longer 'happy', as she was when she was single (line 2). This type of analysis calls for a recognition of the contradictions and pleasures of romantic love, and foregrounds the fact that perhaps being acted upon may be pleasurable but dangerous. It also calls for a recognition that ideologies are not static and are frequently called into crisis.

What often happens in feminist transitivity analysis is that there is a simple replication of the message 'All texts about and by women contain these representations of passivity'. What I am trying to foreground here is that making sense of texts is in fact much more complicated: this text does indeed contain some evidence of the female as passive and as acted upon; however, this analysis alone does not show the contradictory elements that are contained within the text – that being in love is pleasurable, that being in love is not pleasurable. The song does not present these positions as contradictory but tries to mask this by presenting them as if they make sense. What my analysis has tried to foreground is the fact that these choices are contradictory. Listeners to this song have choices to make, in that they have to decide whether they will accept the contradictions within the song, or whether they will in fact only selectively listen to the song, for example, reading only those sections of the text which add up to the message 'romantic love is enjoyable' or those which add up to 'romantic love is a nuisance'. Listeners may feel that these contradictions are so great that they listen to the song critically, or finally listen to some other kind of song. But what this analysis is aware of is that ideology is not simply a representation of a single position, but that it may rather represent a more complex vision of itself in crisis, showing the great pleasures invested in this type of representation, as well as the more negative aspects. Listeners may find pleasure in aligning themselves to the partial representations of women as passive even at the same time that they do not generally see themselves or other women in this way. Feminist analysis of this sort is not concerned necessarily with proposing that this type of song is 'wrong', since it does not see its meaning as singular or univocal, and therefore does not propose as in the 1960s that we should not listen to certain types of music or read certain types of text. But, rather, it is concerned with foregrounding the fact that for many women, some forms of pleasure may be concerned with not being an agent, but that this is set within more critical discourses which recognize that we would be happier in control or 'by myself'. Sandra Harding states that this more complex analysis may be a direction in which feminist theory should go, rather than opting for a simpler form of analysis which sees a particular type of representation as right or wrong. She says:

> Instead of fidelity to the assumption that coherent theory is a desirable end in itself and the only reliable guide to action, we can take as our standard

fidelity to *parameters* of dissonance within and between assumptions of patri-archal discourses. This approach to theorizing captures what some take to be a distinctively women's emphasis on contextual thinking and decision-making and on the processes necessary for gaining understanding in a world not of our own making – that is, a world that does not encourage us to fantasize about how we could order reality into the forms we desire. It locates the ways in which a valuably 'alienated consciousness', 'bifurcated consciousness', 'oppositional consciousness' might function at the level of active theory-making – as well as at the level of scepticism and rebellion. We need to be able to cherish certain kinds of intellectual, political and psychic discomforts, to see as inappropriate and even self-defeating certain kinds of clear solutions to the problems we have been posing.

(Harding 1992: 342)

Although Harding's views were formulated in a discussion of feminist theory as a whole, I have quoted them at length here because of their relevance as to how to make sense of and interpret the text by the Sugar Cubes. If we adhere to the principle of feminist analysis being a clear-cut critique of the ways that women have been represented, then we will offer a reading of this text which is unequiv-ocal and which sees the meaning of the transitivity choices all pointing in one direction. The female character is passive; the transitivity choices are of particular types, and this has some impact on the fact that the woman is represented as passive. We would then go on to argue that this is a general case for represen-tations of women as a whole, and perhaps demand that this situation change. With the more complex model which Harding is proposing, we are able to see that whilst this analysis is correct on one level, it does not explain the power that these types of representations have for women listeners and the reasons why women in particular are subject to this type of representational practice, nor is it aware of the other messages in the text which undercut this dominant passive role for the female character. This more complex form of feminist analysis would set out to explore the way that passivity is constructed as pleasurable, and at the same time analyse the ways that the text displays a number of contradictory forces, which undercut and challenge that pleasure; for example, showing the way that the female character was 'happy' on her own, and in fact does not want or need this type of disruption to her life. Thus, analysis of transitivity is an excellent basis for interpretation, but only when we acknowledge that transitivity like other linguistic features can mean in a variety of different ways, according to the type of context in which it is set and also the set of assumptions which the reader brings to bear on the interpretative process.

   Thus, in summary, this chapter has attempted to examine the larger discursive structures which underlie our constructions and our understandings of texts. I have argued here that analysis of language items in isolation is insufficient, and that stylistics needs to turn to an analysis of these larger-scale features, in order to be able to describe the meanings of texts. The interpretations of text which we can make using this more complex model of feminist analysis are perhaps less clear-cut and because of this complexity are certainly less satisfying, but in some senses they do approximate more to the complexity of the processes whereby we make sense of ideological representations.

Chapter 6

Analysis at the Level of Discourse

This chapter examines the way that feminists can undertake a gendered analysis focusing on the larger-scale structures at the level of discourse, that is, above the level of the sentence. It is the intention of this chapter not to focus on content as if it were a self-evident given, but to see content, the substance of texts, as something which is the negotiation of textual elements and codes and forces outside the text which influence both the way that the text is constructed and the way that we decipher what is written.[1]

This focus on the analysis of language at the level of discourse is often not considered in stylistic analysis, because it does not feel as if it is truly linguistic analysis, since it is not concerned only with individual lexical items (see Carter and Simpson 1989). However, it is very much concerned with the larger structures and patterns which determine the occurrence of these individual lexical items, and it is also concerned with the effect of these items and larger structures on readers; as Carter and Simpson state: 'Discourse analysis should . . . be concerned not simply with micro-contexts of the effects of words across sentences or conversational turns but also with the macro-contexts of larger social patterns' (Carter and Simpson 1989: 16). In this way, the analysis links the word and the phrase with a larger notion of ideology through these textual patterns and structures. Michel Foucault's work on the structure of these discursive frameworks has been of great use here, but it seems as if it is necessary to add to those general ideas about discourse a notion of gender, since it is the argument of this book as a whole that discourse is profoundly gendered (Foucault 1972). I shall term these gendered discursive structures 'gendered frameworks', since they function at a stereotypical level to determine the type of language which is produced.

The first part of the chapter is mainly concerned with the construction of character in texts: I analyse the way that stereotypical notions often inform the language choices which are made when describing characters in fiction and newspapers, and also the way people describe themselves. I also consider the roles that female characters can fill, drawing on a modified version of Vladimir Propp's work on narrative. I then go on to examine particular language choices in terms of the description of the fragmentation of the female body. The second part of the chapter is concerned with larger-scale schemata which determine the roles which women are allocated in much writing. I am interested in the way that there are structures at the level of narrative and at the level of association which are determined by ideologies of gender difference.

CHARACTERS/ROLES

Characters are made of words; they are not simulacra of humans – they are simply words which the reader has learned how to construct into a set of ideological messages drawing on her knowledge of the way that texts have been written and continue to be written, and the views which are circulating within society about how women and men are. Jonathan Culler has shown that reading literature is largely a question of learning a set of conventions in order to decode texts; this he terms 'literary competence' – the set of skills which the reader of literature learns so that certain elements are interpreted in ways which can be predicted (Culler 1975). There seems also to be a set of skills which we as readers have acquired in interpreting the ideological knowledges about women and men which texts provide, particularly at the level of stereotypes. A great number of texts draw on stereotypical knowledge when presenting information about characters, particularly when these characters are not 'fleshed out' but are simply described briefly. In order to summon up a character quickly, a form of shorthand is used which the reader decodes with reference to stereotypical knowledge. The descriptions of clothes and facial characteristics are used to 'point to' the type of overall assessment that the reader is expected to make of the character. These signals are conventional, in that they are signs which the reader learns when she learns to read literature and they constitute part of her 'literary competence'.

Such knowledge might mean that female and male characters are described differently. For example, in *Rewriting English*, Batsleer *et al.* analyse the types of parts of the body which are described in popular fiction, when a writer is trying to present a character (Batsleer *et al.* 1985). They analyse several novels by Desmond Bagley and Gavin Lyall which contain reference to both male and female characters; they note that male characters are almost invariably introduced to the reader with a description of their head – their hair colour and eyes – and a sense of their overall size. Female characters are more likely to be described in terms of their legs and parts of their bodies. They give the following examples.

> I stepped forward to the desk and said, 'Rearden – to see Mr Mackintosh.' The red-headed girl behind the desk favoured me with a warm smile and put down the teacup she was holding. 'He's expecting you,' she said. 'I'll see if he's free.' She went into the inner office, closing the door carefully behind her. She had good legs.
>
> (Bagley 1973: 5)

O'Hara was just leaving when he paused at the door and turned back to look at the sprawling figure in the bed. The sheet had slipped revealing dark breasts tipped a darker colour. He looked at her critically. Her olive skin had an underlying coppery sheen and he thought there was a sizeable admixture of Indian in this one. With a rueful grimace he took a thin wallet from the inside pocket of his leather jacket, extracted two notes and tossed them on the bedside table. Then he went out, closing the door quietly behind him.

(Bagley 1967: 7)

Her legs were long, rather thin and covered with golden sand broken by zig-zag trickles of water. For some reason I like watching a girl's legs covered with sand; psychologists probably have a long word for it. I have a short one.

(Lyall 1967: 38)

He was a sand-coloured man with light gingery hair and invisible eyebrows and eyelashes which gave his face a naked look. If he didn't shave for a week probably no one would notice. He was slight in build and I wondered how he would use himself in a rough-house.

(Bagley 1973: 6)

O'Hara grunted. He did not like Grivas, neither as a man nor as a pilot. He distrusted his smoothness, the slick patina of pseudo good breeding that covered him like a sheen from his patent leather hair and trim toothbrush moustache to his highly polished shoes.

(Bagley 1967: 9)

He hadn't changed much. Broad, stocky, steady, like the hand. A snub square face with a tanned and oddly coarse skin, pale blue eyes, short curly fair hair.

(Lyall 1967: 16)

In these examples, it is clear that the male characters are described in terms of their overall appearance: 'sand-coloured', 'slight in build', 'broad, stocky'. Their heads in particular are described: 'light gingery hair', 'invisible eyebrows', 'a snub and square face with a tanned and oddly coarse skin, pale blue eyes, short curly fair hair'. The males are discussed in terms of their trustworthiness, their strength and whether the narrator likes them or not. Little evaluation is made of the character's body; it does not seem to make a great deal of difference if the hair of the character is red or brown; what is at issue is that these elements signal that the character is a strong person or a person to be trusted; for instance, in example 4, the fact that the character does not need to shave is a signal that he is not strong. Clothes are described in order to evoke a certain type of character: a leather jacket signifying toughness, and highly polished shoes denoting a superficial sophistication. In this sense the parts of the body which are described are very like the clothes which are described since they serve only to denote the type of personality that the character has; with the female characters, the descriptions are concerned with establishing a degree of sexual attractiveness and sexual availability, and there is a concentration on their supposed sexual characteristics; here, for example, there is a great deal of concern with the legs, skin, breasts and hair. These are not simply reported in the way that they are for the male characters, but it is necessary to evaluate them: for example, 'her legs were long, rather thin' and 'she had good legs'; the female characters here are described in relation to the sexual desires of the male character, and the narrator in example 2 draws attention to this convention when he states 'He looked at her critically'.

Furthermore, the detail given in the description of elements of the women's bodies is surprising: in example 2, the woman's skin is described in terms not only of its colour but of the nuances of that colour and its translucent qualities: 'her olive skin had an underlying coppery sheen.' In example 1, the use of the verb 'favoured me' is significant since the women is portrayed as acting in relation to the male narrator, rather than in her own terms. It is significant that the female characters are described as if they were interchangeable; for instance, in example 2, the female is called 'this one' and her racial origin given in the same way as the breeding of a horse or dog: 'there was a sizeable admixture of Indian'; she is also described as a 'sprawling figure' rather than as an individualized character. In example 3 the woman is only a representative of a particular type of response that the narrator enjoys experiencing: 'For some reason I like watching a girl's legs covered in sand.' Paradoxically, although the female characters are described only in terms of their sexual characteristics, they are termed 'girl' (see Chapter 4).

Whilst the elements which are described for the male characters are those which are evident when they are in face-to-face contact, the ones which are described for the female characters are those which have to be observed when the character is portrayed as an object to be seen. The narrator is observing the character without her being aware: in example 2, the female character is asleep and therefore the narrator can appraise her 'dark breasts tipped a darker colour' and 'her olive skin', and in another example the character is viewed from behind, when she is closing the door behind her.

When describing female characters, it seems that there is also a wider range of terms which can be drawn upon than exists for male characters. These terms also seem to have connotations which they do not have for male characters. Consider the range of words that exist for descriptions of hair for women: brunette, blonde, auburn, redhead; ash blonde, peroxide blonde, natural blonde. When describing male characters, it is not possible to use a large number of these terms, and men's hair is conventionally described as ginger, brown, black, etc. These words do not simply refer to hair colour but also have connotations of sexual availability or attractiveness; they seem to always refer to a position of voyeurism – a position of meticulous cataloguing of difference; in this sense, I would like to describe these terms as 'sexualized', that is, despite seeming to be simply descriptive terms, they are in fact terms which are related to the person's sexual attractiveness.

Women are often referred to in a different way from men in newspaper reports; however, not only are women more often referred to in terms of their sexuality, but also often in terms of their relations to others. For example, in the *Sun* newspaper, women are generally described in terms of their relations to other people ('mother of three, Mrs Brandon') or with respect to their appearance ('Mrs Smith, a trim brunette from Woking'), whilst men are referred to with respect to their occupations. For example, the *Herald* reports on road accidents: three people, two men and a woman, are reported to have been killed in accidents on the road. All of their names, ages and addresses are given. However, for the female victim, the fact that she is a grandmother is included, whereas the males' status in terms of their relationship is not given.

In the *Sun* a headline appeared which stated 'MAD GUNMAN HUNT AS WIFE IS SHOT'. The woman who had been shot is identified by the fact that she is married to someone; her profession is not given, and it would be difficult to imagine substituting 'Mad gunman hunt as husband is shot'. It is almost as if there is a stereotype at work: women have relationships and men have jobs. In headlines referring to males – for example, 'SOCCER STAR BARRED FROM NIGHTCLUB' – it is the man's profession which is considered to be his most important attribute. In an article on women and the Gulf War, all of the women are referred to in terms of their appearance and age: 'delightful Diana Macadam, 19'; 'blonde Jackie Brennan, 22'. The one case where the woman's job is mentioned is in 'stunning Michelle Thomas, 17, is a forklift truck driver', but here the newspaper feels it necessary to mention that 'she's definitely not muscle-bound' as if a woman who has a job which is perceived to be within the male domain has both to have this fact mentioned and also to prove her femininity.

As I show later, men's bodies are not fragmented and categorized as women's bodies are because it seems that men are not sexual objects in the same way. For example, in the first extract from Bagley above, it is enough to describe her as 'the red-headed girl' to suggest that she is to be viewed sexually rather than in terms of alliance or competition as the male characters are.

There are also verbs which are used only to describe female characters:

> Here was that awful woman Muriel Campshott coming up to claim acquaintance. Campshott had always simpered. She still simpered. And she was dressed in a shocking shade of green.
>
> (Sayers 1935: 16)

It would be very unusual to use the verb 'simper' for a male character; for a female character it does not seem exceptional and hence forms part of the reader's expectations for representations of women and men in general.

When females and males are represented in a work situation, they often seem to be described in stereotypical jobs. This has been the subject of a great deal of feminist critique of sexist representations in children's books, where women

An old lady interested in retiring to Bournemouth.
A businessman going to a conference there.
A housewife interested in a family seaside holiday.
A student interested in learning English.

A spokesman.   A receptionist in a hotel.
Your boss in an office.   Your secretary in an office.
Your best friend.   Your father-in-law to be.
An elderly stranger.   A child.

Source: Jones (1977) *Functions of English*, Cambridge University Press, Cambridge, pp. 14 and 19.

THE ENGLISH BROADCASTING COMPANY

1

This is the headquarters of the English Broadcasting Company. People call it the EBC for short. This company makes radio and television programmes in English and then sells them to countries all over the world.

2

Hello. My name's David Nelson. I was born in England but I lived in South America when I was a child. I lived there for ten years. Then I came back to England. I'm a journalist. I worked for a London newspaper for five years, and I've been working in television for the past two years. I don't work for the EBC. I work for another company. The EBC has just offered me a job. I'm thinking about the offer. I'm considering it very carefully.

3

My name's Linda Blake. I was born and brought up in a small town. I studied at Cambridge for three years. Then I became a teacher. I was a teacher for three years. For the last year I've been working for a women's magazine. I'm trying to get a job with the EBC. I don't think I'll get it because I have no experience in television. I like my job with the magazine but I'd like one with the EBC even more!

4

My name's Robert Wilson. I'm the director of educational programmes for the EBC. In other words, I direct the programmes and other people write them. I offered David Nelson a job last week. As you see, I'm having an interview with Linda Blake now. She hasn't got any experience in television but I like her. I think she'll probably get the job.

seem to be portrayed in certain stereotypical ways, being described as housewives and mothers, only capable of certain actions, such as washing the dishes and caring for children, and female children seem to be restricted to certain actions, such as helping mother and playing with dolls. Whilst children's books have greatly improved during the last ten years in terms of their representation of women and men, there nevertheless remains a tendency to stereotype male and female characters into traditional white heterosexual roles.

A similar problem arises in English as a Foreign Language textbooks where female characters are often presented according to stereotypes and the language and situations in which they are portrayed lead to a sexualized vision of females. Very often females are presented only as secretaries or as teachers and even here the range of their actions and the type of statements they make are very limited in comparison with the male characters. In the example from *Functions of English* the majority of women characters have children or cats or are secretaries. The male characters are not represented in this way. In the example from *Kernel Lessons Plus* the two male biographies are concerned with their subjects' successful jobs as a cameraman and director. The female is a secretary and is interviewed by one of the males. She is the only one who expresses uncertainty about her job; the male who interviews her is unsure whether to give her the job because she does not have much experience but he states he will do so because he likes her. Thus, the males are represented as having experience and the female is given the job because of her personal qualities rather than her professional skills. These examples on their own mean little, but they do not occur in isolation; they are part of a larger representational structure where women are represented in particular ways in EFL textbooks. This textbook continues with males enjoying their jobs and being well paid and females being nurses and poorly paid.

Consider this example from Dorothy Leigh Sayers's *Gaudy Night* where the narrator Harriet Vane is trying to consider which of the residents of an all-female Oxford college might be responsible for some disturbing acts in the college:

> Then the Old Students in the body of the Hall – all types, all ages, all varieties of costume. Was it the curious round-shouldered woman in yellow djibbah and sandals, with her hair coiled in two snail-shells over her ears? Or the sturdy, curly-headed person in tweeds, with a masculine waistcoat and the face like the back of a cab? Or the tightly corseted peroxide of sixty, whose hat would better have suited an eighteen-year-old débutante at Ascot? Or one of the innumerable women with 'school-teacher' stamped on their resolutely cheery countenances? Or the plain person of indeterminate age who sat at the head of her table with the air of a chairman of a committee? Or that curious little creature dressed in unbecoming pink, who looked as though she had been carelessly packed away in a drawer all winter and put into circulation again without being ironed? Or that handsome, well-preserved businesswoman of fifty with the well-manicured

hands, who broke into the conversation of total strangers to inform them that she had just opened a new hairdressing establishment 'just off Bond Street'? Or that tall, haggard, tragedy-queen in black silk marocain who looked like Hamlet's aunt, but was actually Aunt Beatrice who ran the Household Column in the *Daily Mercury*? Or the bony woman with the long horse-face who had devoted herself to Settlement work? Or even that unconquerably merry and bright little dumpling of a creature who was the highly valued secretary of a political secretary and had secretaries under her? The faces came and went, as though in a dream, all animated, all inscrutable.

(Sayers, 1935: 50–1)

The tone of the piece as a whole is ironical, and Sayers captures some of the statements presumably made by the characters to use against them. But each one of them seems to represent a stereotype of a female. It is interesting that these characters are described in ways which would not be possible for male characters, since they draw on gendered stereotypical knowledges. For example, the attractiveness of the character is of paramount importance: 'tall, haggard', 'face like the back of a cab', 'handsome, well-preserved woman', or 'bony woman with the long horse-face'. Two of the women are described using the word 'little': 'bright little dumpling of a creature', 'curious little creature dressed in unbecoming pink'; along with 'pretty', 'little' is used less as a purely descriptive term meaning physically small than as a diminutive term in the sense that it denotes someone of less importance (see Chapter 4 on endearments). Thus the level and type of description of characters can be seen to be quite different for males and females.

Males and females describe themselves in different ways; for example, in Heartsearch columns, there is a marked distinction between the information which is presented by males and by females.

In the asterisked entries, the males use a generic noun to describe themselves. The women foreground themselves as female, and this is the first element about them that is mentioned. Note how many of the entries describe themselves as 'lady', 'female', or 'woman'. The level of modification for females is higher than for males; so that women tend to describe themselves in terms of their physical and emotional characteristics ('incurable romantic, charming, uncomplicated, attractive woman, not slim, not young, feminine'; 'attractive, intelligent, good-humoured, reasonably solvent woman, 34'). Most of the women are also quite specific about what they want; they do not simply wish to meet any attractive male, but rather a 'personable, caring, retired male, sixty plus, middlebrow'; or 'intelligent caring man', 'interesting, non-chauvinist, unattached male friend with functioning emotions'. Most of the women indicate what sort of interests they would need to have in common with the male: 'homelife, gardening, cinema, theatre, books, boating, swimming, walking, motoring, scrabble, socialising, serenity'. Many of the male advertisers mention that they are interested in sex: for example, 'Cambridge graduate seeks ... sexually alert woman also wanting

HEARTSEARCH

BIRMINGHAM MAN, 31, seeks exceptional woman for long-term partnership. Interests include: arts, cinema, classical music, philosophy. I am tall, attractive, gentle and happy! I would like her to be confident, strong without excess of problems – psychological or historical, for relationship based on reciprocity sense of absurd essential. Box (15)4798.

W15 9

CAMBRIDGE GRADUATE, vaguely academic, likes: films, opera, Europe, old things. Lithe, fit, 6', sporty. Still attractive despite thinning hair, 48 years
✳ and past (hetero)sexual indulgence. Sensitive, honest, complains in restaurants. Own house, etc. Seeks bright, slim, sexually alert woman also wanting to settle and have kids. Photo? Box (15)4786.

W15 10

CAMBRIDGE, LONDON, East Anglia: attractive, intelligent, good-humoured, reasonably solvent woman (34), seeks intelligent, caring man. Interests: theatre, film, books, good conversation, music (jazz and classical), and travel. Box (15)4781.

W15 11

DRAWING DOWN THE MOON – the alternative introduction agency for thinking people. Personal attention. Choose your own contacts. 7–11 Kensington High Street, W8. Phone Mary Balfour on 01–938 1721.

W13 20

DATELINE'S PSYCHOLOGICALLY accurate Introductions lead to pleasant friendships, spontaneous affairs and firm, lasting relationships including marriage. All ages, all areas. Free details: Dateline Computer Dating Dept. (7NS), 23 Abingdon Rd, London W8 Tel. 01–938 1011.

N49 20

FEMALE, 34, graduate, friendly. Likes: books, cinema, music, travel. Seeks kind and intelligent man, for lasting relationship. Photo appreciated. London area. Box (15)4780

W15 12

FEMALE, 45, teacher/journalist, Jewish (n/o). intelligent, unconventional, seeks interesting, non-chauvinist, unattached male friend with functioning emotions. North/West or London. Box (15)4794.

W15 13

GOOD-LOOKING German writer, early 30s, wishes
✳ to indulge voyeuristic fantasy, with young couple or single FORUM minded female. Box (15)4793.

W15 14

I AM an enterprising woman, 45, who wants a romantic, working-class male, who can share music, massage and rides on a bike, river walks, long talks in Central London. 'Swedish Springtime'. Box (15)4802.

W15 15

LADY professional (45), misses sharing life with unattached, compatible gentleman. Enjoys: homelife, gardening, cinema, theatre, books, boating swimming, walking, motoring, scrabble, socialising, serenity. (Photo appreciated). Box (14)4755.

W14 14

LECTURER (non-smoker), seeks woman (40+), hopefully interested in Latin America or labour history, for usual recreation activities. Inner London ✳ resident. Box (15)4796.

W15 16

RICH 1945 vintage Claret with firm strong body, sensuous flavour and adventurous bouquet, handsomely bottled, seeks younger crisp and frisky Chablis, ✳ equally well packaged, for mulled fun, including weekends and holidays abroad, with a view to durable casting. Photo appreciated, anywhere UK. Box (15)4805

W15 24

SENSITIVE HIPPY, 24, seeks sincere and caring female, for loving relationship. Box (14)4756. ✳

W14 10

SINCERE, ATTRACTIVE widow. independent, 58. Continental origin. Interested: travel, theatre, music, seeks man preferably widower, similar age and interests, for companionship. N. London. Box (15)4791.

W15 25

SLIM, ATTRACTIVE, male graduate, 50, artistic cultural interests, wishes meet attractive woman, long-term relationship. Box (15)4784.

W15 26

TWO WOMEN wish to meet two men who value style, wit and real communication, aged between 28 & 45. Photo appreciated. West Midlands area. Box (15)4797.

W15 27

WOMAN, INTELLIGENT, perceptive, witty, keen sailor – seeks committed relationship with man of generous spirit, 45–55, who loves life, food and wine. (South East). Box (15)4779.

W15 28

INCURABLE ROMANTIC, charming, uncomplicated, attractive woman, not slim, not young, feminine, wide interests, seeks personable, caring, retired male, sixty plus, middlebrow, for commitment. Box (19)4904.

W19 12

LADY, ATTRACTIVE, intelligent, independent mind and means, seeks similar man 40–50. Devon-Cornwall only. Loves: art, books, history, music, cooking, DIY. Photo, phone no. please. Box (19)4900.

W19 13

LADY, YOUNG 38, attached, seeks tall, professional man for friendship – talking, dining, theatre, outings. London/South Box (19)4914.

W19 14

LIVERPOOL, 32 year-old bi-sexual graduate seeks gay friends (over 21), for company, and to explore ✳ the horizons beyond the clubs. Usual Statesman interests. Box (19) 4897.

W19 15

New Statesman 8 May 1987

to settle'; and 'lecturer . . . seeks woman', 'slim attractive male . . . wishes meet attractive woman'. The females tend to modify the type of male they wish to meet with adjectives and post-modification, whereas the males seem to use unmodified forms such as 'woman' or barely modified forms such as 'woman 40+', 'attractive woman'. The women, by contrast, often ask for emotional support or care: 'interesting non-chauvinist unattached male friend with functioning emotions'; and stress that they would like 'companionship' or 'friendship'. This difference may be largely to do with the discursive history of these columns, in that there is a certain range of parameters within which we construct ourselves as an advertiser/ heartsearcher. However, it is partly to do with larger discursive structures which present women and men as having different priorities in relationships. Most interesting perhaps is the entry which begins 'Rich 1945 vintage Claret', where there is no reference at all to the gender of the advertiser or the gender of the person which is required. However, because of stereotypical knowledge about females and males it is possible to interpret this entry fairly easily. Therefore, the reader takes the 'vintage Claret' to be male because of our stereotypical knowledge that males are strong and are likely to be older in relationships. 'Handsome' is also a term used mainly for men's attractiveness. 'Mulled fun' and 'durable casting', even if we do not comprehend the terms themselves, can be understood, because of the history of *doubles entendres*, where it is enough to state something within the context of sexual joking, such as this has signalled itself to be because of the metaphorical structure of the wines, for it to be understood to refer to sex (see Chapter 5).

In relation to the analysis of characters and roles, Vladimir Propp's schema for the structure of folk tales is interesting, as, although Propp did not consider gender, he described the different roles that there are for male and female characters in texts (Propp 1968 [1928]). He was interested in the fact that, time after time, he encountered, in his reading of Russian folk-tales, very similar plots and narrative events; he found that these were often cross-cultural and could not be explained in terms of cultural transfer alone, since the stories involved were often from widely different cultures which had little or no contact. Propp suggested that the reason for this similarity was that there are a limited number of narrative roles and what he terms functions (we might consider these to be actions or events) in folk-tales. He located thirty-one functions, each of which entails a specific role for the agent; for example, the hero goes in search of a magical solution, the hero is given a gift, the villain attempts to deceive his victim, and so on.

When we consider these functions it is interesting to examine the roles that female characters play. Females are often the recipients of actions or are the vehicle whereby a problem is solved, either through marriage or through being presented as a gift. If we consider the story of Snow White, this will become clear. In this story, although it is centred around a female character, she herself is not the character whose agency is central to the structure of the narrative. At the end of the story, she is passive and she is awakened from her sleep only by a kiss from a prince; she here is the epitome of the fairy-tale princess, in that she is unable to live without this awakening by the prince.

Joanna Russ has noted that in literature there are similar constraints on female characters. She considers that female heroines can perform only very limited tasks within texts (Russ 1984). She argues that the roles that women characters have are determined by stereotypes of what women are like: that is, concerned with emotion rather than action, relegated to the private sphere rather than the public sphere, seen as the appendages of males rather than characters in their own right. In much nineteenth-century literature, women characters often function as plot mechanisms, that is, they bring about plot resolution or closure by marriage, by dying, or by leaving. Furthermore, Catherine Clement has noted that the only real function which heroines perform in opera is that of dying tragically, usually of consumption or a broken heart (Clement 1989).

It is clear that there are discursive constraints on the roles that women characters are supposed to play in texts, since when these limitations are transgressed, there is usually some controversy. For example, nineteenth-century women travel writers do not, in the main, fit into the narrative roles which are mapped out for women characters of the period.[2] Those women who do take strong narrative roles – for example, Mary Kingsley and Alexandra David-Neel – are often accused of falsifying their accounts. Consider, for example, Mary Kingsley's *Travels in West Africa* (1897), where the narrator describes many elements which do not fit in with the type of stereotypical behaviour considered becoming for women characters within the nineteenth century. She describes a voyage in West Africa, where she travels alone with a group of Fan tribespeople, who are allegedly cannibal. She makes statements which are recognizably masculine; for example, she says about the Fan: 'We each recognised that we belonged to the same section of the human race with whom it is better to drink than to fight. We knew we would each have killed each other if sufficient inducement were offered, and so we took a certain amount of care that the inducement should not arise' (Kingsley 1982 [1897]: 161). Here, Kingsley is claiming a masculine voice – one of solidarity with other males which is affirmed by drinking or fighting. However, it is clear that the constraints on the representation of female characters have an effect on the way that Kingsley presents herself in the text, since she often tries to defuse the seriousness of her text by using humorous remarks. When she sees a herd of elephants at close quarters, she writes:

> I know exactly how I ought to have behaved. I should have felt my favourite rifle fly to my shoulder, and then carefully sighting for the finest specimen, have fired. The noble beast should have stumbled forward, recovered itself, and shedding its life blood behind it, crashed away into the forest. I should then have tracked it, and either with one well-directed shot have given it its quietus, or have got charged by it, the elephant passing completely over my prostrate body; either termination is good form, but I never have these things happen and never will.
>
> (Kingsley 1982 [1897]: 258)

Here Kingsley shows herself to be well aware of the conventions by which male explorers present their heroic behaviour in such situations, but through the consistent use of 'ought to have' and 'should have', she shows that this is a difficult textual position for a female to adopt. Compare this with a more conventional portrait of the fragile Victorian woman traveller such as Nina Mazuchelli who wrote: 'I have no wish to make myself out to be a heroine, being on the contrary the veriest coward; never *entre nous* having yet been able to go into a darkened room alone or pass an open doorway at night, without seeing faces peering at me out of the darkness' (Mazuchelli 1876: 276). Yet, paradoxically, this passage occurs in a description of a journey to the north of India which took over two months; rather than stressing the adventure and danger involved in such a journey, Mazuchelli relates her own personal deficiencies, which are in fact those stereo-typically sanctioned for females as feminine.

There are differences in the way that women from different classes are represented. As Caroline Steedman has shown in her work on the possibilities of representing working-class women, there is a range of constraints which determine the type of language and image which is chosen (Steedman 1986). These constraints make it very difficult to write about a working-class female character without reacting against or resorting to the use of certain stereotypical images. Steedman has shown in her work that the image of the working-class mother dominates representation to the point that when she tried to describe her own mother's life, she was left with very little in the way of ground-rules since her mother did not conform to the stereotypes of the figure of the working-class mother. This sense of constraint on representation can also be seen if we examine representations of working-class life such as Oscar Marzaroli's repre-sentations of the East End of Glasgow; the men are represented at work in occupations which demand heavy manual labour, the women at home, sitting on doorsteps, gossiping to neighbours, leaning out of windows, or pushing prams. In a representation of working-class women in the 1930s this might be possible, but these photographs were taken in Glasgow from the 1970s onwards, when this polarization of gender role was not still viable.

Thus, I have argued in this section that the characters and roles for women and men in fiction and other arenas are informed by stereotypes of what is appropriate according to gender norms. This is extremely restricting on women in particular, since they are restricted to inactivity, sexual attractiveness, or self-deprecation.

FRAGMENTATION

The technique of fragmenting the female body in pornographic literature has been widely noted (see especially Kappeler 1986). This has two primary effects. First, the body is depersonalized, objectified, reduced to its parts. Second, since the female protagonist is not represented as a unified conscious physical being, the scene cannot be focalized from her perspective – effectively, her experience is written out of the text. Fragmentation of the female is therefore associated with male focalization – the female represented as an object, a collection of objects, for the male gaze.

The convention of referring to a protagonist as anatomical elements is not without its defendants. For example, Derek Attridge in *Peculiar Language* (1988) argues that what he terms 'organic liberation' in a text results in 'erotic arousal': 'Sexuality thrives on the separation of the body into independent parts, whereas a sexually repressive morality insists on the wholeness and singleness of body and mind or soul' (Attridge 1988: 167). This argument, however, totally ignores the gender inequalities of such representations. Representations of women fragmented into anatomical elements occur far more frequently than do such representations of men – this is true not only of pornographic material, but advertising images, romances and love poetry, amongst other genres. We should also remember that there are different legal restrictions on the representation of male and females, so that females may be photographed in great detail and in sexually provocative poses, the camera focusing on their sexual characteristics, whereas male sex organs may be represented only if they are not erect, that is, if they are specifically not sexual.

First I will consider a 'traditional' love sonnet, 'Her real worth', written by Thomas Nabbes in the seventeenth century. This poem is typical of the way the female is 'dismembered' by the text, her physical attributes described as if they were separate entities:

> What though with figures I should raise
> Above all height my Mistress' praise,
> Calling her cheek a blushing rose,
> The fairest June did e'er disclose,
> Her forehead lilies, and her eyes
> The luminaries of the skies;
> That on her lips ambrosia grows,
> And from her kisses nectar flows?
> Too great hyperboles! unless
> She loves me, she is none of these,
> But if her heart and her desires
> Do answer mine with equal fires
> These attributes are then too poor;
> She is all these and ten times more.

Poems of this kind – the female identified by anatomical elements such as cheeks, forehead, eyes and lips as here – are so familiar that it is difficult to imagine them otherwise, and so conventional that it is difficult to see their consequences as representations of the world. For each element of the woman's body which is fragmented, a natural object is drawn upon to serve as a comparison, as in this section from a poem by Thomas Carew (1595–1639):

Aske me no more where love bestowes,
When June is past, the fading rose;
For in your beauties, orient deepe,
These Flowers, as in their causes, sleepe.

Aske me no more whither doe stray
The golden Atomes of the day:
For in pure love heaven did prepare
Those powders to enrich your haire.

The poem continues in a similar vein for three further stanzas as elements from the natural world – roses, sunlight, nightingales, stars – are compared to the woman's beauties and parts of her body. This has a number of effects: women's bodies are seen to be fragmentable and composed of a number of separate objects which may be considered beautiful in their own right; women's bodies begin to assume the qualities of the elements to which they are compared: that is, natural, passive and consumable. Thus, it is not simply the process of fragmentation which seems to be gendered but the objects which are compared to the body parts are also different. We would find it very difficult to imagine the same process being applied to the depiction of male characters.

The Hidden Target by Helen McInnes (1982), the work of a well-known novelist in the spy-thriller genre, reveals in passages the kind of fragmentation found in the poems above, associated by Kappeler with pornography and by Attridge with 'erotic arousal':

> She raised her head, let her eyes meet his. . . . She held out her hand.
>
> He grasped it, took both her hands, held them tightly, felt her draw him near. His arms went around her, and he kissed her mouth, her eyes, her cheeks, her slender neck, her mouth again – long kisses lingering on yielding lips. Her arms encircled him pressing him closer.
>
> (McInnes 1982: 314–15)

In this extract, anatomical elements of the male are referred to only twice in the expressions 'her eyes met his' (nominal ellipsis of 'his eyes') and 'his arms'. References are made to anatomical elements of the female twelve times, however: 'her head', 'her eyes', 'her hand', 'her hands', 'them', 'her mouth', 'her eyes', 'her cheeks', 'her neck', 'her mouth', 'lips', 'her arms'. The marked difference in this distribution reflects the conventions of representation of male and female protagonists. Focalization in the poem 'Her real worth' obviously resides with the male narrator; it also resides with the male in the McInnes extract above, although apparently not so inevitably. In the McInnes passage, the narrator is external to the text and so could theoretically give an impartial account of the scene, not prioritizing the experience of either protagonist over the other's. However, such adjectives as 'slender', and 'yielding' to describe the female indicate that the male, rather than the female is focalizing the scene, coinciding as predicted with female fragmentation.

Having commented that fragmentation of the female tends to co-occur with male focalization, it is perhaps worth illustrating what a text which exploits different forms of representation might look like. The following is from *The Vagabond*, by Colette, first published in 1911, and first published in English in 1954. The eroticism of this text does explore the 'organic liberation' to which Attridge refers, but the effect differs because focalization is with the female character rather than the male, and the distribution of anatomical elements referred to is roughly equal:

> I move my head imperceptibly, because of his moustache which brushes against my nostrils with a scent of vanilla and honeyed tobacco. Oh! . . . suddenly my mouth, in spite of itself, lets itself be opened, opens of itself as irresistibly as a ripe plum splits in the sun. And once again there is born that exacting pain which spreads from my lips, all down my flanks as far as my knees, that swelling as of a wound which wants to open once more and overflow – the voluptuous pleasure that I had forgotten.
>
> I let the man who has awakened me drink the fruit he is pressing. My hands, stiff a moment ago, lie soft and warm in his, and my body, as I lie back, strives to mould itself to his. Drawn close by the arm which holds me, I burrow deeper into his shoulder and press myself against him, taking care not to separate our lips.
>
> (Colette 1954: 126–7)

The eight references to anatomical elements of the female ('my head', 'my nostrils', 'my mouth', 'my lips', 'my flanks', 'my knees', 'my hands', 'my body') are accompanied by five equivalent references to the male ('his moustache', 'his [hands]', 'his [body]', 'the arm', 'his shoulder'), and focalization is totally that of the female narrator.

Visual examples of fragmentation are very common in advertisements, which often show women's legs or mouths independently of the rest of their bodies. One perfume advertisement (Rive Gauche) appeared to exploit the concept of fragmentation, showing the image of a woman in a broken mirror, so that the effect was literally one of fragments of the female form.

The process of fragmentation is further used in the practice of juxtaposition which has been widely discussed in the construction of advertisements (see Montgomery *et al.* 1992). It is quite common to find advertisements blatantly using women's bodies in juxtaposition with products in order to make the readers infer that they will be able to attain the qualities of the female if they buy the product. Consider the accompanying advertisement for Chanel No. 5.

The simple juxtaposition of elements in the advertisement means that the reader is led to assume that each of the objects – the woman and the perfume – takes on the other's positive qualities, and that she herself will become like the model in the image through buying and wearing the perfume. In this image, the perfume somehow absorbs the qualities of the beautiful, assured, relaxed and

An image from an advertisement for Coco perfume was to have appeared on this page. It was a close-up image of a woman's face and a bottle of Coco perfume. Chanel were approached for permission to reproduce the image, which they refused. After several months of negotiations they offered another, more recent image from an advertisement for Chanel No. 5, which also showed a close-up of a woman's face and a bottle of perfume. I rewrote the text and sent a copy to Chanel so that they could grant permission to use the image. At a very late stage in the production of this book they refused to grant permission unless I deleted a sentence: 'But this has the effect of making the woman into an object whose colour-toning is simply manufactured to match the product'. Since I was not prepared to write this analysis to conform to the wishes of advertisers I have had to take the decision to withdraw the image. You will have to find an advertisement for yourselves which features a woman's face in close-up and a bottle of perfume.

wealthy woman – she is wearing understated elegant makeup, a chic thin-strapped black dress and expensive gold jewellery. The woman takes on some of the qualities of expense and simplicity characterized by the understated design of the bottle of perfume. Chanel No. 5 has a reputation for being a very expensive perfume and most readers will share this background knowledge. The woman and the bottle of perfume contribute to an image of uncluttered elegance and wealth: there is after all no overt statement on the part of the advertiser urging the reader to buy this product. An equivalence is set up between the perfume and the woman through the use of colour: the perfume in this advertisement is a shade of gold which is echoed in the woman's earrings. But this has the effect of making the woman into an object, whose colour-toning is simply manufactured to match the product. Similarly, if we analyse the sight-lines in the image, the woman's head, outstretched arm and shoulder form a triangle whose apex is the bottle of perfume; it is almost as if she serves the purpose of leading the reader's eye to the label on the bottle.

Cruder advertisements use semi-clad women's bodies to similar effect in selling anything from cars to drain-cleaner. In the following advertisements for high technology, women's sexuality and bodies are used in a form of *double entendre* in order to promote machines. In the first, an advert for Triumph Adler computers, the text starts with a sentence where the rules of collocation are violated: 'She looks like the type of woman who sleeps with her *micro-computer*' whereas the seemingly obvious collocation would be 'boss'. The use of the *double entendre* 'sleep with' here plays on either the woman's total professional commitment or her sexuality. This is reinforced by posing the woman as a sexual object seen by the 'I' of the narrator, and by the sub-headings which all have a double sexual meaning, and which refer to the woman and the computer at the same time: 'warmed up quickly', 'lovely shape', 'perfect figure' and so on. While describing the woman as a business woman who owns a health club, the text still manages to trivialize her in the comments that she makes to the narrator about the computer. Instead of her praising the computer for its efficiency, she praises the fact the 'the characters are nice and large' and that it is 'much less complicated to operate'. The phrase 'nice and large' seems to be the sort of naive approach to the computer which stereotypes of women have promoted. The computer also 'has a wrist-rest'. One can imagine that this advertisement would have been very different had the object of juxtaposition been a male. Thus, here feminist critiques of representation are clearly evident; the main representation is of a cool, level-headed, competent woman manager, but the text incorporates that feminist critique to present the woman as sexualized.

In the same way, the advertisement for Audioline answering machines opens with a *double entendre*: 'beautiful, slender, responsive', as if the narrator is referring to the woman pictured in the advertisement, and then 'and that was just her answerphone' where the woman and the machine are elided. Here again the process of juxtaposition takes place between the female whose pictures can be obliquely seen in the advert and the answerphone against which her image is

She looks like the type of woman who sleeps with her micro-computer.

I first met Joanna at a new health club I'd just joined. Seeing her perched at the bar, the membership fee seemed entirely justified.

I offered her an apple juice. Opting for white wine, she explained she was there not to work out her body, but the final details of buying the club.

Joanna, it emerged, runs a health empire. Everything from gymnasia to the clothes people wear in them.

Or rather, almost wear in them.

A beautiful business.

"I keep it all in my new Alphatronic," she announced.

"Keep what?", I enquired, feigning ignorance of this, one of the most exciting steps forward in business micro-computers for years.

"All my accounts," she continued, "all of the information I need to run my companies."

Well, having just bought one of the new Alphatronics for my own firm, I knew that there was a micro which wasn't just a copy of everything else.

Impressively IBM compatible, it's anything but one of those trendy machines that date quickly and won't run the programme you need to run your business.

"Apart from making people beautiful, my business helps them relax," she said, "so, I didn't see why I should get tense and lose sleep buying a computer which is supposed to help me achieve all that."

Warmed up quickly.

"Which is why you went for the Alphatronic," I said.

"Precisely. It's much faster and better," she enthused, "thanks to one of the new Intel 80186 16-bit processors. And with a capacity large enough to easily accommodate my plans for expansion."

"Others," she continued, "take up to two minutes to warm up. But with that 16-bit processor, the Alphatronic's ready to use in seconds.

"Then it reacts faster to your instructions, racing through the data you feed it."

Lovely shape.

"The characters are all nice and large," she went on, "clearly readable, with pin-sharp resolution."

"But being so concerned with aesthetics, surely looks were important to you, too," I ventured. "And don't all micro's look the same?"

"Not my Alphatronic," she replied, "lovely shapes, soft, relaxing colours and ergonomically designed, so it fits

the human body perfectly. Triumph Adler is part of VW-Audi, and they apply the same design principles to their computers as VW-Audi do to their cars."

Reflecting on this, I pushed her for more.

The human body.

"Triumph Adler probably know more about keyboards than anyone," she said, "and this one has eighteen function keys where others only have ten, so it's much less complicated to operate."

At this point, I recalled the Alpha Key. One touch instantly suspends any program you're running turning the Alphatronic into a type-writer, with everything you type appearing on the screen.

"Mmmm." I said, "but how does that affect the human body?"

"Well, everything about the Alphatronic is designed to be totally accessible," she replied, "and with everything so quickly and easily reached, it's far less stressful to use.

"They've even gone so far as to include a wrist-rest."

Perfect Figure.

Her mention of rest reminded me I should be doing precisely the opposite back in the gym.

"Good luck with your take-over," I said to Joanna as I excused myself.

"Oh, I just have to reduce a certain figure" she said.

"Something she'll find very easy," I thought, "with her Alphatronic."

"BEAUTIFUL. SLENDER. INSTANTLY RESPONSIVE. AND THAT WAS JUST HER ANSWERPHONE!"

I've shot a few fancy models in my time but never one quite like this.
The Audioline 910.

The fact is you just don't expect trim proportions with a dual recording system. Oversized and overweight is the usual order of the day.

The 910, however, is built for speed, thanks to technology that actually contributes to the art of conversation rather than getting in the way of it.

Your personal message to callers is recorded on a micro-chip thus leaving the micro-cassette free to record incoming messages instantly. A single tone and no frustrating hanging on. The list of Audioline 910 features goes on (you'll find them all in the specification panel). But its really outstanding features are staring you in the face and (at £99.99) soothing you in the wallet.

juxtaposed. These advertisements and many other texts pose women as essentially sexual and sexually available: that is seen as women's defining feature.

When we compare these advertisements with adverts for male cosmetics a surprising difference exists, because when we examine the adverts for Gillette we find that there are no representations of men: only representations of the product. I have been unable to find an advertisement for any product marketed targeting female consumers which did not contain a representation of a female. In a similar way, the advertising series by the Meat Marketing Board which aims to promote meat, represents men in a variety of vigorous activities, all of them involving the whole of the male body. There was no fragmentation, and no juxtaposition of the body with the objects which were being promoted.

Thus, fragmentation seems to be an element which comes into play when women are described; this is obviously a strategy which is located at a higher level than the lexical item, but it does determine the type of language which will be used.

FOCALIZATION

There has been a great deal of work in narratology on point of view and focalization: position relative to the story, and degree of persistence. With regard to position relative to the story, focalization can be either external or internal to the story. External focalization 'is felt to be close to the narrating agent'

Introducing The Gillette®
Series

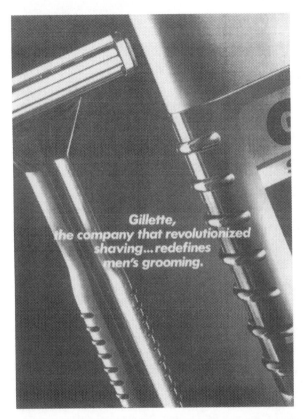

Gillette,
the company that revolutionized
shaving... redefines
men's grooming.

*A Complete Line
of High
Performance
Personal Care
Products for Men.*

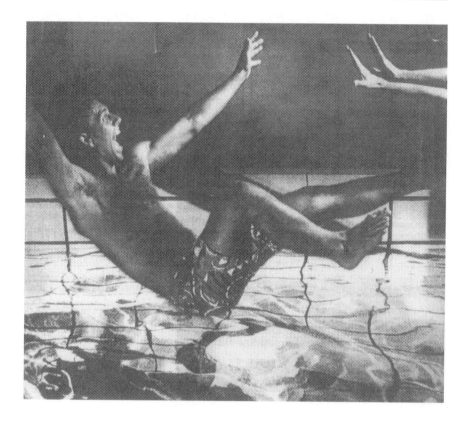

(Rimmon-Kenan 1983: 74) and is termed 'narrator-focalizer' (Bal 1985: 37). Examples of texts relying on 'narrator-focalizer' are *Tom Jones* and *A Passage to India* where the narrator is the sole source of vision, information and judgement on the characters and events. However, according to Rimmon-Kenan, external focalization can also occur in narratives told in the first person 'either when the temporal and psychological distance between narrator and character is minimal (as in Camus's *L'Etranger*) or when the perception through which the story is rendered is that of the narrating self rather than the perceiving self' (Rimmon-Kenan 1983: 74). One test which Rimmon-Kenan advises might be employed to disclose whether a text is internally or externally focalized is to attempt to 'rewrite' the extract in the first person. 'If it is feasible – the segment is internally focalized, if not – the focalization is external' (ibid.: 75). This test is also of significance when we attempt to locate those focalizations which are in fact male-oriented, yet posing as neutral, as I show later.

With regard to the degree of focalization, Rimmon-Kenan proposes three distinctions, between fixed, variable and multiple focalization, depending on whether focalization remains fixed throughout the narrative, alternates between two predominant focalizers, or shifts amongst several. The important point to extract from this is that focalization need not remain with a single character, or narrator-focalizer, but can shift in the course of a text.

Other aspects of focalization to be considered are those of the time and space the focalizer inhabits, and controls, in the text. Spatially, there are many positions the focalizer might take up. The classic position of the narrator-focalizer is the bird's-eye view, which has omniscient access to the activities of all characters, wherever they occur within the universe of the narrative. If the focalization is attached to a character or to an unpersonified position internal to the story, however, only those events perceived by the focalizer can be represented in the text. Focalization is not necessarily fixed as was stated above, so the reader may be introduced to an event through the perception of an internal focalizer, and then be transferred to another focalizer, internal or external, so as to obtain another 'vision' of the event.

It is common to find that an external focalizer can function across all the temporal dimensions of the narrative, past, present and future, while the internal focalizer is limited to the 'present' of the characters. This argument is strongly supported by texts in which the narrator and the focalizer are the same 'character' in the text, but operate independently to disclose the story as, for example, in Daphne du Maurier's *Rebecca*. The character of the narrator 'knows' the entire history of events in the novel from the opening, but reveals them as they are revealed to her younger self at the time of their occurrence. Hence the reader experiences the partial understanding of the character contemporary with events and undergoes with the character the process by which she achieves the total knowledge of the narrator. This permits the device of suspense, as the narrator withholds information from the reader which was unknown to her younger self, until the moment of revelation when the character and the reader discover the truth about Maximilian and Rebecca's marriage.

Other aspects of focalization are examined by Rimmon-Kenan, but little has shown how gendered point of view is. I will analyse here the way that supposedly neutral narration is gendered and I will point to specific ways in which this process of gendering can be located. Analysing a range of texts, both literary and non-literary, where the focalization appears to be neutral will enable the reader to locate where the 'voice' of the text is coming from and to specify the gender of that point of view. I will particularly examine markers such as free indirect speech in male- and female-authored texts as a marker of gendered focalization.

The purpose of the concept 'focalization' is to provide a means of identifying the consciousness through which a fictional event is presented in a text. This is most likely to be a fictional character within the text, or an external narrator. Mieke Bal, who coined the term, describes its textual effect, and the value of an analytical practice which can handle it as follows: 'As any "vision" presented can have a strongly manipulative effect, and is, consequently, very difficult to extract from the emotions, not only from those attributed to the focalizer and the character, but also from those of the reader, a technical term will help us to keep our attention on the technical side of such a means of manipulation' (Bal 1985: 102). Focalization may manipulate the reader's sympathies by means of the vision which is presented and the evaluation which is implicit in that representation. I will consider first the mechanics of focalization, and then texts in which focalization becomes an issue in a feminist analysis. The term is intended to give priority to the source of vision of events which is presented, while preserving the distinction between the process of seeing and the process of verbalizing in a text.

Rimmon-Kenan poses two criteria for distinguishing different kinds of heading of 'psychological facets'. Aspects of texts embraced by this heading include the partial knowledge an internal focalizer has of events witnessed and their significance. Also included under this heading is the 'emotive transformation', which produces a subjective representation of a scene or an incident rather than an objective one, as when a description is strongly coloured by the focalizer's state of mind or emotions. The third and last aspect referred to under 'psychological factors' is the ideology of the text, also known as the 'norms of the text'. This consists of 'a general system of viewing the world conceptually' (Uspensky 1973: 8), and in accordance with this 'world-view', characters and events in the story are evaluated. Rimmon-Kenan observes that 'the norms of narrator-focalizer may be implicit in the orientation he gives to the story, but they can also be formulated explicitly' (ibid.: 82).

There may also be lexical or syntactic indicators of focalization, where the lexis or syntax seems peculiarly appropriate to the consciousness of a particular character. Alternatively, there may be a syntactic or lexical signpost which suggests that a scene is represented as focalized by the narrator at a particular age, and not necessarily the one the narrator appears to be on the whole throughout the text. This may either be because it betrays knowledge acquired after the events narrated, thus implying the event is focalized by the older narrator with hindsight, or because the statement seems immature, or is childish in its simplicity, suggesting it is a 'memory', a description focalized by the younger narrator.

Robert Scholes has shown the way that in Ernest Hemingway's 'A very short story' the focalization at first glance appears to be fairly neutral and equally distributed between the two main characters.[3] The story recounts a love-affair between a nurse, Luz, and her patient during the war in Italy, which ends with the breakdown of that relationship when the solider is posted back to the war. Scholes shows that at first sight each of the characters seems to have a similar number of verbs allotted to their actions, so that in the first paragraph we find 'One hot evening in Padua they carried him up on to the roof and he could look out over the top of the town' which is followed later by 'Luz sat on the bed'. However, Scholes shows that here is a fundamental difference in the way that the actions of the female are viewed by the reader since they are mediated through the consciousness of the male character. The male character seems to be much closer to the position of narrator. Scholes tries to rewrite some of the clauses in the text from the point of view of the female by using the pronoun 'I' rather than the pronoun 'she' or her name, Luz, in much the same way as Rimmon-Kenan suggests may be done to discover whether the focalization is

A VERY SHORT STORY

(Ernest M. Hemingway)

One hot evening in Padua they carried him up on to the roof and he could look out over the top of the town. There were chimney swifts in the sky. After a while it got dark and the searchlights came out. The others went down and took the bottles with them. He and Luz could hear them below on the balcony. Luz sat on the bed. She was cool and fresh in the hot night.

Luz stayed on night duty for three months. They were glad to let her. When they operated on him she prepared him for the operating table; and they had a joke about friend or enema. He went under the anaesthetic holding tight on to himself so he would not blab about anything during the silly, talky time. After he got on crutches he used to take the temperatures so Luz would not have to get up from the bed. There were only a few patients, and they all knew about it. They all liked Luz. As he walked back along the halls he thought of Luz in his bed.

Before he went back to the front they went into the Duomo and prayed. It was dim and quiet, and there were other people praying. They wanted to get married, but there was not enough time for the banns, and neither of them had birth certificates. They felt as though they were married, but they wanted everyone to know about it, and to make it so they could not lose it.

Luz wrote him many letters that he never got until after the armistice. Fifteen came in a bunch to the front and he sorted them by the dates and read them all straight through. They were all about the hospital, and how much she loved him and how it was impossible to get along without him and how terrible it was missing him at night.

After the armistice they agreed he should go home to get a job so they might be married. Luz would not come home until he had a good job and could come to New York to meet her. It was understood he would not drink, and he did not want to see his friends or anyone in the States. Only to get a job and be married. On the train from Padua to Milan they quarrelled about her not being willing to come home at once. When they had to say good-bye, in the station at Milan, they kissed good-bye, but were not finished with the quarrel. He felt sick about saying good-bye like that.

He went to America on a boat from Genoa. Luz went back to Pordenone to open a hospital. It was lonely and rainy there, and there was a battalion of 'arditi' quartered in the town. Living in the muddy, rainy town in the winter, the major of the battalion made love to Luz, and she had never known Italians before, and finally wrote to the States that theirs had been only a boy and girl affair. She was sorry, and she knew he would probably not be able to understand, but might some day forgive her, and be grateful to her, and she expected, absolutely unexpectedly, to be married in the spring. She loved him as always, but she realized now it was only a boy and girl love. She hoped he would have a great career, and believed in him absolutely. She knew it was for the best.

The major did not marry her in the spring, or any other time. Luz never got an answer to the letter to Chicago about it. A short time after he contracted gonorrhoea from a sales girl in a Loop department store while riding in a taxicab through Lincoln Park.

internal or external. Scholes finds it to be impossible, since the female is described from the point of view of the man. He gives as an example: 'Luz sat on the bed. She was cool and fresh in the hot night.' The first phrase is neutral, although it should be noted that only the female is given a name; this leads us to consider that maybe the unnamed male character and the narrator may somehow be elided. But the second phrase is difficult to rewrite from the woman's point of view or even from a neutral position: 'I was cool and fresh in the hot night' sounds strange since these words are ones which we use to describe the way that other people appear to us; they are not words which we use to describe our own experience. Thus, this story, whilst appearing at first sight to be neutrally focalized, is in fact focalized from the male point of view.

Focalization is not something which occurs only in literature, since most information which is presented to us is from someone's point of view. In a linguistic textbook, focalization can also be seen to be male, since in the following list of Australian euphemisms, the two sets of terms for urinating and for having intercourse are entirely from a male point of view. Despite the clear male orientation, the text poses itself as neutral.

urinate:	drain the dragon
	syphon the python
	water the horse
	squeeze the lemon
	drain the spuds
	wring the rattlesnake
	shake hands with wife's best friend
	point Percy at the porcelain
	train Terence on the terracotta
have intercourse:	shag
	root
	crack a fat
	dip the wick
	play hospital
	hide the ferret
	play cars and garages
	hide the egg roll (sausage, salami)
	boil bangers
	slip a length
	go off like a beltfed motor
	go like a rat up a rhododendron
	go like a rat up a drain pipe
	have gin on the rocks
	have a northwest cocktail

In summary, there are signals in texts as to the centre of focalization, and this does not necessarily coincide with the narrative voice, although it may. Neither is the focalizer necessarily static, but may shift from one internal character to another, or to an external narrator. The importance of the concept of focalization is that it slants the emotive and ideological content of a text, and represents the experience of the protagonists partially. Below are some examples of how a feminist analysis of texts could utilize focalization.

As an illustration, consider the following passage from *A Woman of Substance*:

> Paul finally took her to him with flaring passion, his ardour gentled but in no way muted by his tenderness. Silken arms and legs entwined him, fluid and weightless, yet they pulled him down . . . down . . . down.
>
> (Taylor Bradford 1981: 667)

The narrative voice is external and omniscient. It is not present in the text as a fictional character but is external, yet can reveal the characters' motivations and thoughts to the readers. So, theoretically, the narrative is reported by a disembodied, impersonal voice which can record objectively the course of events and the psychology of the characters. However, the 'vision' is Paul's: it is his experience of the event which is narrated. The woman Emma is presented not as her own consciousness, but as Paul experiences her – as disembodied limbs, 'silken arms and legs', without weight or form, 'fluid and weightless'. A further linguistic signal that it is Paul's consciousness from which the event is focalized is that the pronouns 'him' and 'his' suggest a subject which has unity of mind and body. For Emma, however, the pronoun 'her' is replaced by 'they', referring to her limbs. By this linguistic device, her body has been separated from her consciousness: her body is present as focalized by Paul. Her unified consciousness is not available to the reader. The focalizing of the scene through the male's experience inevitably represents the female as the object of the male gaze. Mediating her textual representation by the male's perception of her subordinates her sexual pleasure to his, or means that hers may be created as a result of his. Furthermore, whilst the text seems to be narrated by an external narrator, there are points where the narrative voice and Paul's consciousness seem to merge even more fully. For example, through the use of free indirect speech, Paul's thoughts are not represented as such, but his thoughts and the narrator's seem to become the same as, for example, in 'down . . . down . . . down' where the sensations of Paul are described by the narrator in words which could be Paul's own thoughts. Where this happens, the focalization seems to be at one and the same time that of an internal character and that of an external narrator.

Heterosexual sex in literature of course does not have to be focalized from the perspective of the male. Exactly the opposite occurs in the following passage from Toni Morrison's *Sula*:

> There in the pantry, empty now of flour sacks, void of row upon row of canned goods, free for ever of strings of tiny green peppers, holding the wet

milk bottle tight in her arm she stood wide-legged against the wall and pulled from his track-lean hips all the pleasure her thighs could hold.

(Morrison 1982: 113)

Focalized from Sula's centre of consciousness, not only is the female represented as unified ('she stood'), while the male is reduced to anatomical elements ('his track-lean hips'), but the whole environment is evidence of the domestic life which coexists with Sula's sexual life. However, within this novel, it is while Sula's sexual power is in the ascendancy that she is the focalizer, and this perhaps gives us another indication of the effect of focalization. Sula later loses the authority she held in her relationship with her lover, which came from the absence of claims each made on the other. As she inclines towards the security of domesticity, dependency and monogamy, the centre of focalization shifts from Sula to Ajax, her lover.

> He stood up and mounted the stairs with her, and entered the spotless bathroom where the dust had been swept underneath the claw-foot tub. He was trying to remember the date of the air show in Dayton. As he came into the bedroom, he saw Sula lying on fresh white sheets, wrapped in the deadly odour of freshly applied cologne.
>
> He dragged her underneath him and made love to her with the steadiness and intensity of a man about to leave for Dayton.
>
> (Morrison 1982: 120)

Focalization has reverted to the male. It is his, rather than Sula's, mental activities which are revealed to the reader, and his emotions which colour the scene. Ajax tries to remember the date of the air show; he is planning to leave. Sula's thoughts and intentions can only be speculated upon, being unknown to Ajax, and thus to the reader. It is he who 'does' the actions ('He stood up and mounted the stairs'); Sula accompanies him, an accessory to his actions. He 'sees' Sula lying on the sheets, she is perceived by him – a third indication of where focalization lies. Yet perhaps the clearest signal that Ajax is the focalizer, is the word 'deadly'. Only so far as Ajax is concerned is the cologne 'deadly', because for him it indicates the threat Sula poses of freedom curtailed. From Sula's perspective the perfume is intended to attract, not repel, and thus the word would be impossible if she were the focalizer of the scene. Therefore, there does seem to be a correlation between focalization and the power relations which occurs in these two extracts from *Sula*. A further example could be considered here – an advertisement for Tennant's lager. This was part of a campaign for the lager based around the catch-phrase 'I've got mine' where the 't' of 'got' was represented as the same as the 't' in the word 'Tennant's'. In each of the settings of the advertisement a man was generally at work in an industrial setting, hard manual labour in the main, and he would be shown with a can of Tennant's lager beside him. In the advert in question, and there were two like this, the man is shown not only to have his can of lager but to have a female with him and therefore the

phrase functions to say not only does he have a can of lager but also his female. In this advertisement it is the male whose eyes meet the reader's, whilst the female gaze is averted and she simply nestles into his coat. Focalization which poses as neutral can on closer analysis be shown to be that of the male.

SCHEMATA

Having considered character focalization as gendered frameworks I would now like to examine some even larger discursive frameworks which seem to operate over a wide range of texts to produce different visions of male and females.[4] These large-scale frameworks I shall refer to as schemata.

The ideas developed in this section arose when I was reading a new novel by Martin Amis, *London Fields* (1989). Apart from feeling intensely irritated, depressed and bored by the book, because of the way female and male characters are represented, I also had a strange sensation of *déjà vu* whilst I was reading it – as if I had already read the book, or the plot had been borrowed from another novel. I felt irritated by what I perceived as the book's sexism, which seemed to me to pervade it as a whole: the female characters seemed to be portrayed as objects, usually sexual, and they seemed to be actively working towards their own destruction. The male characters also seemed to be lifeless vehicles of an ideology of macho behaviour. I was quite shocked that the options that the author had chosen for the female characters in particular were so retrograde, and yet at the same time I began to wonder why these characters seemed so familiar.

The book opens in the following way:

Line 1   This is a true story but I can't believe it's really happening.
2   It's a murder story, too. I can't believe my luck.
3   And a love story, (I think), of all strange things, so late in
4   the century, so late in the goddamned day.
5   This is the story of a murder. It hasn't happened yet. But it
6   will. (It had better.) I know the murderer. I know the
7   murderee. I know the time, I know the place, I know the
8   motive (*her* motive) and I know the means. I know who will be
9   the foil, the fool, the poor foal, also utterly destroyed. And
10 I couldn't stop them, I don't think, even if I wanted to. The
11 girl will die. It's what she always wanted. You can't stop
12 people, once they *start*. You can't stop people, once they
13 *start creating*.

(Amis 1989: 1; emphasis in original)

The novel thus opens with a very knowing narrator who addresses the reader in a direct, intimate and informal way, letting the reader in on his plans. The short simple sentences imitate spoken discourse and the phrases in parentheses suggest an intimate tone of disclosure to the reader. At the same time that this passage signals itself as intimate, it also signals to the reader that it is a highly literary text, because of its playful use of language; for example: 'the foil, the fool, the poor foal' (line 9). The tone of this opening passage is also very reminiscent of passages in John Fowles's work, where the narrator draws attention to the fictiveness of the story, but at the same time he suggests that he himself is not entirely in control of the story.

But what struck me most of all was the phrase 'murderee' (line 7). I had never encountered this phrase before and yet as soon as I read it I knew that it referred to a female character and not a male, and as I read further on in this opening paragraph my expectations were shown to be right, since the narrator refers to 'the girl' who will die (lines 10–11) and her death is described as 'what she always wanted' (line 11). I was interested by the fact that when describing the murder of this female character certain linguistic choices were made around the question of agency.

There are many ways of representing actions and who is responsible for them; take, for example, the following phrases:

1 [The murder] hasn't happened yet (line 5)

In this example, the murder is described using the verb 'to happen'; this is a verb which does not reveal who has performed the action (the agent) and, further, the verb makes the murder seem more like an event than an action, since generally things which 'happen' are those which are not motivated or decided upon, for example:

2 The motorway accident happened because of fog. (i.e. the drivers involved were not responsible for the accident)

If we rewrite the sentence in example 1 to reveal who is plotting the murder, it is clearer that the agency in the text has been obscured:

3 X hasn't murdered her yet.

In example 3, there is a human agent who appears at the front of the phrase (rather than the action itself appearing in this position) and he has responsibility for this motivated act. Phrases in close proximity to example 3 back up this feeling that the murder is being described as if the person who is planning to commit the crime is not the person responsible; for example, the narrative continues 'But it will. (It had better.)' (lines 5–6). Here, it seems as if the narrator knows more about the murder than the murderer himself and it is he who wishes the murder to happen. If we consider another phrase from this paragraph:

4 The girl will die (lines 10–11)

we also see a similar kind of grammatical structure being used. Generally, when we are describing actions, the agent comes at the front of the phrase and the person who is affected by the action comes after the verb. Thus, in example 5, the person who performs the action is put in the position of the agent:

5 X will kill the girl.

However, the choice which is in fact made in example 4 is to place the woman who is murdered in the position normally reserved for the agent, and this often has the effect of making the person who takes up this position seem in some sense to be the agent and to bear responsibility for the action. Here again, a verb is chosen which does not foreground the agent – the girl will simply die, as if no one brought about her death; it simply happened. Compare this with passive constructions which could have been used:

6 The girl will be killed.

7 The girl will be shot.

In examples 6 and 7, although the verbs do not reveal to us who has performed the action, they do suggest to us that the action was motivated – someone killed the woman, her death was not simply due to natural causes as the words 'she will die' might suggest. Further to this, the phrase which follows example 4 in the text is:

8 It's what she always wanted. (line 11)

which again focuses on the girl and her wishes rather than the real agent of the murder. Thus, the opening passage of this book seems to signal to the reader that she is responsible for her own murder, and that the murderer is actually only a poor 'foil' or 'fool'. In essence, the book is about the male protagonists and the lead-up to the murder of the 'girl', Nicola Six. Nicola herself does not feature a great deal in the book and she is not described in anything more than very vague terms, but the fact that she is described as wanting her own death began to remind me of a large number of other plots, specifically Muriel Spark's short story 'The driver's seat' where a female protagonist prepares herself for her own murder in a way which suggests that she had planned for it and wished for it. Numerous other plots which seemed to display women as wanting harm to come to themselves came to mind. I remembered an American advertisement I had seen which seemed to back up this way of representing women – where a woman is shown smiling and as about to kiss the man at the same time as the message 'No' is emblazoned on the top of the advert. The advertisers would presumably claim that the No in the advert refers to 'No sweat', but the advert seems to play on the possibility of their product bringing about the situation where a woman may say 'no' but actually mean 'yes'. Thus, in a wide range of cultural images and texts there seems to be a message that women want things which are not in their interests – they are 'asking for it'.

There also seem to me to be a large number of plots in films where women are the victims of murders; often a film opens with the murder of a woman as the problem which it then goes on to 'solve'. Women characters are routinely stalked through empty office buildings and car parks and even their own homes in a way which does not seem to happen for male characters, who when they are presented being killed do at least have the means to fight back on equal terms with their killers. I found that this complex of ideas around women being agents and being acted upon particularly in their own murders coalesced in the analysis of this passage from Amis. It is for this reason that I have turned to the analysis of schemata to explain the preponderance of narratives which seem to work in similar ways.

Robert Hodge and Gunther Kress, in their book *Social Semiotics*, have attempted to look beyond a simple analysis of language items; they argue that 'a concentration on words alone is not enough' (Hodge and Kress 1988: vii). By this they mean that language items cannot be studied in isolation from the other language items with which they co-occur and also that language items, phrases, or grammatical structures themselves cannot be seen as containing ideological meaning. They argue that 'to capture the contradictory characteristic of ideological forms, we will talk of ideological complexes, a functionally related set of contradictory

versions of the world, coercively imposed by one social group on another on behalf of its own distinctive interests or subversively offered by another social group in attempts at resistance in its own interests' (ibid.: 3). This notion of contradictory ideological complexes seemed to me to be of some value, since it is clear that the passage from Martin Amis does offer a message about the female character; but rather than thinking about it in terms of statements, it is possible to think of it in terms of a complex of statements which, taken together, combine to form an ideological viewpoint.

Hodge and Kress's book pointed out to me the necessity of some mediating structure between language items and ideology at a conceptual level. Although many theorists of ideology seem to feel that ideology works on individuals in a fairly straightforward way, it seemed useful to me to specify the way that there were many different elements within the ideology of sexism. Wareing has shown that it is possible for there to exist in a text two conflicting messages about female characters, one of which is an older ideology which presents women as acted upon and passive within sexual relations, and the other which presents women characters as strong and active in the public sphere (Wareing 1990). It is clear therefore that sexism as an ideology is more complex than a simple representation of women in terms of a negative difference in relation to men.

What concerns me here is the way in which there may be certain narrative structures which lead to particular representations of women, and these narratives or schemata are the interface between language choice and ideology. In the instance under discussion, Martin Amis's narrator's choice of language items is certainly clearly brought about by the initial decision to present the female character as acting to bring about her own murder. Thus, it is not simply the case that the female character is acted upon, although that is important, but the fact that she wishes to be acted upon and paradoxically strives to bring that about. This seems to me to constitute a schema or narrative pattern which once embarked on entails in its wake all manner of linguistic choices and decisions. It is a schema which is familiar through a wide range of texts and it is perhaps the familiarity and the repetitive nature of the narrative which intrigue me.

In the study of artificial intelligence, the schema or scenario is a model or narrative format which individuals use to structure their thought and action sequences; these are stereotypical models for the processing of thought (see Brown and Yule 1983). Thus, the schema for going to a restaurant will involve opening moves such as entering the restaurant, being greeted by a waiter and asking for a table, and will map out the possibilities for ordering, eating and paying for food within the constraints of behaviour appropriate in restaurants. We do not need to think about the sequence of events within this train of actions; they form part of a larger structure which is familiar to us, because it is stereotypical. In some sense it is an idealized lowest common denominator of all the times we have been to restaurants. In the same way, there are schemata for other events, and this makes it easier for us to deal with unexpected deviations from the schema, because we are able to deal with the general run of events automatically rather than having to consider each move in the narrative before proceeding. The notion of a narrative schema is obviously simplistic but it does help to explain the way in which there are certain plots which seem to us familiar and those which present themselves as marked or unfamiliar. Lynne Pearce has examined how the narrative constraints of the romance determine the way that many people think about their relationships (Pearce 1994, pers. comm.). She has found that it is difficult for people to think beyond the narrative frameworks which to them seem self-evident; for example, that one lives with someone that one falls in love with, that this entails monogamy and a downgrading of relationships with one's friends, and so on. However, her work is an attempt to try to analyse the choices that people make in terms of their relationships in order for them to see that there are other choices that they could make. Similarly,

I was interested in the way that the narrative choices made by Amis which seemed to be part of an ideological complex were difficult to 'see around' to find alternative roles for female characters.

Brown and Yule note that in some strong versions of schema theory, 'schemata are considered to be deterministic, to predispose the experiencer to interpret his [sic] experience in a fixed way. We can think of racial prejudice, for example, as the manifestations of some fixed ways of thinking about newly encountered individuals who are assigned undesirable attributes and motives on the basis of an existing schema for members of the race' (Brown and Yule 1983: 247). What I am arguing is that sexism is precisely operating at this level of schemata, but that in addition to there simply being ways of thinking about members of other groups, in this case women, there are *narratives* which involve certain ways of thinking about them. This does not mean that this is all that can be thought about women, but that these schemata are likely to be chosen in certain circumstances, even when there are other schemata which are more productive.

I would like now to consider what these narrative pathways or schemata might consist of. We can plot out the schema in the following way:

- An attractive female is described.
- A male is described (the narrative takes his point of view).
- The male follows the female without her knowledge.
- The male plans to murder/rape the female.
- The male manoeuvres/lures the female to an isolated place.
- The male murders/rapes the female.

The basic schema has a number of additional features which are optional; for example, it can continue:

- The narrator/detective/policeman hunts the murderer.

In some plots based on this schema, more time is spent on the plans to murder than the actual murder itself: *London Fields* is a good example of this, as is John Fowles's chilling novel *The Collector* where a female character is stalked, held captive and then killed by someone who 'collects' her in the same way that one collects butterflies.

Several features are interesting: first, that the plot necessarily has to be focalized on the male protagonist, that the female character has to be attractive, and that the murder/rape needs to be planned meticulously. If we follow Michael Hoey's narrative model and assume that narratives are constructed on the basis of a problem followed by its solution, we can see that the problem which the narrative proposes is the murder/rape of a female which is solved by the murderer being hunted and caught (Hoey 1983). However, a variant on the basic schema which can be seen in *London Fields* is that the problem is perhaps the female herself and the solution to this problem is that she assents to her own murder. There are various degrees of intensity of this narrative, so that women can be seen to be asking for intimacy, rape, or murder when in fact their outward behaviour seems to signal that this is not what they want.

In much the same way as with racist knowledges, the reader has certain choices to make about these narrative schemata: whether to accept them as part of his/her knowledge and as commonsense or whether to react against them. This decision will depend on the reader's interests (in Hodge and Kress's sense) and their familiarity with other ways of thinking about the issues. There are some male readers who feel that it is in their interests to accept this schemata knowledge as part of their own knowledge; some male readers may not have come across knowledge which conflicts with this narrative in order to challenge it and think through alternatives; other males will reject the narrative, because they take pleasure in other narrative pathways for female and male characters, or because they have read feminist work and find some narratives retrograde and unchallenging. What feminist analysis needs to do is to focus on the way that this acceptance of sexist schemata works in the interests of some readers. Rather than simply dismissing the plot out of hand, it is necessary to map out in detail its constructed nature, so that building blocks of thought are shown to be only one choice amongst many others. In this way, rather than readers feeling comfortable with this type of ideological complex, they will perhaps recognize it as a construction which they have the choice whether to accept or not.

But this schema is not the only one which is drawn upon to represent women in texts. For example, a further common framework is the one where women are viewed as having problems which they need to be advised about. A vast number of texts produced in women's magazines conform to this pattern. For example, most women's magazines contain problem pages where questions are asked of an expert who gives advice to the individual woman reader but also indirectly to the readers of the magazine.

The representation of women as having problems and as writing to someone to ask for advice means that the image of women becomes one of 'there to be advised'. Throughout women's magazines, even in the less traditional ones, there is a tone of advice which pervades all of the information which is given, from cookery to cosmetics. There is no such tone in magazines which are aimed specifically at males. In fact there is no real equivalent of women's magazines. What are termed 'men's magazines' generally are considered to be soft pornography or special interest magazines on such subjects as photography or motor-cycles. There is no text which systematically advises men on their personal conduct and appearance in the same way as women, or which implicitly carries the message that they have problems which need to be resolved.

. A similar framework can be seen in the 'before and after' structure where women are seen to be improved by work done by the magazine. In the pictures which are taken of the women before they are given a 'makeover' they are shown to be drab and unattractive, but when they have worked at their appearance they are shown to be suddenly attractive. This presents an image of women as sites of transformation. Again there is no male equivalent for this type of structure

Dear Sue

Don't just sit there and worry alone—if you've got a problem and you need some help, write to Sue Frost

My marriage is over

I'm 32 and very unhappily married. I feel I'm wasting my life and need a way out. My husband accepts that the marriage is over but he doesn't want us to separate as he's been divorced before and knows it'll cost him a lot financially. He also doesn't want to lose our two lovely boys, aged nine and five, as he lost two children from his first marriage. I feel so very sorry for him but no love—only pity. We met when my parents had split up and when he was going through his divorce and I suppose we were both feeling upset and lonely. I've got a lovely home and a husband who doesn't go out womanising or drinking and who's quite a good father now that the children are older. But I feel for the children's sake we'd be better apart. I'd be so much happier if it were just me and the boys together. But I can't get a council house as I haven't any points in my favour (he doesn't abuse me). If I were to rent a house, who would pay for it? Please don't suggest Relate. It's over.

I think your husband would be better off without you but I can't see why he should readily give up his sons and support you all in another home. This is worth pondering. Women locked in bitter, destructive marriages have rights which enable them to escape but husbands have rights, too, if they choose to pursue them. What's to stop him battling for custody of the boys and meanwhile leaving you to pay your own rent? Try to turn your pity for your husband into something more constructive. It doesn't have to be love but friendship might be a good start. Talk with him about the future and what would be best for the children. And if there's no future for you as a family, look to your own life and ways of securing your financial independence. You'll feel better for it.

He won't leave her

I'm 52, still fairly attractive and I've been a widow for the past 11 years. For some time now I've been seeing a married man who's three years older than me. He visits me every Saturday night and we go to bed for a couple of hours, which is great. He says I'm the best thing to happen to him in all his life. But he also says he'll never leave his wife, although he doesn't love her any more. They've been married for 32 years and have a 24-year-old daughter who lives at home. I'm always telling him that I couldn't bear to live without him but he never says anything about moving in with me. I'm sure his wife must know about us, because I'm always buying him things like socks, underwear and shoes. Do you think there's any hope for me in this situation?

Your lover has no reason to stay with his wife. No reason, that is, apart from all the things they've shared over the past 32 years

and all the emotional ties that inevitably bind such a long relationship. So if he won't leave her it's because their history as a married couple matters more to him than you do. I know you're in love and I can understand how lonely you've been. But if you could put yourself in the position of this man's wife, you couldn't fail to see how badly he's behaving. Whatever the truth of their marriage, she doesn't deserve this. And you deserve better, too. Recognising this would be a very hopeful sign for your future.

I'm so confused

I'm 19 and live with my boyfriend who's 24. We rushed into buying this house as I really had nowhere else to live. The problem is that I've just come into contact with my ex-boyfriend again and when our eyes met, we knew what was happening. He's told me he wants us to get involved. But I don't want to hurt my present boyfriend who's been very good to me and I admit I'm scared of losing my house. I know this is just a material thing and, if I follow my heart, it's my ex-boyfriend I want. I feel so confused. Please help. I don't know what to do.

You'll have to tell your present boyfriend how you feel. Not that you love someone else more than him but that you're deeply confused, worried about the future and anxious not to hurt him. Tell him about your ex, but make it clear that you're seeking help in making a decision. It may be that when you talk things through, your feelings for both men will become clearer. There's no painless way out of this situation but by being honest about your doubts you can limit the damage. Try not to worry about the house. The practical details will improve once you have the emotional situation under control.

How can I tell her?

I'm a married woman with four children and a loving husband whom I care for deeply. My problem started when we moved house to a larger property. My husband works continental shifts and most weekends he's working. My mother is a lonely lady who's always complaining about being on her own. Since we moved and have had the room to put her up, she's come to stay with us every weekend. Last weekend my husband was off work and was very annoyed that my mother was there yet again. I have a sister—who tells me I'm a fool—but I work full time and Mum's a great help to me when my husband isn't there. How can I tell her that we need a weekend on our own without hurting her feelings?

This is very difficult and needs to be handled with great care. Your mother could hardly be blamed for feeling that she's welcome when she's needed but not at other times. I think the answer lies in encouraging new activities

for her, trying to set up new friendships and asking your sister, quite frankly, to do her share. Your mother would benefit from being less dependent on you, although you'd have to accept that she mightn't be able to help out quite so readily. Talk this over with your husband and get him to see that as the whole family is helped by your mother, it's a joint problem for you both to sort out.

I feel so hurt

My fiancée of two years is seeing a married man behind my back. She's 20 and he's 40 with two children. When I found out, she said she still loved me but couldn't stop seeing him. The problem is that I live with her family and we all get on together very well. I'm 21 and serving an apprenticeship, so I don't have much money and I've nowhere else to stay. I've got no family and no other friends. His wife knows about the affair because I told her. But although she's said she'll divorce him, nothing has happened. I can't understand why she's treating me this way.

Your fiancée may be infatuated, she may be rebelling against the restriction of being engaged, or she may just be very confused. But none of that really matters. She'll have to work it out for herself. You, on the other hand, must decide whether you're prepared to endure this situation for the sake of a roof over your head, or whether you want to deliver an ultimatum. You've already made a bad mistake in telling his wife (who probably knew anyway and was trying to cope as best she could) and you should certainly not confront your fiancée's parents, who must make their own enquiries if the two of you split up. Talk it over with your fiancée again, and if she still can't make up her mind, then consider moving out. There'll be somewhere you can go. It's madness to live in misery for the sake of convenience.

Pregnant 15 year olds, Belfast, Sheffield and Fort William: if you really can't approach your parents or your family doctor, then ring the Samaritans for a confidential talk, anonymously, if you prefer. They talk to lots of young people with problems, and they'll know how to help. Look in your local telephone directories for numbers. Ring The British Pregnancy Advisory Service on 056 423225 and LIFE on 0926 421587 who'll also give advice. Don't despair. There are people willing to help.

Sorry, but in our August 28 issue we printed the wrong number for ChildLine. The correct number is 0800 1111.

SUE'S NEW ADDRESS
■ If you have a problem, please write to Sue Frost at WOMAN, ADMAIL 13, London SE1 9XA, enclosing a large sae.

WOMAN OF THE WEEK

Meet 38-year-old Lynne Newman, from North London

■ LYNNE'S MAKE-UP

"What a treat to be made up by a professional . . . I feel so well groomed and glowing . . . the colours are lovely." Yanina showed Lynne how to achieve a more balanced neutral make-up using Kanebo's exclusive Bio Line cosmetics range from Japan. She used a light powder foundation in shade F4 to compliment Lynne's attractive olive complexion. While shades of rose (BE-24) and taupe (BE-23) subtly opened out Lynne's hazel coloured eyes. Rich brown mascara was applied to the top lashes only, for a more natural result. A rosy blusher was applied in shade BC-14. Lynne adored the lipstick—a lovely pinky red called Primula.

■ LYNNE'S HAIR

Lynne has lovely dark, naturally wavy hair—and the style she wears it in suits her well. "I like my hair to look "curly" she told us "without resembling Angie in EastEnders—severe hair styles just don't suit me." So our hair stylist Yanina set to and created this special look for the evening by gently tonging Lynne's hair to create extra body and delicate wispy ringlets. It's a very sophisticated style and looked great with the beautiful ballgown Lynne chose.

For a more casual everyday look, Yanina showed Lynne how to experiment with lots of different, pretty hair combs and slides to compliment the soft, natural hair styles she likes to wear.

which occurs frequently in women's magazines. When we consider the elements which are aimed at males and those which are aimed at females we can see that they add up to furthering the stereotyping of women and men as always different.

A further element which is often found in women's magazines is the story which can be described as 'triumph over tragedy'. In this type of plot, women are presented as victims of terrible accidents or difficult circumstances which they then go on to conquer, because of their own personal strength. These stories are uplifting in the sense that they show individuals who have survived difficult circumstances but they have the added message that women should have to survive these things on an individual basis, rather than there being any more general strategy for dealing with inequality.

What I have been arguing in this chapter is that language analysis alone cannot help us to make the link between language and ideology, because if we focus on individual language items we risk both excluding the context of the text and also the polyvalence of language items themselves. What is necessary is some inter-mediate stage or structure which determines the choice of language items. In this chapter I have tried to demonstrate that one of these structures might be gendered frameworks. These structures are well-trodden pathways, which because of their familiarity, take on an air of commonsense knowledge. It is only by describing these seemingly commonsense structures that we will begin to expose their constructed nature and at the same time their perniciousness. This type of feminist analysis will, I hope, move us forward from blanket accusations of political incorrectness towards an analysis which is detailed enough to demon-strate to readers the way that certain texts offer us constructions which are retrograde; once those constructions have been described and 'made strange', it is to be hoped that readers will see them as not being in their interests.

Conclusions

Feminist Stylistics has suggested ways in which those concerned with the repre-sentation of gender relations might draw on linguistic and language analysis to develop a set of tools which could expose the workings of gender at a range of different levels in texts. Because of the nature of feminist analysis, it has been necessary to question the seemingly self-evident boundaries of the text itself, arguing that the text is permeated by discourses and ideologies, and that the distinction between textual and extratextual cannot really be held to. That is not to say like Derrida 'Il n'y a pas d'hors texte', there is nothing but textuality – there is nothing but text – there is nothing outside the text; but rather to say almost the opposite. Texts are invaded by sociocultural norms, by ideologies, by history, by economic forces, by fashions, by gender and racial stereotyping, and so on. That is not to say that authors have no control whatsoever about what they write, but that authors themselves are also subject to interpellation and interaction with these discursive forces.

This might be a cause of pessimism – if texts are the sites of ideological deter-mination, then there is nothing that we can do, but submit to the barrage of ideology. However, if we take our model of power relations from Michel Foucault, it is quite clear that 'where there is power there is resistance' (Foucault 1981: 36). Thus power has implicit within it the notion of resistance. Authors and readers are not passive, but rather can take a role in actively negotiating and thus redefining the scope and nature of these larger discursive structures. As Foucault states: 'We must not imagine that the world turns towards us a legible face which we would only have to decipher. The world is not the accomplice of our knowl-edge: there is no pre-discursive providence which disposes the world in our favour' (Foucault, 1981: 67). Thus, although accepting this view of reality may seem quite daunting, in some sense it is tremendously liberating to realize that we can intervene in the process of shaping the boundaries of discourse.

The book as a whole has argued that it is necessary to analyse a wide range of factors such as the role of the reader and gendered frameworks. This focus on macro- and micro-structures makes for a more complex analysis, one which is perhaps more unwieldy than the simple lexical analyses beloved of formalist stylistics. However, in this way, it is possible to consider the relationship between lexical items and discourse frameworks. It is clear that the relationship is not one of simple determination – i.e. lexical items are determined by discursive structures; there is a certain level of interaction and contestation, simply because these lexical items are *used* and inhabited by individuals, who through their use and analysis of terms bring about changes to the larger structures.

Analysis which relies on this model of discourse and practice will necessarily be concerned to change structures and ways of thinking. This is the purpose of this book: to document the ways in which gender difference is represented in texts in order to change the way that this happens. Taking on board Foucault's views means that we can recognize that there is no reason why we should represent gender differences in this way rather than in other ways; rather than this seeming naturally and self-evidently the way that all nations represent gender, it can be seen as particular to dominant forces within our culture at this point in time. Precisely because it is possible to see this form of representation as so particular, it is also possible to see the potential for change. Feminist work has been active in bringing about change in representational practices through critique, through teaching and through developing new models of writing practice.

It might be useful at this point to summarize the skills which I have detailed in this book, to try to distil them down to a list of possible questions which can be addressed to a text. In this way, it will be possible for any text to be subjected to a thorough analysis of its representations of gender relations.

SUMMARY

Context and Theoretical Model

 1   What sort of text is it?
1.1 What genre does it belong to? (novel, advertising, newspaper, song)
1.2 Is it a text which has status? (canonical, literary, popular)
1.3 Is there a tendency for women or men to be associated with this type of text? (as readers, as writers, as representational objects)
1.4 How is it produced? (Is it authored or produced anonymously?)
1.5 What is the history of the text? How did you come to read it? (Is it on a reading list; did you buy it, were you given it?)
1.6 Why are you analysing it? (within an educational institution, for assessment, for pleasure)
1.7 What general expectations do you have in relation to the text and gender representation? (Consider what expectations the genre and context of the text set up; how stereotypical do you expect the text to be?)

Gender and Writing

2   Is the style of this genre considered to be feminine or masculine?

2.1 Are the sentences short or long? Are they composed of subordinate clauses or co-ordinate clauses? How are they linked? By conjunctions such as 'however' or 'nevertheless', or by 'but' and 'and'?

2.2 Are the verbs used concerned with action, with doing, or with reporting feelings, emotions and what is said?

2.3 Is the narration first person or third person, and is that narration from the point of view of a character within the text or is it narrated by a voice external to the text?

2.4 What style does the text most approach – scientific reports, colour supplement journalism, intimate confessional autobiography?

2.5 What makes you assume that the voice of the author is female or male? Is it intuition (and thus probably drawing on stereotype) or is there some evidence for your assumption?

2.6 What purpose does knowing that the author is male or female serve for you?

Gender and Reading

3   Does the text address you as male or female? What sort of male or female? White or Black? Straight or gay? Married or single? Young or old? Middle-class or working-class? What language items convey this information to you?

3.1 Does the text use pronouns such as 'you', 'I' and 'we'?

3.2 Do you feel that the position which you are reading from is aligned with one of these pronoun positions?

3.3 Does the text address you directly in other ways, by referring to your assumed profession, marital status, age, race, interests, 'life-style', wishes/desires? Are these linked to your supposed gender identity?

3.4 Does the text assume that you have certain elements of background knowledge? Make explicit what the text assumes that you know or agree to.

3.5 Is this background knowledge drawing on stereotypical assumptions about men and women? Are these stereotypical assumptions about all men and women or only certain groups of men and women?

3.6 Does the text assume that you will agree with certain of its statements? Are these statements about gender?

3.7 Do you have to work to make sense of the text? What elements do you have to supply in order for the text to make sense?

3.8 Does the text address you in a way which does not include you? Does it implicitly or explicitly address a 'universal' audience, which in fact is only a white male heterosexual audience or a white female heterosexual audience?

3.9 Does the text contain information which could be coded as stereo-typically feminine or masculine? Specify what exactly this information is. (technical, emotional, concerned with particular spheres of activity: work, home)

Gender and Individual Lexical Items

4 Are the words which are used gender-specific?

4.1 Is the generic pronoun 'he' used to refer to males in general?

4.2 Are generic nouns used to refer to males?

4.3 Is the suffix '-man' used to refer to males?

4.4 How are males and females named in the text? (surname, first name, diminutives, title)

4.5 Do any of the terms used to describe males or females have sexual connotations?

4.6 Do any of the terms used to describe males or females have positive or negative connotations?

4.7 Do any of the terms used to describe males or females have taboos associated with them?

Gender and Clause Level/Sentence Level

5 Are there statements in the text which are gender-inflected?

5.1 Are there ready-made phrases which refer to gender difference?

5.2 Does the text assume you hold certain gendered assumptions? Make explicit what this information consists of.

5.3 In order to make sense of certain statements do you have to make a bridging assumption drawing on stereotypical gender information?

5.4 Are metaphors or figurative language used which draw upon gendered assumptions? Are males and females compared with different elements?

5.5 Is the text humorous? What propositions do you have to agree to in order to find the text funny? Why is the text using humour? Is it a difficult area? Is the text addressing you as a male? What type of male?

5.6 Does the text use *doubles entendres*? Why does it use them?

5.7 Analyse the transitivity choices. Are they predominantly material action intention, supervention, material event, mental, or relational? Are they different for males and females represented in the text?

5.8 Who acts in the text? Examine the use of passive voice. Are females acted upon more than males or vice versa?

Gender and Discourse Level

6 Are there larger structures in the text which seem to be gendered?

6.1 Analyse the male and female characters. Are they described in the same way? Are certain words used which are gender-specific? What sort of female or male characters are represented? Are they predominantly white or black? Are they predominantly young or old? What sort of relationships are they represented as having? Are there power hierarchies in the test? Do these relate to gender, race, class, or sexual orientation?

6.2 Are there narrative pathways which seem to be gender-specific? Do males perform in different ways from females? Are these pathways ones that you have encountered in other texts? Is the text resolved in certain ways which seem to have implications for gender?

6.3 Are the bodies of males and females represented as whole or as fragmented parts? As clothed or unclothed?

6.4 Whose point of view does the text emanate from? Who is speaking? Who is telling you this? Who does the text focus on? Does the focalization shift at any point in the text? Whose interests does the text seem to be working in? Whose information does the text seem to be endorsing as true?

6.5 What elements are associated with males and females in the text?

By working through these questions in a systematic way, it will be possible to track down the ways that texts encode gender and the ways that representations of gender may form part of the logic of the text. It may also help us to investigate ways in which gender is dealt with by our society as a whole. This checklist approach is not about providing an index of political correctness, but rather about enabling readers to work through a range of factors which might point up and make more clearly visible some of the implicit or hidden assumptions about gender. Focusing on language either at the level of the word or at the level of discourse can enable us to track down some of these hidden assumptions.

Whilst it is clear that stylistic analysis as a simple formal analysis is a thing of the past, this type of analysis – where language analysis is enmeshed with a concern with the representation of sexual difference, and/or racial difference, and/or sexual orientation – may hold a way forward for the analysis of text. As Carter and Simpson state: 'At the risk of overgeneralization and simplification, we might say that if the 1960s was a decade of formalism in stylistics, the 1970s a decade of functionalism and the 1980s a decade of discourse stylistics, then the 1990s could well become the decade in which sociohistorical and sociocultural stylistic studies are a main preoccupation' (Carter and Simpson 1989: 17). It is to be hoped that this concern with the sociohistorical and the sociocultural will pervade future work in this field.

Glossary

These definitions are necessarily simplifications of complex terms; in order to understand the terms themselves in their complexity you will need to follow up some of the further reading.

actor: the person who performs an action

address: the way that a text calls on you or talks to you as a **reader**

adjective: a word which modifies a noun; for example, a *good* book, a *long* walk, an *interesting* play

adverb: a word which modifies a verb; for example, she walked *slowly*, she played *well*, they argued *violently*

adverbial: a phrase which has the same function as an adverb in that it modifies a verb; for example, she played the piece *in a very apathetic way*

aesthetic effect: an effect on the reader which is brought about by elements in the text, usually a literary or artistic text

affiliation: the links that are made between yourself and a larger group

affix: an element which is fixed to the front or back of words; for example, *anti*-sexist, poet*ess*

agency: a concern with who acts and who is acted upon

androcentric: reflecting a world-view which is male-oriented

androgyny: the idealized state where sex differences are not important

Anglo-American: primarily used of a school of feminist literary theory where the focus was on content analysis

anti-sexist: a strategy to combat sexism

apposition: a phrase or clause which is not essential to the structure of the sentence, and which usually modifies the force or meaning of the main clause; for example, 'etymology, *the study of the history of words*, is very useful for students of English'

archaeological: in text analysis, the process whereby one 'unearths' the process of production and reception of a text

asymmetric power relation: a relation between people who are not in similar positions of power: one has power over the other

author function: a term used by theorists to make the author seem less a person with intentions and a development, but rather something which is used to group a set of disparate texts together

avant-garde: those writers who experiment with language and form in literature, usually in reaction to a previous school of writing

background assumptions: the knowledge which someone needs in order to make sense of a statement

bidirectional: moving in two directions

binary opposition: a pair of terms which are seen to be in complete contrast to one another; for example, good/bad, hot/cold, man/woman; not many of these seeming contrasts are in fact really in complete opposition

canon: a group of texts which is given high status within a society

canonical: the position given to texts in the canon

classic realism: those writers, such as George Eliot, whose writing is seen to 'reflect' or 'mirror' reality, since they give very detailed descriptive accounts of settings and characters

clause: a group of words which contains a finite verb; for example, 'Klein *worked* as a psychoanalyst', 'Foucault *wrote* a great many books'

close reading: a practice where the reader concentrates on small sections of text and analyses the language very closely in order to help her come to an interpretation

closure: the way that narratives pull together various strands of the plot in order to come to a satisfying end

code model: a model of language which sees communication as a process of transferring information from the speaker to the hearer

coherent: a sentence or text is coherent if the ideas within it are judged to be unified by, or make sense to, a reader/speaker

collocation: the occurrence of words in the company of certain other words; for example, with the phrase 'all day . . .' we can predict that the missing word is 'long' because the words often co-occur

commonsense: the set of ideological knowledge which a society assumes can be understood as background knowledge for its members

competitive strategy: a strategy used by participants in conversation, whereby their own needs take precedence over the needs of the others in the group; for example, they interrupt and change the topic at will, rather than attending to other people in the group

connective: a word which links clauses together; for example, 'The accident happened *because* conditions on the road were very poor'

connotation: words often have an overlaid meaning which modifies the dictionary definition; for example, the word 'scab' in industrial disputes has strong negative connotations

consciousness-raising: in the 1960s in Britain and America many women joined groups to discuss their condition; talking about their lives and realizing that the causes of difficulties and problems which they had experienced were

in fact not simply personal but social, caused many women to become politically aware. This process of becoming aware of the political dimension to
personal difficulties is consciousness-raising

consensus reading: a reading which a group of people can agree on

content analysis: analysis of the plot and characters with no reference to
language

contextual stylistics: linguistic analysis of text which tries to situate the texts
in their socioeconomic environment

contiguity: the condition of being close to something

co-operative strategy: a strategy used by participants in conversation,
whereby they show their concern more for the good of the group than for
their own personal needs; therefore, they will ask questions to stimulate
discussion, rather than simply say what they want to say

co-ordination: the linking of clauses by 'and', 'but', 'or'

covert prestige: prestige which is gained through unusual means; for example,
some working-class men gain a form of prestige through emphasizing their
regional accent, rather than by adopting a middle-class RP accent

critical discourse analysis: a form of discourse analysis which is informed
by political concerns

critical linguistics: a form of linguistics which is informed by political
concerns

critical reception: the way that a text is evaluated by critics

critique: to criticize in order to find constructive solutions to problems

cultural code: the set of background knowledge which it is assumed that each
member of a society will have

dead metaphor: a metaphor which has been used so often that it no longer
appears to be one but seems instead like a stock phrase; for example, 'shivers
ran down my back'; 'ran' is used metaphorically but we have become habitu-
ated to its use and no longer see it as a metaphor

decoding: in the code model of language, the hearer of a message decodes the
signal in order to decipher the message

deconstruct: this is often used loosely as meaning to 'unpack' or to take to
pieces critically an idea, a text, a binary opposition, in order to expose its
workings

deconstruction: a form of philosophical and rhetorical enquiry whose aim is
to analyse the logic of texts in order to expose their workings

deixis: words which indicate space and time in relation to the speaker; for
example, 'here/there'; 'now/then'; 'this/that'

descriptive linguistics: linguistics whose aim is to describe language without
evaluating

determinism: a view of language which sees language as being an important
factor in the way that we think; for example, if our language makes a categorical
distinction between green and blue, we will be able to perceive the distinctions
between these colours more easily than if our language contained no such terms

deviation: in stylistics terms, a deviation assumes a norm which is transgressed for a purpose; for example, rules are broken in a collocation, or a seemingly inappropriate word is used

dialectical: a form of reasoning where conflict between two propositions or ideas is resolved by a solution which transcends both of them

diminutive form: a form of language which is used for people and things which are considered smaller/younger than yourself. The addition of 'y' or 'ie' will often make a word diminutive; for example, John/Johnnie; Penelope/Penny

direct address: when a text addresses the reader by the use of 'you'

direct speech: in a text when a character's speech is reported in inverted commas; for example, 'I have a dream,' said Martin Luther King

discourse: this is a very complex term. It has two main meanings: the first used in linguistics and the second in literary and cultural theory. The first one refers to a group of sentences which form an extended text; this is how it is used in the phrase 'discourse analysis', where relations beyond the sentence are examined. The second usage is more complicated: discourse refers to a much wider grouping of statements which can be seen to have some homo-geneity; it also refers to the set of rules which brought these statements into existence. Thus the 'discourse of advertising' refers to the statements which are generated within advertising and also the rules which generated those sentences rather than other ones. The study of this form of discourse is called 'discourse theory'.

discourse stylistics: a form of stylistics which analyses language above the level of the sentence

discursive framework: a framework which determines what can be said within a particular field

discursive parameters: the limits of a discourse

dominant reading: the reading which presents itself as self-evident

double entendre: a sexual play on words

écriture féminine: an experimental writing practice which French feminist theo-rists assert is potentially subversive in that it disrupts the status quo in language

encoding: in the code model of language, the process of finding words for ideas

endearment: a term which is used to intimates to express emotion

epistemic modality: a form of modification which softens the force of a state-ment; for example 'I *may* have lost it' rather than 'I have lost it'

essentialism: the notion that identity is based on essences; that is, male and females behave and dress differently because they are biologically different

etymology: the history of a word's constituent parts

euphemism: a word or phrase which is used in place of one which is tabooed or socially unacceptable; for example, 'I'm going to the *bathroom*' instead of 'I'm going to the *lavatory*'

experimental writing: that writing style which tries to play with and subvert the rules of meaning and making sense

external focalizer: when a story is focused on the events through the consciousness of a character external to the action in the story

extratextual: those elements which are seen to be outside the text

female affiliation: the signals which some women writers display in texts to show that they are writing for a primarily female audience

femininity: the set of socially constructed stereotypical behaviour which is supposed to be acquired by females

feminist: a person who would like to improve the range of possibilities for women

feminist stylistics: a form of politically motivated stylistics whose aim is to develop an awareness of the way gender is handled in texts

finite verb: a verb which changes to show time and person; for example, 'I *bought* a paper today; I'll *buy* one tomorrow as well'

focalization: the process whereby the events in a story are related to the reader through the consciousness of a character or narrator

foregrounding: the positioning of an element in a prominent place in a text which it does not usually occupy, thus drawing attention to it

formalism: the analysis of features of the form of texts; for example, language patterning or structures

fragmentation: the process whereby characters in texts are described in terms of their body-parts instead of as people

free indirect speech: a form of speech where the style of language of a character and that of the narrator are difficult to disentangle, and where there are few formal clues to tell the reader who is speaking; for example, 'She looked again. Was that the man she had seen yesterday?' Here it is unclear whether the second sentence is spoken by the character or reported by the narrator, since it is not marked by inverted commas or by a phrase such as 'she wondered'

French feminism: a form of feminism which developed in France but which has been very influential in many countries; it is primarily a form of theoretical work which tries to carve out a space for feminist work within mainstream psychoanalysis and philosophy

gatekeepers: those institutions which often prevent change from occurring

gender: the sexualized identity of each individual

gender bias: the bias which is shown towards one gender

gender-blind: the seeming blindness to the implications of gender on an issue

gender-free language: policies which try to discourage discrimination against a gender group, particularly women, in language

genderlect: language-choices which are made more frequently by one gender than another

gender-neutral: a form of language which tries not to make unnecessary reference to gender

generative grammar: grammatical theory developed by Noam Chomsky

generic: used in a general way to refer to women and men

generic noun: a noun which purports to refer to men and women, whilst in fact only referring to males; for example, 'The *inhabitants* had to leave their wives behind'

generic pronoun: a pronoun which purports to refer to both men and women, whilst in fact referring only to males: 'he'

grammatical analysis: analysis which focuses on quantifying and evaluating the use of particular grammatical items within a text; for example, pronouns, nouns or verbs

heterogeneous: composed of unrelated parts, or composed of elements which are not of the same type

heterosexual: having sexual and emotional relations with a member of another gender (often termed the 'opposite' sex)

hierarchical: a system of persons arranged in a graded order because of power relations

homogeneous: composed of similar elements

homosexual: having sexual and emotional relations with a member of the same gender/sex

hypothesis: an idea which is tested against data

ideal reader: an idealized construct to whom the text is addressed

ideolect: the personal 'dialect' of each individual

Ideological State Apparatus: the institutions such as the Church, the education system, the press and media which ensure the circulation of certain ideological knowledge

ideology: a set of seemingly coherent ideas which represent our experience to us in stereotypical ways

indirect address: the way that texts address the reader by assuming certain knowledge is shared

inference: to deduce a message from a statement when that message is not explicitly given

internal focalizer: where the events of a story are focused through the consciousness of a character in the story

interpellation: the process whereby individuals are called upon to internalize ideological knowledge as their own thoughts

intransitive verb: a verb which does not take an object; for example, 'The car *backfired*', 'The snow *fell*'

irony: the humorous use of words to imply the opposite of what they normally mean

juxtaposition: the process whereby two elements are put into close contact with each other and each takes on some of the other's qualities

Leavisite: a reading of literature which is concerned to evaluate a text's literary and philosophical qualities

lexical gap: a gap in the language where there appears to be no word for a concept

lexicalization: the process whereby experience is encoded in language

lexicographer: someone who writes or compiles dictionaries

lexis: vocabulary, words

liberal feminism: a form of feminism which aims to achieve equal rights for women

linguistic determinism: see determinism

linguistic stylistics: a form of stylistics which is focused on the language used in literary texts in order to make wider claims about language as a whole

linguistics: the theoretical study of language

literariness: the quality which is supposed to mark literary texts off from other texts; usually it is assumed to be a special use of language

literary theory: the theoretical study of literature and other texts

literary language: see literariness

literary stylistics: the form of stylistics which focuses on the analysis of literary texts, drawing on linguistics, in order to aid interpretation and evaluation

logonomic system: a larger-scale grouping of statements which, at the level of discourse, have some coherence

man-made language: for some feminists, language has developed so that it favours men's interests: this is reflected in the phrase 'man-made language': the language we speak seems to be made in men's interests

marked: a form which is seen to be deviant or different from a norm

masculinity: the social construct of stereotypical behaviour which men are supposed to acquire

material action process: an action which has effects on others

material action intention process: an action which has effects on others and where the actor intends to perform it; for example, 'She stole the car', 'They went on holiday'

material action supervention process: an action which has effects on others and where the actor does not intend the particular outcome to happen; for example, 'He fell over the cliff', 'They crashed their car'

material event process: often the action of an inanimate object; for example, 'The ship sank', 'The sun shone'

mediation: a situation where there is no direct access to something; rather it is filtered through an intermediary

members' resources: the knowledge which it is assumed you have

mental externalized process: an action which takes place mentally but which is externalized; for example, 'She talked about the war'

mental internalized process: an action which takes place mentally; for example, 'He noticed the change'

metaphor: a word or phrase which uses analogy to suggest similarity in one respect between two things; for example, 'She *cut* me when she saw me in the street the other day' (meaning to pointedly ignore)

minority writing/literature: writing by a group which because of its ethnic or gender position in the larger society tends to write in a politically informed way

modal verb: a word which modifies a verb; for example, 'She *can* drive', 'I *may* help you'

modernist: the style of writing associated with a school of experimental writing at the turn of the century

modification: the changing of statements or words, often lessening their force; for example, from 'Do it now' to 'Could you do it now'

narrative: a sequence of events which has a structure

narrator: the character who mostly focalizes the story

nominalization: the turning of verbs into nouns and thus deleting agency; for example, from 'The terrorists exploded the bomb at night' to 'The *explosion* happened at night'

non-sexist: a strategy which aims not to discriminate against women

non-transactive verb: a verb which does not take an object; see intransitive

noun: a word which refers to an object/person/concept; for example, 'book', 'teacher', 'justice'

obviousness: commonsense ideological knowledge often has this quality of presenting itself as necessarily obvious and available to all without reflection

onomatopoeia: words whose sounds seem to imitate the sound of a noise or action; for example, 'hiss', 'zap', 'woof'

overdetermined: caused by several different factors

parataxis: the juxtaposition of clauses without co-ordination

parenthesis: the marking-off of a phrase by the use of brackets

parler femme: in French feminist thought a form of writing which is potentially subversive of the status quo in language

passive: a form of the verb where it is not necessary to specify the agent; for example, in 'The people were shot' we do not know who shot the people; it is possible to add to 'The people were shot' the words '*by an intruder*', but often the passive is used to avoid specifying agency

patriarchy: a society which is organized largely in men's interests

pedagogic: educational

phallocentric: criticism which has an overt or covert bias against women

poetics: the study of the way literature works

point of view: the consciousness from which the story is related

politically correct: a view of language which assumes that if a sexist person uses a gender-neutral language form they will change the way that they think. The term 'politically correct' is generally used only as a term of disparagement; it is not used by theorists who are trying to change the language in positive ways

polyvalence: multiple meanings

positioning: the way that a text addresses the reader

poststructuralist: theorists such as Jacques Lacan, Julia Kristeva, Jacques Derrida, Michel Foucault

pragmatics: the study of language-use in context

prefix: an affix which is added to the beginning of a word; for example, *uneasy*

preposition: a word which generally indicates position; for example, '*in* the road', '*on* the table'

prescriptive linguistics: linguistics which attempts to evaluate language performance and to judge the correctness of utterances

presupposition: an idea or a statement which it is necessary to already know in order to make sense of a given statement

private sphere: primarily the home

production of texts: the complex process whereby texts are published

protagonist: the principal character in a story

psychoanalysis: the analysis of the unconscious

public idiom: the speech which newspapers use, as an imitation of the way they believe their readers speak

public sphere: all space outside the home

radical feminism: a form of feminism which believes that women and men are fundamentally different and that women are better

radical stylistics: a stylistics which is politically motivated

reader response: the study of the way that groups of readers respond to texts

ready-made phrases: those phrases which are preconstructed; for example, proverbs and advertising slogans

reception of texts: the processes whereby a text is evaluated and received by critics and readers

referent: the thing/concept to which a word refers

resisting reader: a reader who refuses the dominant reading and produces a critical reading of a text

Russian Formalists: a group of theorists who were particularly interested in formal patterning in texts and also in literariness

samizdat: a subversive 'underground' publication

Sapir–Whorf hypothesis: the hypothesis that the language you speak determines the way that you think and divide up reality

schemata: a set of preconstructed narrative choices

semantic derogation: the process whereby words associated with women begin to have negative connotations

semantics: the study of meaning

semiotic: this word has a number of different meanings; it is used in psychoanalysis to refer to deviations in language which seem to disrupt the whole linguistic order

sentence: a group of words containing one or more clauses

sexism: irrelevant and derogatory reference to gender; sexism usually consists of statements which are derogatory to women

sex-preferential usage: see genderlect

sex-specific language: language which is restricted to representing one gender; for example, the so-called 'generic pronoun' 'he'

signification: the process of making sense/meaning

slack reading: a quick reading of a text without analysing in detail

social stratification: the process whereby people in societies are graded according to their position in the power hierarchy

sociolinguistics: the study of language in relation to its social context

soft pornography: pornographic images which are supposed to be less offensive than others

speech-acts: the theory which sees language in terms of the acts which are performed in and through it

speech community: a group of people who share a language

stereotypical: preconstructed ideas

stream-of-consciousness: a form of writing best exemplified by Virginia Woolf and Dorothy Richardson which attempts to depict interludes of unstructured thinking

subject: a word with two meanings: first, the person or object who performs an action (agent, actor); second, the individual from a psychoanalytical perspective

subjective reading: a reading which is particular to the individual

subjectivity: the state of recognizing yourself as an individual

suffix: an affix which is added to the end of a word; for example, soft*ness*

syntax: word order

systemic linguistics: the grammatical theory developed by Michael Halliday

taboo: forbidden or stigmatized by society

tag-question: a question which is formed from a statement by using a 'tag'; for example, 'It's too hot in here, *isn't it?*'

task-based approach: an approach to teaching and analysing texts which encourages engaging with the texts, by performing small tasks, generally in groups; by focusing on small facets of the text it is possible to begin to engage with the structure of the text as a whole

text-immanent: a view of texts which sees meaning as residing in the text

totem: the symbol which is used to stand for a group

transactive verb: a verb which takes an object; for example, in 'She *ate* the meal', the object is 'the meal'

transitive verb: see transactive verb

transitivity: the analysis of who does what to whom

trope: a literary figure, such as metaphor or metonymy

turn-taking: in conversation, one speaker speaking after another

unmarked: a form which is seen to be the norm (see marked)

variable: a factor which plays a major role in the way something is determined

verb: a word which represents an action or event; for example, 'She *took* them to the station', 'They *understood* the question'

vocative: a form of a noun used to call people, often strangers; for example, 'mate' and 'darling'

world-view: the total set of ideas which a person has which determines the way that that person will think in the future

Notes

INTRODUCTION

1 This introduction was written initially by Sara Mills; Shan Wareing provided some revisions and suggested others; Sara Mills revised it overall.

   To get some idea of possible approaches which come under the umbrella term 'stylistics', and the full breadth and complexity of the field, see Katie Wales's (1989: 437–8) definition.

2 *The Linguistics of Writing*, edited by Nigel Fabb, is a good example of the diversity of the kind of work which has been done in this new stylistics (Fabb *et al.* 1987).

3 The Poetics and Linguistics Association is an organization which tries to combine an analysis of texts from a linguistics perspective with a concern for the type of questions that literary theory has asked.

4 For example, Traugott and Pratt (1980: 169–77) analyse syntactic structures in the prose of Ernest Hemingway and Henry James, to illustrate characteristic choices in their writing styles. For further examples of attempts to demonstrate what is special about the styles of certain writers, see Freeman's *Linguistic and Literary Style* (1970).

5 The Poetics and Linguistics Association conference on Radical Stylistics at the University of Sheffield Hallam, was a notable exception.

6 Shan Wareing initially wrote this paragraph on feminist sociolinguists and it was revised by Sara Mills.

7 Burton's work will be discussed in greater detail in Chapter 5.

8 As an illustration of this process, think of the way that animals and birds are used to symbolize football teams. Football teams are not very different, one from the other, but because of competition, it is essential to emphasize their difference; therefore animals which are clearly different are used to symbolize this difference.

9 Shan Wareing provided this advertisement for analysis; Sara Mills wrote the analysis.

1 FEMINIST MODELS OF TEXT

1 This chapter was initially written by Sara Mills; Shan Wareing added some revisions and wrote some additional sections, such as the section on onomatopoeic words; Sara Mills then revised the chapter as a whole.

2 There are too many types of feminist literary analysis to describe here (for example, feminist theories based on psychoanalysis, reclaiming women's writing, Marxist feminist, deconstructive feminist and so on). For a selection of critical feminist

approaches to texts, see *Feminist Readings, Feminists Reading* (S. Mills *et al.* 1989). For an introduction to different types of stylistics, see the journal *Language and Literature.*

3 As Alan Durant showed in a series of lectures at Strathclyde University in 1990 on the nature of language and communication in modern technology, this face-to-face model of communication is very rarely the norm. See his *Soundtrack and Talkback: Language Communication and Education* (1994).

4 Parts of this discussion have appeared in an earlier form in sections of an essay entitled 'Knowing y/our place: towards a Marxist feminist contextualised stylistics', in Toolan 1992 (S. Mills 1992c).

5 Winterson quoted in *Cosmopolitan,* July 1992: 173; this example was supplied by Shan Wareing.

6 See my *Discourses of Difference* (S. Mills 1992b) which attempts to analyse the conditions both of production and of reception in order to try to approximate to some sense of the range of meanings which texts might be said to hold.

7 Throughout this book, I will be using a range of generic references, such as 's/he' and also 'she'. In this context, I am using 'herself' to refer in a generic way to all readers.

2 THE GENDERED SENTENCE

1 This chapter is a substantially revised version of a short section of a paper by Sara Mills (1987).

2 One notable exception to this is the work of Makiko Minow-Pinkney in *Virginia Woolf and the Problem of the Subject* (1989).

3 Despite being based on very different theoretical premises, it is surprising that more recent theoretical work, for example, Jennifer Coates's work on female groups in 'Gossip revisited' (Coates and Cameron 1988) and Deborah Tannen's work on female/male misunderstanding in conversation in *You Just Don't Understand* (1991), is based on similar assumptions that males and females differ fundamentally in their use of language. However, neither takes the male as the norm from which women's speech deviates. Coates revalues co-operative strategies and Tannen, rather unsuccessfully, tries to argue that female and male speech-patterns and styles should be equally valued. For a critique of this see Cameron's essay in Mills's *Language and Gender* (1995).

4 Some work has attempted to survey males' usage of certain items: for example, Woods analyses males' use of tag-questions (Woods in Coates and Cameron 1988). Cameron and Coates have drawn attention to the fact that William Labov's work in Harlem has dealt with the language-use of male single-sex groups, but he presents his findings as if they were not from a segregated sex group (Labov 1972).

5 The distinction between formal/public and informal/private spheres is an important one in analysing language, particularly in relation to gender. Several theorists, such as Kaplan (1986), have argued that women are largely excluded from the language of the public sphere. Many theorists have remarked upon the special problems which confront women when engaging in public speaking. However, as Margaret Thatcher, Betty Boothroyd, Benazir Bhutto, Cory Aquino, Brenda Dean and many other women have shown, these boundaries cannot be clearly mapped on to gender divisions. (See Wendy Webster's analysis of Margaret Thatcher's language in Webster 1990).

6 An illuminating analogy here is with the work of Marianne Grabrucker on non-sexist child-rearing; she describes in her book *There's a Good Girl* (1988) the way that girls can be reared as boys, and this would be seen as a move towards androgyny, but boys would not be allowed a reciprocal arrangement. Therefore, girls can wear dungarees *and/or* dresses, but boys can only wear dungarees. Any activity which is

encoded as male can be performed by girls, in addition to their own female-encoded activities, but such an arrangement is not available to boys. Androgyny means, in essence, that women can perform male tasks; the same flexibility is not open to men.

7 Consider, for example, Gertrude Stein, H. D., Dorothy Richardson, Virginia Woolf and many others. For accounts of experimental women's writing, see Hanscombe and Smyers 1987.

8 See Leith's *A Social History of English* (1983) for an alternative interpretation of the derogation of parataxis and co-ordination.

9 One has only to consider the wide range of texts written by men focusing on women's experience: for example, *Madame Bovary*, *The Taming of the Shrew*, *The Bostonians*, *Tess of the d'Urbervilles*, *The French Lieutenant's Woman*, *Women in Love*, *Moll Flanders* and so on.

10 I would like to thank the MLitt in Linguistics students in the Programme in Literary Linguistics, University of Strathclyde, particularly Mairi, Ilham, Zaidi, Mazlan, Nora, Luce and Qu.

11 This analysis of *Moll Cutpurse* was written by Shan Wareing.

12 See the introduction for a brief discussion of Lévi-Strauss's work on totem. Male and female gender difference seems to be very much based on the same need to differentiate when the difference in essence is extremely small. (For an excellent discussion of the paucity of biological sex difference see Gisel Kaplan and Lesley Rogers, 'The definition of male and female: biological reductionism and the sanctions of normality', in Gunew 1990.)

3 GENDER AND READING

1 This chapter is a substantially reworked version of a section of a chapter by Sara Mills entitled 'Knowing y/our place: towards a Marxist feminist contextualised stylistics', in Toolan 1992.

2 In this article, Althusser describes two main mechanisms which bring about the maintenance of the status quo in capitalist societies: the repressive state apparatuses, consisting of the police, the army and the state, which achieve this aim through force or violence; and the ideological state apparatuses, whose effect is more subtle but equally effective.

3 Althusser's notion of obviousness has remarkable similarity to Roland Barthes's 'cultural code' (Barthes 1975).

4 However, it is important that we do not simply consider gender in isolation from other variables in analysis, since as Howard and Allen have demonstrated, in certain reading contexts, age and relative knowledge base are more important. Despite problems with their analyses, their work shows both the necessity of not assuming a homogeneous female reading community, and also the importance of realizing that gender is not always the most important factor (Howard and Allen 1990).

5 I deal with background knowledge, presupposition and assumptions in more detail in Chapter 6.

6 Both Showalter and Fetterley have rather a simplistic model of the relation between literary texts and reality, for they both consider that literary texts reflect reality and this runs the risk of flawing their argument about address (see Mills *et al.* 1989 for a full discussion of this). A further problem with both Showalter's and Fetterley's work is that they simply assert that texts address the reader as male on the basis of content analysis and do not provide any language analysis to prove their assertions. It is clear from an analysis of texts which are written by males that there are a large number of elements which can be focused upon which signal to the reader that this is a man-to-man dialogue and it is these elements which I focus on in the analysis here.

4 ANALYSIS AT THE LEVEL OF THE WORD

1 This chapter was originally written by Sara Mills; Shan Wareing contributed the section on Sapir and Whorf, Spender on field dependence, the Royal Mail text and the example from the *Observer*: 'Top people told: take a mistress' and also the analysis of Haden-Elgin's *Native Tongue* (1985).

2 The notion of politically correct language-use seems to be almost entirely a media invention; for an example of a particularly trivializing account of attempts to change language usage and promote awareness of discrimination in language in America, see a *Guardian* article entitled 'Mind your language' (11–12 May 1991: 14) by Mike Bygrave, where such strategies are parodied: 'Politically correct people look for "racism" and "fascism" everywhere and they find them everywhere.'

3 Daly's method of countering sexism is novel; she believes that since language is so important in the way we form our sense of selves, we must struggle over meanings within the sign itself. So she reclaims words which describe women in negative ways, she splits words up to show their underlying meanings and she capitalizes words for women thus giving them the status of many words within the mainstream. Daly's work is discussed in more detail later in this chapter.

4 In a joint Strathclyde/Glasgow University training course for lecturers in 1986, this gender-specific pronoun was systematically used, despite complaints from both female and male participants. In a further course in 1989, the same usage was continued by a different tutor, again despite complaints. Many people seem to feel that it is extremely difficult to alter your language-use, as if it were an integral part of your personality or nature, and cite this as the reason for not changing.

5 The asterisk is used to signal that the example is incorrect or inappropriate.

6 It has also been suggested that in terms such as 'craftsman', since we do not pronounce the 'man' as we would the noun 'man' (that is, in 'craftsman', it is pronounced /m[ə]n/ and in 'man' it is pronounced /m[a]n/), we should therefore see the 'man' in 'crafts-man' and other terms as being substantively different; although it has derived from the same etymological source, it should now be seen to have differentiated itself from its origin, and to be a true generic (Sunderland 1994). However, context determines the meaning, and either such terms will be modified when they refer to women – 'lady/woman craftsman', 'craftsperson', or 'craftswoman' – or a different and specific term will be used instead, for example, 'seamstress'.

7 Although it must be noted that the plural of this word is probably 'walkmans' rather than 'walkmen'; I assume that the term was invented by the Japanese makers and therefore this new usage may not be the same as the word 'man' but a new type of reference.

8 However, there are terms such as 'ombudsman' where a truly generic term has not yet been developed. It should be noted that the Post Office's decision to call all people who deliver the post 'postie' has been met with widespread derision, since for many people this term is too informal a word to be used to describe a profession.

9 I have used the term 'gender-free language' rather than 'anti-sexist language' because the former seems to be less accusatory when trying to change someone's language-use.

10 It is interesting that chairperson is used almost exclusively in the media to refer to women, and chairman is retained for men. Veach (1979) has shown that 'chairperson' is used in American universities to refer to low-status males and all females, whereas higher male faculty staff are termed 'chairman', thus foregrounding the lower prestige of the term 'chairperson'.

11 It may be argued that example 4 does not signal to male students that they are included in the address. For many (Cameron 1985; Fairclough 1989) it is used as a short-term strategy to draw reader's attention to gender-specific usage.

12 In reviews of Kramarae and Treichler's *A Feminist Dictionary* (1985), it was surprising to see such stereotypes still very much in circulation.

13 Sara Mills originally wrote this section. Shan Wareing and Sara Mills then worked on this section together to the extent that it is impossible to disentangle those contributions which belong to each writer. Both of us revised this chapter and added sections. The sections on Haden-Elgin, Carol Cohn and the names for sexual organs are Shan Wareing's. These were then revised by Sara Mills.

14 It should also be remembered here that only women writers have considered it necessary to use male pseudonyms when writing (perhaps with the exception of the male writers who adopt women's names when their work is published by Mills & Boon).

15 This example was written by Shan Wareing.

16 The power relation which is being signalled here by the use of T/V forms does not necessarily feel like a power relation because of the use of these so-called endearments; it may also not be perceived as such by participants. However, it should be noted that it is one of the most difficult elements of sexist language to counter, in the same way as chivalric behaviour is difficult to resist without appearing to be impolite. It should also be noted that although perceived power relation is being signalled, it is possible to challenge that perception.

17 See Chapter 1 on information sources in Montgomery *et al.*, *Ways of Reading* (1992) for a discussion of the partiality of dictionary definitions.

5 ANALYSIS AT THE LEVEL OF THE PHRASE/SENTENCE

1 This chapter was initially written by Sara Mills. The first part of the Essex girl jokes section was written by Shan Wareing and revised by Sara Mills. The first section of the analysis of transitivity was written by Shan Wareing; the analyses of Helen McInnes and Barbara Taylor Bradford were written by Shan Wareing (see Wareing 1994).

2 There are Essex man jokes which seem to dwell on stupidity, but they do not elide vulgarity, stupidity and sexuality as these jokes do and are merely a by-product of Essex girl jokes (and possibly a reaction to them by women from Essex). It should also be remembered that there are no male equivalents of the mother-in-law joke.

3 The analysis here is based on Deirdre Burton's 1982 paper, discussed later. There are a range of different models, but Burton's is possible the most flexible.

4 This section is a revised part of an essay which appears in Wales (ed.), *Feminist Linguistics in Literary Criticism* (1994).

6 ANALYSIS AT THE LEVEL OF DISCOURSE

1 This chapter was initially written by Sara Mills; Shan Wareing provided the section on focalization and fragmentation; she provided the analyses of Taylor Bradford and Morrison. Sara Mills revised the chapter as a whole.

2 See for a full discussion *Discourses of Difference: An Analysis of Woman's Travel Writing and Colonialism* (S. Mills 1992b).

3 Martin Montgomery introduced me to this analysis in his teaching and I am indebted to him for pointing out the focalization in this story and the detailed way in which it works.

4 A version of this section appears in Verdonck and Weber (1995).

Bibliography

Abbott, F. (1990) *Men and Intimacy: Personal Accounts Exploring the Dilemmas of Modern Male Sexuality*, Freedom, CA: Crossing Press.

Adamsky, C. (1981) 'Changes in pronominal usage in a classroom situation', *Psychology of Women Quarterly* 5: 661–9.

Althusser, L. (1984) *Essays in Ideology*, London: Verso.

Amis, Martin (1989) *London Fields*, London: Jonathan Cape.

Attridge, D. (1988) *Peculiar Language: Literature as Difference from the Renaissance to James Joyce*, London: Methuen.

Atwood, M. (1979) *Surfacing*, London: Virago.

Bagley, D. (1967) *High Citadel*, London: Fontana.

Bagley, D. (1973) *The Freedom Trap*, London: Fontana.

Bal, M. (1985) *Narratology: Introduction to the Theory of Narrative*, Toronto/London: University of Toronto Press.

Barthes, R. (1975) *S/Z*, London: Jonathan Cape.

Barthes, R. (1977) *Image, Music, Text*, trans. S. Heath, London: Fontana.

Batsleer, J., Davies, T., O'Rourke, R. and Weedon, C. (1985) *Rewriting English: Cultural Politics of Gender and Class*, London: Methuen.

Battersby, C. (1989) *Gender and Genius: Towards a Feminist Aesthetics*, London: Women's Press.

Belsey, C. and Moore, J. (eds) (1989) *The Feminist Reader: Essays in Gender and the Politics of Literary Criticism*, London: Macmillan.

Bem, S. *et al.* (1973) 'Does sex-biased job advertising "aid and abet" sex discrimination?', *Journal of Applied Social Psychology* 3: 6–18.

Berry, M. (1975) *An Introduction to Systemic Linguistics*, vol. 1, London: Batsford.

Betterton, R. (ed.) (1987) *Looking On: Images of Femininity in the Visual Arts and Media*, London: Pandora.

Black, M. and Coward, R. (1990) 'Linguistic, social and sexual relations', in D. Cameron (ed.) *The Feminist Critique of Language*, London: Routledge, pp. 111–33.

Bloom, H. (1975) *The Anxiety of Influence*, Oxford: Oxford University Press.

Boone, J. and Cadden, M. (1990) *Engendering Men: The Question of Male Feminist Criticism*, London: Routledge.

Bowles, G. and Klein, R. (eds) (1983) *Theories of Women's Studies*, London: Routledge.

Bradby, B. (1990) 'Do-talk and don't talk: the division of the subject in girl-group music', in S. Frith and A. Goodwin (eds) *On Record: A Rock and Pop Reader*, London: Routledge, pp. 341–68.

Bradby, B., and Torode, B. (1984) 'Pity Peggy Sue', *Popular Music* 4: 183–206.

Brannon, R. (1978) 'The consequences of sexist language', paper given to American Psychological Association, Toronto.

Bristow, J. (ed.) (1992) *Sexual Sameness: Textual Differences in Lesbian and Gay Writing*, London: Routledge.

Brookner, A. (1984) *Hotel du Lac*, London: Jonathan Cape.

Brown, G. and Yule, G. (1983) *Discourse Analysis*, Cambridge: Cambridge University Press.

Brown, R. and Gilman, A. (1972) 'The pronouns of power and solidarity', in P. Giglioli (ed.) *Language and Social Context*, Harmondsworth: Penguin, pp. 253–76.

Burchfield, R. (1980) 'Dictionaries and ethnic sensibilities', in L. Michaels and C. Ricks (eds) *The State of the Language*, Berkeley and London: University of California Press, pp. 15–23.

Burton, D. (1982) 'Through dark glasses, through glass darkly', in R. Carter (ed.) *Language and Literature*, London: Allen & Unwin, pp. 195–214.

Butler, J. (1990) *Gender Trouble: Feminism and the Subversion of Identity*, London: Routledge.

Butturff, D. *et al.* (1978) *Women's Language and Style*, Ohio: L & S Books.

Bygrave, M. (1991) 'Mind your language', *Weekend Guardian* (11–12 May): 14–15.

Cameron, D. (1985) *Feminism and Linguistic Theory*, London: Macmillan.

Cameron, D. (ed.) (1990a) *The Feminist Critique of Language: A Reader*, London: Routledge.

Cameron, D. (1990b) 'Demythologising sociolinguistics: why language does not reflect society', in J. E. Joseph and T. J. Taylor (eds) *Ideologies of Language*, London: Routledge, pp. 79–96.

Carter, R. (ed.) (1982) *Language and Literature: An Introductory Reader in Stylistics*, London: Allen & Unwin.

Carter, R. (1989) *Teaching Literature*, London: Longman.

Carter, R. and Nash, W. (1990) *Seeing Through Language*, Oxford: Blackwell.

Carter, R. and Simpson, P. (1989) *Language, Discourse and Literature: An Introduction to Discourse Stylistics*, London: Unwin Hyman.

Cixous, H. (1976) 'Le sexe ou la tête', *Les Cahiers du GRIF* 13: 1–16.

Cixous, H. (1981a) 'The laugh of the Medusa', in E. Marks and I. de Courtivron (eds) *New French Feminisms*, Brighton: Harvester, pp. 245–64.

Cixous, H. (1981b) 'Sorties', in E. Marks and I. de Courtivron (eds) *New French Feminisms*, Brighton: Harvester, pp. 90–9.

Cixous, H. (1986) *The Newly Born Woman*, Manchester: Manchester University Press.

Clement, C. (1989) *Opera, or the Undoing of Women*, London: Virago.

Coates, J. (1986) *Women, Men and Language*, Cambridge: Cambridge University Press.

Coates, J. and Cameron, D. (eds) (1988) *Women in Their Speech Communities*, Harlow: Longman.

Colette (1954) *The Vagabond*, Harmondsworth: Penguin.

Coupland, N. (ed.) (1988) *Styles of Discourse*, Beckenham, Kent: Croom Helm.

Coward, R. (1984) *Female Desire*, London: Paladin.

Crawford, M. and Chaffin, R. (1986) 'The readers' construction of meaning', in E. A. Flynn and P. P. Schweickart (eds) *Gender and Reading*, Baltimore, MD: Johns Hopkins University Press, pp. 3–30.

Crowther, B. and Leith, D. (1995) 'Feminism, language and the rhetoric of TV wildlife programmes', in S. Mills (ed.) *Language and Gender: Interdisciplinary Perspectives*, Harlow: Longman.

Crystal, D. (1988) *Cambridge Encyclopaedia of Language*, Cambridge: Cambridge University Press.

Culler, J. (1975) *Structuralist Poetics*, London: Routledge & Kegan Paul.

Culler, J. (1983) 'Reading as a woman', in *On Deconstruction*, London: Routledge & Kegan Paul, pp. 43–64.

Dale, C. (1986) *A Personal Call*, Harmondsworth: Penguin.

Daly, M. (1981) *Gyn/Ecology*, London: Women's Press.

Davies, K., Dickey, J. and Stratford, D. (eds) (1987) *Out of Focus, Writings on Women and the Media*, London: Women's Press.

Day, A. (1988) *Joker Man: Reading the Lyrics of Bob Dylan*, Oxford: Blackwell.

Deleuze, G. and Guattari, F. (1986) 'What is a minor literature', in *Kafka: Towards a Minor Literature*, trans. D. Polan, Minneapolis, MN: Minnesota University Press.

Dollimore, J. (1991) *Sexual Dissidence*, Oxford: Oxford University Press.

Durant, A. (1995) *Soundtrack and Talkback: Language Communication and Education*, London: Macmillan.

Durant, A. and Fabb, N. (1989) *Literary Studies in Action*, London: Routledge.

Eagleton, M. (ed.) (1986) *Feminist Literary Theory: A Reader*, Oxford: Blackwell.

Eagleton, T. (1991) *Ideology: An Introduction*, London: Verso.

Eberhardt, O. M. V. (1976) 'Elementary students' understanding of masculine and neutral generic nouns', unpublished PhD thesis, Kansas State University.

Eco, U. (1979) *The Role of the Reader: Explorations in the Semiotics of Text*, Bloomington, IN: Indiana University Press.

Edelsky, C. (1977) 'Acquisition of an aspect of communicative competence: learning what it means to talk like a lady', in S. Ervin-Tripp and C. Mitchell-Kernan (eds) *Child Discourse*, New York: Academic Press.

Ellman, M. (1968) *Thinking about Women*, New York: Harcourt Brace.

Fabb, N. *et al.* (eds) (1987) *The Linguistics of Writing*, Manchester: Manchester University Press.

Fairclough, N. (1989) *Language and Power*, Harlow: Longman.

Fetterley, J. (1978) *The Resisting Reader*, Bloomington, IN: Indiana University Press.

Fish, S. (1980) *Is There a Text in This Class?*, Cambridge, MA: Harvard University Press.

Flynn, E. and Schweickart, P. (eds) (1986) *Gender and Reading: Essays on Readers, Texts and Contexts*, Baltimore, MD/London: Johns Hopkins University Press.

Foucault, M. (1972) *The Archaeology of Knowledge*, trans. A. Sheridan Smith, New York: Harper.

Foucault, M. (1980) 'What is an author?', in J. V. Harari (ed.) *Textual Strategies: Perspectives in Poststructuralist Criticism*, London: Methuen.

Foucault, M. (1981) *The History of Sexuality*, vol. 1, Harmondsworth: Penguin.

Fowler, R. (1981) *Literature as Social Discourse*, London: Batsford.

Fowler, R. (1986) *Linguistic Criticism*, Oxford: Oxford University Press.

Fowler, R. (1991) *Language in the News: Discourse and Ideology in the Press*, London: Routledge.

Fowler, R. *et al.* (1979) *Language and Control*, London: Routledge & Kegan Paul.

Freeman, D. (ed.) (1970) *Linguistics and Literary Style*, New York: Holt Rinehart & Winston.

Frith, G. (1991) 'Transforming features: double vision and the female reader', *New Formations* 15 (Winter): 67–81.

Frith, S. (1988) 'Why do songs have words' in *Music for Pleasure: Essays in the Sociology of Pop*, Oxford: Polity, pp. 105–28.

Frye, M. (1981) 'Male chauvinism: a conceptual analysis', in M. Vetterling-Braggin (ed.) *Sexist Language: A Modern Philosophical Analysis*, Totowa, NJ: Littlefield Adams, pp. 7–22.

Furman, N. (1980) 'Textual feminism', in S. McConnell-Ginet *et al.* (eds) *Women and Language in Literature and Society*, New York: Praeger, pp. 63–88.

Fuss, D. (1990) *Essentially Speaking: Feminism, Nature and Difference*, London: Routledge.

Galford, E. (1993) *Moll Cutpurse*, London: Virago.

Gamman, L. and Marshment, M. (eds) (1988) *The Female Gaze: Women as Viewers of Popular Culture*, London: Women's Press.

Gibbons, T. (1980) *Language and Awareness*, London: Batsford.

Gilbert, S. and Gubar, S. (1988) *The War of the Worlds*, vol. I, *No Man's Land*, New Haven, CT: Yale University Press.

Goldberg, S. (1992) 'Going the whole hog', *GQ* (August): 22–3.

Grabrucker, M. (1988) *There's a Good Girl*, London: Women's Press.

Gunew, S. (ed.) (1990) *Feminist Knowledge: Critique and Construct*, London: Routledge.

Haden-Elgin, S. (1985) *Native Tongue*, London: Women's Press.

Halliday, M. A. K. (1971) 'Linguistic function and style: an inquiry into the language of William Golding's *The Inheritors*', in S. Chatman (ed.) *Literary Style: A Symposium*, London/New York: Oxford University Press, pp. 330–68.

Halliday, M. (1976) 'Notes on transitivity and theme in English – part 1', *Journal of Linguistics* 3: 37–81.

Hanscombe, G. and Smyers, V. (1987) *Writing for Their Lives*, London: Women's Press.

Harding, S. (1992) 'The instability of the analytical categories of feminist theory', in H. Crowley and S. Himmelweit (eds) *Knowing Women*, Cambridge: Polity/Open University Press, pp. 338–54.

Haugg, F. (1988) *Female Sexualisation*, London: Verso.

Hiatt, M. (1977) *The Way Women Write*, New York: Teachers' College Press, Columbia University.

Hobby, E. and White, C. (eds) (1991) *What Lesbians Do in Books*, London: Women's Press.

Hodge, B. and Kress, G. (1988) *Social Semiotics*, Oxford: Polity/Blackwell.

Hoey, M. (1983) *On the Surface of Discourse*, London: Allen & Unwin.

Holder, R. W. (1989) *The Faber Dictionary of Euphemisms*, London: Faber.

Horner, A. and Zlosnick, S. (1990) *Landscapes of Desire: Metaphors in Modern Women's Fiction*, Hemel Hempstead: Harvester Wheatsheaf.

Howard, J. and Allen, C. (1990) 'The gendered context of reading', *Gender and Society* 4(4) (December): 534–52.

Humm, M. (1989) *The Dictionary of Feminist Theory*, Hemel Hempstead: Harvester Wheatsheaf.

Hyams, R. (1990) *Empire and Sexuality: The British Experience*, Manchester: Manchester University Press.

Hymes, D. (1971) *Directions in Sociolinguistics*, New York: Holt, Rinehart & Winston.

Irigaray, L. (1985) *This Sex Which Is Not One*, ed. C. Porter, New York: Cornell University Press.

Jakobson, R. (1960) 'Linguistics and poetics' in T. Sebeok (ed.) *Style in Language*, Cambridge, MA: MIT Press, 350–77.

Jardine, A. and Smith, P. (eds) (1987) *Men in Feminism*, London: Methuen.

Jones, A. R. (1985) 'Inscribing femininity: French theories of the feminine', in G. Greene and C. Kahn (eds) *Making a Difference*, London: Methuen.

Joyce, J. (1922 [1960]) *Ulysses*, London: Bodley Head.

Kamuf, P. (1980) 'Writing like a woman', in S. McConnell-Ginet *et al.* (eds) *Women and Language in Literature and Society*, New York: Praeger, 284–99.

Kaplan, C. (1986) *Sea Changes: Culture and Feminism*, London: Verso.

Kaplan, G. T. and Rogers, L. J. (1990) 'The definition of male and female: biological reductionism and the sanctions of normality', in S. Gunew (ed.) *Feminist Knowledge: Critique and Construct*, London: Routledge, pp. 205–28.

Kappeler, S. (1986) *The Pornography of Representation*, Cambridge: Polity Press.

Kappeler, S. *et al.* (eds.) (1983) *Teaching the Text*, London: Routledge & Kegan Paul.

Karpf, A. (1985) 'Nukespeak for old', *Guardian* (20 Nov.): p 15.

Kidd, V. (1971) 'A study of the images produced through the use of the male pronoun as the generic', in *Moments in Contemporary Rhetoric and Communication* 1(2): 25–30.

Kingsley, M. (1982 [1897]) *Travels in West Africa*, London: Virago.

Kolodny, A. (1975) 'Some notes on defining a feminist literary criticism', *Critical Inquiry* 2(1) (Autumn): 63–80.

Kramarae, C. *et al.* (eds) (1980) *The Voices and Words of Women and Men*, Oxford: Pergamon.

Kramarae, C. and Treichler, P. (1985) *A Feminist Dictionary*, London: Pandora.

Kristeva, J. (1981) 'Oscillation between power and denial', in E. Marks and I. de Courtivron (eds) *New French Feminisms*, Brighton: Harvester, pp. 165–8.

Kuhn, A. (1982) *Women's Pictures*, London: Routledge & Kegan Paul.

Labov, W. (1972) *Language in the Inner City*, Philadelphia, PA: University of Pennsylvania Press.

Lakoff, G. (1987) *Women, Fire and Dangerous Things: What Categories Reveal about the Mind*, Chicago: Chicago University Press.

Lakoff, G. and Johnson, M. (1980) *Metaphors We Live By*, Chicago: University of Chicago Press.

Lakoff, R. (1975) *Language and Woman's Place*, New York: Harper & Row.

Laws, S. (1990) *Issues of Blood: Politics of Menstruation*, London: Macmillan.

LeCercle, J. (1990) *The Violence of Language*, London: Routledge.

Lee, D. (1992) *Competing Discourses: Perspective and Ideology in Language*, London: Longman.

Leech, G. (1973) *Linguistic Guide to English Poetry*, Harlow: Longman.

Leech, G. and Short, M. (1981) *Style in Fiction*, London: Longman.

Leigh, R. and Wood, B. (1991) *The Essex Girl Jokebook*, London: Corgi.

Leith, D. (1983) *A Social History of English*, London: Routledge & Kegan Paul.

Leonardi, S. (1986) 'Bare places and ancient blemishes: Virginia Woolf's search for new language in *Night and Day*', *Novel* (Winter): 150–64.

Levinson, S. (1983) *Pragmatics*, Cambridge: Cambridge University Press.

Lévi-Strauss, C. (1967) *The Structural Study of Myth and Totemism*, ed. E. R. Leach, Harmondsworth: Penguin.

Lowry, M. (1984) *Under the Volcano*, London: Jonathan Cape.

Lyall, G. (1967) *Shooting Script*, London: Pan.

Lyons, J. (1981) *Language and Linguistics: An Introduction*, Cambridge: Cambridge University Press.

McCabe, C. (1981) 'Realism and cinema: notes on some Brechtian theses', in T. Bennet *et al.* (eds) *Popular Film and TV*, London: Oxford University Press and British Film Institute, pp. 216–35.

McConnell-Ginet, S. *et al.* (eds) (1980) *Women and Language in Literature and Society*, New York: Praeger.

Macdonnell, D. (1986) *Theories of Discourses*, Oxford: Blackwell.

Macherey, P. (1978) *A Theory of Literary Production*, trans. G. Wall, London: Routledge & Kegan Paul.

McInnes, H. (1982) *The Hidden Target*, Glasgow: Collins/Fontana.

MacKay, D. (1983) 'Prescriptive grammar and the pronoun problem', in B. Thorne *et al.* (eds) *Language Gender and Society*, Rowley, MA: Newbury House, pp. 38–53.

MacKay, D. *et al.* (1979) 'On the comprehension and production of pronouns', *Journal of Verbal*

Learning and Verbal Behaviour 18: 661–73.

Mandelbaum, D. (ed.) (1949) *Selected Writings of Edward Sapir*, San Francisco, CA: University of California Press.

Marks, E. and de Courtivron, I. (eds) (1981) *New French Feminisms*, Brighton: Harvester.

Marshment, M. *et al.* (eds) (1988) *The Female Gaze*, London: Women's Press.

Martin, J. R. (1986) 'Grammaticalizing ecology: the politics of baby seals and kangaroos', in T. Threadgold *et al.* (eds) *Language, Semiotics, Ideology*, Sydney Studies in Society and Culture, no. 3, pp. 225–68.

Martyna, W. (1978) 'What does "he" mean: use of the generic masculine', *Journal of Communication* 28: 131–8.

Martyna, W. (1980) 'The psychology of the generic masculine', in S. McConnell-Ginet *et al.* (eds) *Women and Language in Literature and Society*, New York: Praeger.

Martyna, W. (1983) 'Beyond the he/man approach: the case for non-sexist language', in B. Thorne *et al.* (eds) *Language, Gender and Society*, Rowley, MA: Newbury House, pp. 25–37.

Mazuchelli, N. (1876) *The Indian Alps and How We Crossed Them*, London: Longman.

Miall, D. (ed.) (1982) *Metaphor: Problems and Perspectives*, Brighton: Harvester.

Middleton, P. (1992) *The Inward Gaze: Masculinity and Subjectivity in Modern Culture*, London: Routledge.

Miller, C. and Swift, K. (1979) *Words and Women*, Harmondsworth: Penguin.

Miller, C. and Swift, K. (1980) *The Handbook of Non-Sexist Writing*, New York: Lippincott & Crowell; revised edn (1989) London: Women's Press.

Millett, K. (1977) *Sexual Politics*, London: Virago.

Mills, J. (1989) *Womanwords*, London: Longman.

Mills, S. (1987) 'The male sentence', *Language and Communication* 7(3): 189–98.

Mills, S. (1989a) 'No poetry for ladies: Gertrude Stein, Julia Kristeva and modernism', in D. Murray (ed.) *Literary Theory and Poetry*, London: Batsford, pp. 85–107.

Mills, S. (1989b) 'Poetics and linguistics: a critical relation?', *Parlance* 2(1): 25–35.

Mills, S. (1991) 'Feminist futures', *News from Nowhere* 8: 64–75.

Mills, S. (1992a) 'Negotiating discourses of femininity', *Journal of Gender Studies* 1(3) (May): 271–85.

Mills, S. (1992b) *Discourses of Difference: An Analysis of Women's Travel Writing and Colonialism*, London: Routledge.

Mills, S. (1992c) 'Knowing y/our place: towards a Marxist feminist contextualised stylistics', in M. Toolan (ed.) *Language, Text and Context: Essays in Stylistics*, London: Routledge, pp. 182–207.

Mills, S. (1992d) 'Feminist literary theory', in *Year's Work in English Studies*, vol. 70 (for the year 1989), Oxford: Blackwell, pp. 47–57.

Mills, S. (ed.) (1994) *Gendering the Reader*, Hemel Hempstead: Harvester Wheatsheaf.

Mills, S. (ed.) (1995) *Language and Gender: Interdisciplinary Perspectives*, Harlow: Longman.

Mills, S. and Pearce, L. (1993) 'Feminist literary theory', in *Year's Work in English Studies*, vol. 71 (for the year 1990), Oxford: Blackwell, pp. 64–90.

Mills, S., Pearce, L., Spaull, S. and Millard, E. (1989) *Feminist Readings/Feminists Reading*, Hemel Hempstead: Harvester.

Minow-Pinkney, M. (1989) *Virginia Woolf and the Problem of the Subject: Feminine Writing in the Major Novels*, Hemel Hempstead: Harvester Wheatsheaf.

Modleski, T. (1991) *Feminism Without Women: Culture and Criticism in a 'Postfeminist' Age*, London: Routledge.

Moi, T. (1985) *Sexual/Textual Politics*, London: Methuen.

Montgomery, M. (1986a) *Introduction to Language and Society*, London: Methuen.

Montgomery, M. (1986b) 'DJ talk', *Media Culture and Society* 8(4): 421–40.

Montgomery, M. (1988) 'Direct address, mediated text and establishing co-presence', discussion paper, Programme in Literary Linguistics, University of Strathclyde.

Montgomery, M., Fabb, N., Durant, A., Furniss, T. and Mills, S. (1992) *Ways of Reading*, London: Routledge.

Morgan, F. (1989) *A Misogynist's Source Book*, London: Jonathan Cape.

Morris, M. (1989) *The Pirate's Fiancée*, London: Verso.

Morrison, T. (1982) *Sula*, London: Triad, Grafton.

Mukarovsky, J. (1970) 'Standard language and poetic language', in D. Freeman (ed.) *Linguistics and Literary Style*, New York: Holt, Rinehart & Winston, pp. 40–56.

Mulvey, L. (1981) 'Visual pleasure and narrative cinema', in T. Bennett *et al.* (eds) *Popular Film and TV*, London: Oxford University Press and British Film Institute, pp. 206–15.

Murdoch, I. (1971) *An Accidental Man*, London: Chatto & Windus.

Murray, D. (ed.) (1989) *Literary Theory and Poetry: Extending the Canon*, London: Batsford.

Naipaul, V. S. (1973) *Mr Stone and the Knight's Companion*, Harmondsworth: Penguin.

Nilsen, A. P. (1972) 'Sexism in English', in N. Hoffman *et al.* (eds) *Female Studies VI*, New York: Feminist Press.

Nilsen, A. P. *et al.* (1977) *Sexism and Language*, Urbana, IL: NCTE.

Oates, J. C. (1986) 'Is there a female voice?', in M. Eagleton (ed.) *Feminist Literary Theory: A Reader*, Oxford: Blackwell.

Ortony, A. (1979) *Metaphor and Thought*, Cambridge: Cambridge University Press.

Pearce, L. (1991a) 'Dialogic theory and women's writing', paper given at the Women's Studies Network conference London.

Pearce, L. (1991b) *Woman/Image/Text*, Hemel Hempstead: Harvester.

Pecheux, M. (1982) *Language Semantics and Ideology*, London: Macmillan.

Pratt, M. (1977) *Towards a Speech-Act Theory of Literary Discourse*, Bloomington, IN: Indiana University Press.

Pratt, M. (1987) 'Linguistic utopias', in N. Fabb *et al.* (eds) *The Linguistics of Writing*, Manchester: Manchester University Press, pp. 48–66.

Pribram, D. (ed.) (1988) *Female Spectators: Looking at Film and Television*, London: Verso.

Propp, V. (1968 [1928]) *The Morphology of the Folktale*, Austin, TX: University of Texas Press.

Rajan, R. S. (1994) *Imagined Women: Women, Gender, Culture and Postcolonialism*, London: Routledge.

Ricks, C. and Michaels, L. (eds) (1980) *The State of the Language*, London: Faber.

Rimmon-Kenan, S. (1983) *Narrative Fiction: Contemporary Poetics*, London: Methuen.

Rivkin, J. (1986–7) 'Resisting readers and reading effects: some speculations on reading and gender', *Narrative Poetics: Papers in Comparative Studies* 5 (ed. J. Phelan): 11–23.

Robertson, S. (1990) 'Generics', unpublished MLitt dissertation, Programme in Literary Linguistics, University of Strathclyde.

Rochefort, C. (1981) 'Are women writers still monsters?' in E. Marks and I. de Courtivron (eds) *New French Feminisms*, Brighton: Harvester, pp. 183–7.

Russ, J. (1984) *How to Suppress Women's Writing*, London: Women's Press.

Saporta, S. (1964) 'The application of linguistics to the study of poetic language', in T. Sebeok (ed.) *Style in Language*, Cambridge, MA: MIT Press, pp. 82–93.

Sayers, D. L. (1935) *Gaudy Night*, London: Gollancz.

Scholes, R. (1982) 'Decoding papa', in *Semiotics and Interpretation*, Yale University Press.

Schultz, M. (1990) 'The semantic derogation of women', extract in D. Cameron (ed.) *The Feminist Critique of Language*, London: Routledge, pp. 134–47.

Searle, J. (1979) *Speech-Acts*, Cambridge: Cambridge University Press.

Shepherd, S. and Wallis, M. (eds) (1989) *Coming on Strong: Gay Politics and Culture*, London: Unwin Hyman.

Short, M. (1989) *Reading, Analysing and Teaching Literature*, Harlow: Longman.

Short, M. and Leech, G. (1981) *Style in Fiction: a Linguistic Introduction to English Fictional Prose*, London: Longman.

Showalter, E. (1971) 'Women and the literary curriculum', *College English* 32: 855–70.

Showalter, W. (1978) *A Literature of Their Own: British Women Novelists from Brontë to Lessing*, London: Virago.

Shute, S. (1981) 'Sexist language and sexism', in M. Vetterling-Braggin (ed.) *Sexist Language: a Modern Philosophical Analysis*, Totowa, NJ: Littlefield Adams, pp. 23–33.

Shuttle, P. and Redgrove, P. (1980) *The Wise Wound: Menstruation and Everywoman*, Harmondsworth: Penguin.

Simpson, P. (1992) 'Teaching stylistics: analysing cohesion and narrative structure', *Language and Literature* 1(1): 47–67.

Sinclair, J. (1966) 'Taking a poem to pieces', in R. Fowler (ed.) *Essays on Style and Language*, London: Routledge & Kegan Paul, pp. 68–81.

Smith, D. (1990) *Texts, Facts and Femininity: Exploring the Relations of Ruling*, London: Routledge.

Spender, D. (1980) *Man-Made Language*, London: Routledge & Kegan Paul.

Sperber, D. and Wilson, D. (1986) *Relevance: Communication and Cognition*, Oxford: Blackwell.

Spivak, G. C. (1987) *In Other Worlds: Essays in Cultural Politics*, London: Methuen.

Stanley, L. (ed.) (1990) *Feminist Praxis: Research, Theory and Epistemology in Feminist Sociology*, London: Routledge.

Steedman, C. (1986) *Landscape for a Good Woman*, London: Virago.

Steen, G. (1989) 'How empirical are the British?', *Parlance* 2(1): 55–77.

Strainchamps, E. (1971) 'Our sexist language', in V. Gornick *et al.* (eds) *Woman in Sexist Society*, New York: Basic Books.

Suleiman, S. *et al.* (eds) (1980) *The Reader in the Text: Essays on Audience and Interpretation*, Princeton, NJ: Princeton University Press.

Sunderland, J. (ed.) (1994) *Exploring Gender: Questions and Implications for English Language Education*, Hemel Hempstead: Prentice-Hall.

Tallentire, D. (1986) 'Confirming intuition about style using concordances', in A. Jones (ed.) *The Computer in Literary and Linguistic Studies*, Cardiff: University of Wales Press.

Tannen, D. (1991) *You Just Don't Understand: Women and Men in Conversation*, London: Virago.

Taylor Bradford, B. (1981) *A Woman of Substance*, London: Grafton.

Thorne, B. and Henley, N. (eds) (1975) *Language and Sex: Difference and Dominance*, Rowley, MA: Newbury House.

Threadgold, T. (1986) 'Stories of race and gender: an unbounded discourse', discussion paper.

Threadgold, T. (1988) 'Language and gender', *Australian Journal of Feminist Studies* (May): 56–71.

Tong, R. (1989) *Feminist Thought: A Comprehensive Introduction*, London: Unwin Hyman.

Toolan, M. (1988) *Narrative: A Critical Linguistic Introduction*, London: Routledge.

Toolan, M. (ed.) (1992) *Language, Text and Context: Essays in Stylistics*, London: Routledge.

Traugott, E. and Pratt, M. (1980) *Linguistics for Students of Literature*, New York: Harcourt Brace Jovanovich.

Treneman, A. (1988) 'Cashing in on the curse: advertising and the menstrual taboo', in L. Gamman and M. Marshment (eds) *The Female Gaze: Women as Viewers of Popular Culture*, London: Women's Press, pp. 153–65.

Trudgill, P. (1972) 'Sex, covert prestige and linguistic choice', *Language and Society* 1: 179–95.

Uspensky, B. (1973) *A Poetics of Composition*, Berkeley, CA: University of California Press.

Veach, S. (1979) 'Sexism in usage', paper given at Language and Gender Conference, California University at Santa Cruz.

Vetterling-Braggin, M. (ed.) (1981) *Sexist Language: a Modern Philosophical Analysis*, Totowa, NJ: Littlefield Adams.

Verdonck, P. and Weber J.-J. (1995) *Literary Stylistic Criticism of Nineteenth- and Twentieth-Century Prose*, London: Routledge.

Viner, K. (1992) 'Sweet FA', *Guardian* (9 July): 21.

Voloshinov, V. (1973 [1930]) *Marxism and the Philosophy of Language*, trans. L. Matejka and I. Titunik, New York: Seminar Press.

Wales, K. (1989) *Dictionary of Stylistics*, Harlow: Longman.

Wales, K. (ed.) (1994) *Feminist Linguistics in Literary Criticism*, Woodbridge: Boydell & Brewer.

Ware, V. (1992) *Beyond the Pale: White Women, Racism and History*, London: Verso.

Wareing, S. (1990) 'Women in fiction: stylistic modes of reclamation', *Parlance* 2(2): 72–85.

Wareing, S. (1994) 'And then he kissed her: the reclamation of female characters to submissive roles in contemporary fiction', in K. Wales (ed.) *Feminist Linguistics in Literary Criticism*, Woodbridge, Sk: Boydell & Brewer.

Warhol, R. R. and Herndl, D. P. (eds) (1991) *Feminisms: An Anthology of Literary Theory and Criticism*, New Brunswick, NJ: Rutgers University Press.

Webster, W. (1990) *Not a Man to Match Her*, London: Women's Press.

Wetherell, M. and Potter, J. (1992) *Mapping the Language of Racism: Discourse and the Legitimation of Exploitation*, Hemel Hempstead: Harvester Wheatsheaf.

Whorf, B. (1956) *Language, Thought and Reality*, Cambridge, MA: MIT Press.

Wilcox, H., McWatters, K., Thompson, A and Williams, L. (eds) (1990) *The Body and the Text: Hélène Cixous, Reading and Teaching*, Hemel Hempstead, Herts: Harvester Wheatsheaf.

Williams, P. (1989) 'Difficult subjects: Black British women's poetry', in D. Murray (ed.) *Literary Theory and Poetry: Extending the Canon*, London: Batsford, pp. 108–26.

Williams, R. (1988) *Keywords*, London: Fontana (4th impression).

Williamson, J. (1978) *Decoding Advertisements: Ideology and Meaning in Advertising*, London: Marion

Boyars.

Winterson, J. (1992) *Written on the Body*, London: Jonathan Cape.

Wittig, M. (1981) 'One is not born a woman', *Feminist Issues* 1(2) (Winter); reprinted in (1992) *The Straight Mind and Other Essays*, Hemel Hempstead: Harvester Wheatsheaf, pp. 9–20.

Wittig, M. (1983) 'The point of view: universal or particular?', *Feminist Issues* 3(2) (Fall); reprinted in (1992) *The Straight Mind and Other Essays*, Hemel Hempstead: Harvester Wheatsheaf, pp. 59–67.

Woolf, V. (1929 [1966]) 'Women and fiction', in *Collected Essays*, vol. II, London: Hogarth Press.

Woolf, V. (1965) *Contemporary Writers*, London: Hogarth.

Woolf, V. (1977) *A Room of One's Own*, London: Granada.

Woolf, V. (1979) *Women and Writing*, intro. Michele Barrett, London: Women's Press.

Index